Data Types
and Data Structures

Prentice-Hall International
Series in Computer Science

C.A.R. Hoare, Series Editor

Published

BACKHOUSE, R.C., *Syntax of Programming Languages, Theory and Practice*
de BAKKER, J.W., *Mathematical Theory of Program Correctness*
BJORNER, D. and JONES, C., *Formal Specification and Software Development*
CLARK, K.L. and McCABE, F.G., *micro-PROLOG: Programming in Logic*
DROMEY, R.G., *How to Solve it by Computer*
DUNCAN, F., *Microprocessor Programming and Software Development*
ELDER, J., *Construction of Data Processing Software*
GOLDSCHLAGER, L. and LISTER, A., *Computer Science: A Modern Introduction*
HEHNER, E.C.R., *The Logic of Programming*
HENDERSON, P., *Functional Programming: Application and Implementation*
HOARE, C.A.R., *Communicating Sequential Processes*
HOARE, C.A.R., and SHEPHERDSON, J.C., (eds) *Mathematical Logic and Programming Languages*
INMOS, LTD., *The Occan Programming Manual*
JACKSON, M.A., *System Development*
JOHNSTON, H., *Learning to Program*
JONES, C.B., *Software Development: A Rigorous Approach*
JOSEPH, M., PRASAD, V.R. and NATARAJAN, N., *A Multiprocessor Operating System*
LEW, A., *Computer Science: A Mathematical Introduction*
MacCALLUM, I., *Pascal for the Apple*
MacCALLUM, I., *UCSD Pascal for the IBM PC*
MARTIN, J.J., *Data Types and Data Structures*
REYNOLDS, J.C., *The Craft of Programming*
TENNENT, R.D., *Principles of Programming Languages*
WELSH, J. and ELDER, J., *Introduction to Pascal, 2nd Edition*
WELSH, J., ELDER, J., and BUSTARD, D., *Sequential Program Structures*
WELSH, J. and McKEAG, M., *Structured System Programming*

Data Types
and
Data Structures

Johannes J. Martin

University of New Orleans
Computer Science Department

Prentice/Hall International

ENGLEWOOD CLIFFS, NEW JERSEY   LONDON   MEXICO   NEW DELHI
RIO DE JANEIRO SINGAPORE SYDNEY TOKYO TORONTO WELLINGTON

British Library Cataloguing in Publication Data

Martin, Johannes J.
  Data types and data structures.—(Prentice-Hall
  International series in personal computing)
  1. Data structures (Computer sciences)
  I. Title
  001.64'42   QA76.9.D35

  ISBN 0-13-195983-2
  ISBN 0-13-195975-1 Pbk

Library of Congress Cataloguing-in-Publication Data

Martin, Johannes J., 1934–
  Data types and data structures.

  Bibliography: p.
  Includes index.
  1. Data structures (Computer science)
  I. Title
  QA76.9.D35M37   1986   005.7'3   85-12373
  ISBN 0-13-195983-2

PRENTICE-HALL, INC., *Englewood Cliffs, New Jersey*
PRENTICE-HALL INTERNATIONAL, (UK), Ltd., *London*
PRENTICE-HALL OF AUSTRALIA PTY., LTD., *Sydney*
PRENTICE-HALL CANADA, INC., *Toronto*
PRENTICE-HALL HISPANO AMERICANA, S.A., *Mexico*
PRENTICE-HALL OF INDIA PRIVATE LIMITED, *New Delhi*
PRENTICE-HALL OF JAPAN, INC., *Tokyo*
PRENTICE-HALL OF SOUTHEAST ASIA PTE., LTD., *Singapore*
PRENTICE-HALL DO BRASIL LTDA., *Rio de Janeiro*
WHITEHALL BOOKS LIMITED, *Wellington, New Zealand*

Printed in Great Britain at the University Press, Cambridge.

1 2 3 4 5 90 89 88 87 86

ISBN 0-13-195983-2
ISBN 0-13-195975-1 PBK

to Robert and Elisabeth

CONTENTS

Preface

This book presents a rigorous treatment of the specification and implementation of user defined (abstract) data types. In an undergraduate course on data types and data structures, the entire material can be covered in one semester or two terms.

The way in which the field of data structures has been treated in the past reminds us of the Linnaean classification system of species in biology. In earlier text books, we find the data forms are identified, their properties, relationships, and implementations are discussed and their usefulness illustrated by examples. However, with the discovery of data abstraction, data structures (or more accurately, data types) have become more than a system of useful objects. In fact, creating and implementing new data types has become a most powerful tool for separating levels of concern in large programs. In order to use this tool, programmers must learn:

to recognize which objects in their programs are candidates for new data types:
to identify primitive operations for the objects;
to specify these operations precisely; and
to select a good implementation.

Consequently, of central interest are the concept of data abstraction and methods for the specification and implementation of new types while the significance of the classical data types (stacks, queues, trees, etc.) has shifted. Instead of being fixed elements in a fundamental taxonomy, they have become (excellent) examples for illustrating specification and implementation techniques at different levels of complexity.

Another crucial issue not yet treated systematically in other texts is the distinction between *values* and *mutable objects,* two different interpretations of data items. While the usual techniques of algebraic specification treat data items as values, which are created by functions and can be discarded but not modified, the usual techniques of implementation treat these items (e.g. stacks or trees) as mutable objects, processed by procedures and modified whenever convenient. In this book we try to present a balanced account of both the value and the object interpretation, and we offer formal specification methods and discuss implementation techniques for both interpretations.

For any textbook on programming in general and on data types in particular, the choice of the programming language is of fundamental importance. An ideal language for a book on data structures would, of course, be one that is widely used and that supports abstract data types. Unfortunately, such a language does not yet exist. We could use this as a perfect excuse for creating our own notation (as other authors have done). Instead, we use Pascal for the following reasons:

Pascal is widely accepted especially as an instructional language.
It has been made the basis of many other languages including ADA, a language that may become a major programming language of the future.

Hence, the reader should have a working knowledge of Pascal. Nevertheless, the book is equally valuable in courses that are based on other languages than Pascal (especially Modula-2 or ADA) since only very basic features of Pascal, common to most modern programming languages, have been used.

Furthermore, in an effort to unify and thereby simplify the presentation, we use Pascal not only for the implementation of new data types but, enriched by conditional expressions, also for their specification.

Our use of Pascal follows the definition given by Jensen and Wirth [JW74]*. As the only extensions to this definition we allow the "underscore" to be used in identifiers, and we assume that a standard HALT procedure is provided for the termination of execution.

Throughout this book, short slogans run along with the text in an extra column to the left of the text, summarizing the contents of the right column. The reader may find this left column useful in different ways: as an outline for scanning ahead, for getting an overview of the material to come, as excerpts for reviewing or as landmarks for finding wanted details more quickly.

Finally, I would like to add a personal word about the use of pronouns. I am very sympathetic and in every way supportive of the cause of equal rights for women. However, in order to avoid distractive phrases such as "he or she" I have used the pronoun "he", which the reader may kindly interpret as genderless.

I am very grateful to the many people who gave their suggestions and comments on earlier drafts, most of all Maurice Clint. He persuaded me to write the book and he helped me at all stages to see the project through. With his thoughtful comments and observations he contributed to the book in a fundamental way. I am indebted to Ronald Knott for his excellent suggestions that led to the eradication of errors and to many other improvements. Also, I wish to thank Tony Hoare for his kind and encouraging comments. He suggested the inclusion of material on the implementation descriptors.

* See Bibliographical Note p.274.

J.J.M.

Data Types
and Data Structures

Introduction

Data structures,

The field of study concerned with the use and implementation of data objects is usually called "Data Structures". As it was coined, some years ago, when methods for implementing nonnumerical algorithms were developed, the term "data structure" still evokes associations of boxes connected by arrows and of other diagrams explaining storage organization. These notions, dear and familiar to many programmers, are so closely connected with the word "data structures" that attempting to assign a new, more mathematical meaning to the term does not seem to be prudent. We therefore use "data structure" and "implementation structure" interchangeably.

data types,

Data structures serve to implement complex data objects. These objects are classified into types according to the way they are used. Therefore, depending on the point of view, a data object is characterized by its type (for the user) or by its structure (for the implementer). The author of a large program is always both user and implementer; many of the data types that he uses are defined and implemented by himself. In fact, when working with several layers of routines he must often change from the role of the user to that of the implementer and *vice versa*.

and
levels of concern

The main virtue of programmer defined types is that they help to effectively separate different levels of concern. Hence, creating new types begins with identifying levels of concern.

are the topics
of this book.

In this book, we will deal with the user's and the implementer's view of data; we will study data types and data structures. We will learn to recognize when it is appropriate to create new data types, with which qualities to endow them, and how to implement them. Further, levels of concern, their identification and separation will be a recurring theme.

1.1 SEPARATING LEVELS OF CONCERN

Separating levels
of concern is describing
different things
separately.

A program where levels of concern have been carefully separated deals with a task one problem at a time. It does not suffer from what writers call unnecessary shifts in subject or confusing accumulations of details. Different activities are described separately.

Intermixing levels
of concern...

What is meant by "different activities" is best explained by means of examples. The first example demonstrates the negative effects of intermixed levels of concern. The example involves the directions given to a person who wants to know how to get to a bank. This person, a young farmer visiting town, knows how to drive his tractor around his farm but, since he does not need a driver's licence for operating his vehicle, does not know the traffic rules. The description given to him attempts to describe, at the same time, two things that are clearly on different levels of concern: the way to the bank and the traffic regulations. It reads as follows:

...leads to obscure
programs...

> Follow this road, stay on its right side at all times unless there is an obstruction. When you see the street sign for Palmer Drive, then turn left; make sure that you do not cut the corner and that you end up on the right hand side of Palmer. At some intersections on Palmer you will see octagonal signs with the word "stop" printed on them. Here you have to stop your car. Wait until there is no car on the cross-road approaching the intersection; then proceed. If the sign says "4-way stop", then await your turn before proceeding. At the intersection with Sunset Drive turn right. Again, make sure you wind up on the right hand side of Sunset and stay there. At the traffic light Sunset intersects with Main Street. Turn left if the light is green. Otherwise stop and wait until the light turns green; then proceed . . . etc.

... that are overly
complex
and
prone to be incorrect, ...

If our friend has superhuman abilities so that he is not in the least confused by the complexity of this description, he will probably follow it accurately step by step. Nevertheless, it still seems to be unwise to give directions of this sort for the following reason. In order for the instructions to be effective, that is to say, to lead our friend safely to the bank, it is necessary not only that they are followed accurately but especially that they are correct and complete. For this second requirement, our friend's abilities are irrelevant, it is ours that matter. Unfortunately, ordinary humans are known to perform less than outstandingly if things get too complicated. Details are easily overlooked, conclusions are drawn that are incorrect and so forth. In our description, for example, we forgot to tell our friend to use turn signals and to observe the right-of-way rules when going around an obstruction on his side of the road, to name only two.

... while separating
levels of concern leads
to clear programs, ...

Much clearer is the following text!

How to get to the bank

Follow this road, take a left on Palmer, a right on Sunset, and a left on

Main. Take a left at the third traffic light into College Avenue. At this point you will see the XYZ Bank 200 feet ahead of you on your left.

How to drive along a road

Drive on the right hand side at all times. If there is an obstruction in the right lane (e.g. a parked car) then do the following: if there is no oncoming traffic or if you do not need the left side of the road, then pass the obstruction on its left. If there is oncoming traffic and you need the left side of the road in order to pass the obstruction, stop and wait until the road is clear.

The other partial descriptions are similarly simple and straightforward.

... that are more likely, to be correct, and easy to modify ...

So, the proper separation of levels of concern promotes initial correctness of descriptions (programs). But it does more. To see this, we follow the farmer on his way to the bank. To his dismay, turning left at the third traffic light leads him neither to College Avenue nor to a bank. In desperation, he shows the paper with the directions to a passerby (suppose it was the second, improved version) who realizes immediately that the description is correct except that the turn should have been taken at the fifth light instead of the third. The problem is easily corrected and the farmer finds the bank. Now imagine you were the passerby handed the first type of description for clarification!

... and to maintain.

We conclude that the simplicity gained by separating levels of concern makes it easier to correct (or possibly modify) descriptions later if an error has remained undetected. In the technical jargon of programmers this is called "program maintenance".

Organizing a sequence of actions *not* in the order they occur ...

Now let us compare the two different sets of directions with the sequence of actions that our friend performs as he drives to the bank. Clearly, a record of what actually goes on resembles the first set of directions much more closely than the second one. Thus, although a description of intermixed activities is difficult to comprehend it seems to be easy to carry out. In fact, a more detailed record would show that what is carried out is even more complex than the first description. In addition to seeking the bank and obeying traffic rules there is (at least) a third level of activities, namely the technicalities of operating the tractor: turning the wheel, operating the accelerator, the brake and the clutch, and so forth. All these things are easily managed by the same person at the same time.

... but in detached levels of concern ...

We learn from this observation that the order in which activities happen in the course of a process and the order in which they should occur in an understandable description of the process are profoundly different. In a good description, the whole process is taken apart by identifying different levels of concern. These levels are described, detached from each other, one at a time.

... is *abstraction*.

This activity of detaching levels is called abstraction. When we describe the way to the bank, we abstract this description from the concerns about traffic rules; and when we describe the traffic rules, we abstract from concerns about operating the wheel, the pedals and the gear shift.

Abstraction not only simplifies descriptions, it also makes them more general and thus more useful. For example, the abstract directions to the bank (those that do not address the traffic rules) are equally useful to the driver of a car, a cyclist, and a pedestrian. The traffic rules abstracted from the technicalities of driving a car are equally correct for a motorcyclist.

Abstraction makes descriptions simpler and more general.

1.2   A PROGRAMMING EXAMPLE FOR DATA ABSTRACTION

Data abstraction facilitates total separation of levels of concern.

The next example deals with programming. It will show how user defined data types facilitate the complete separation of levels of concern by what is called data abstraction.

NOTE: The language Pascal allows its users to define new types. However, the concept of (abstract) data types as developed in this book, goes beyond Pascal's notion, which views types simply as collections of objects. For clarity we shall use the terms "data type" and "type" as synonyms of "abstract data type" and refer to collections specified by Pascal type definitions as "Pascal types".

The data type that we shall eventually introduce is that of "dates".

In an accounting program, for example, ...

We consider a program — referred to below as "the accounting program" — that computes the interest earned by the sum C of money deposited in a bank on the date $d1$ and withdrawn on the date $d2$. This simple programming problem should be considered as a representative of all those problems that involve money, interest (possibly changing over time) and dates. The ideas below gain importance as they are applied to more complex problems.

... interest computations can be separated ...

If we know the number of days, Nd, between $d1$ and $d2$ and the current interest rate (assuming that it does not change between $d1$ and $d2$), then the interest is computed by

$$interest := C*(Nd/365)*interest\_rate$$

It turns out that the program needed is not quite as simple as one might assume. The reason is that dates are usually given by triples (day, month, year) or (month, day, year) and that the computation of the distance between two dates — the number of days between the dates — amounts to programming the Gregorian Calendar. For this, we need the number of days in each month and the rules that govern the occurrence of leap years.

... from calendar computations by functional abstraction, ...

We can see immediately that the program segment which computes the distance of two dates is more complicated than that needed to compute the interest itself once the distance between the dates is known. We therefore separate the subtask of computing the distance from the rest of the task by writing a function procedure, *DISTANCE*, that computes the distance. Removing details from a program by writing procedures is called procedural (functional) abstraction. With this procedure, our formula reads

$$interest := C * (DISTANCE(d1,d2)) / 365 * interest\_rate$$

... which separates WHAT to do from HOW to do it.

By means of the *DISTANCE* function we can express that we want the distance between two dates without bothering — at this level — with the details of how this distance is computed. Generalizing we conclude that abstraction can help us to separate the concern of *what* needs to be done from the concern of *how* to do it.

NOTE: Going back to the first example we observe a clean separation of the *what* and the *how* in the improved version of the directions. The description of "how to get to the bank" requires *that* we follow (drive along) a road, take a left turn and so on, deferring the description of "*how* to drive along a road" and "*how* to take a left turn" to a separate part of the description detached from the first one.

The details of the representation of dates, ...

It seems that before we can finish the accounting program we must choose a method for representing dates. We apparently need this information since we must declare the variables $d1$ and $d2$ and assign values to them and, in case the program does more than compute the interest, we might need to compute other facts about dates (for example, such things as the date of the first Friday of next month).

... which depend on details of programs on lower levels, ...

Now, the obvious storage structure for dates seems to be a record of the form

record
    day:1..31; *month*:1..12; *year*:integer
end.

Yet, if we have to evaluate the *DISTANCE* function frequently, then this representation may be too costly. Searching for a solution we observe that dates follow each other like integer numbers; given any date we can always compute the date of the next day. So, perhaps we should represent dates by integers. Then the *DISTANCE* function is merely a subtraction. Also other operations such as "compute the date of 12 days from today" become very simple. If dates are integers then there must be a particular date that is represented by zero. Which date should that be?

... are kept out of the accounting program ...

Wait! — Do these details really belong on the present level of concern (the level of the accounting program)? The question of how to store dates is clearly of the *how*-variety. This seems to indicate that the answer to it should be deferred to a lower level. Which of the two arguments above is correct? Do we need to know the exact representation of dates in the accounting program or can we defer the decision to a lower level?

... by the user-defined
data type *"Date"*.

The answer is that we can, indeed, defer the decision by what is called "data abstraction". We accomplish this by removing from the accounting program all expressions that refer to the inner structure of a date. In order to do this we must do a little planning, however. We must identify a (hopefully) small set of operations on dates on which all other conceivable operations on dates can be based. Such a set is called a set of "primitive operations". Only these primitive operations need to know the actual structure of dates; for the programs that use these primitives, it is sufficient to know that dates form a set of objects, given as a (Pascal) type (which we shall call A_DATE), so that variables etc. can be declared properly.

*Abstract
data type
= objects
  + primitive
    operations.*

By identifying this set of objects (A_DATE) and specifying the set of primitive operations we define, in fact, a new abstract data type. An abstract data type is, basically, a pair consisting of: a set of objects (a Pascal type) and a set of operations that manipulate the objects. A more precise definition will be given later.

*The primitive
operations of the
data type Date ...*

We now wish to identify this set of primitive operations on dates.

The *DISTANCE* function is, of course, one of the candidates.
SUM, the counterpart of *DISTANCE*, takes a date d and a number n and computes the date n days beyond d.
DATE, given a day, a month, and a year, returns a date.
DAY, *MONTH*, and *YEAR*, given a date, return the day, month, and year.
WEEKDAY computes the day of the week from a given date.
F_DATE computes the date of the first occurrence of a given weekday in a given month and year, for example, the first Sunday in March of 1985. This function, given a weekday, a month and a year, returns a date.

This seems to be a sufficient set of operations. We shall not worry too much about sufficiency, because we can always add more operations later if we find out that any are missing.

*... obey certain rules of
syntax ...*

The syntax rules that specify how to use these functions are given by the following Pascal code.

With the Pascal types

```
integer;
A_DAY = 1..31; A_MONTH = 1..12; A_YEAR = integer;
A_WEEKDAY = (sun, mon, tue, wed, thu, fri, sat);
and A_DATE {note that no further definition is given here};
```

we have

```
function DISTANCE (dt1, dt2: A_DATE):integer;
function SUM (dt:A_DATE; i:integer):A_DATE;
function DATE (d:A_DAY; m:A_MONTH; y:A_YEAR): A_DATE;
function DAY (dt:A_DATE):A_DAY;
```

function *MONTH (dt:A_DATE):A_MONTH*;
function *YEAR (dt:A_DATE):A_YEAR*;
function *WEEKDAY (dt:A_DATE):A_WEEKDAY*;
function *F_DATE (d:A_WEEKDAY; m:A_MONTH;*
   y:A_YEAR):A_DATE;

... and have several simple properties.

The above operations have some simple properties.

For all *i* in *Integer*;
*dt*1,*dt*2 in *A_DATE*
d in *A_DAY*; *m* in *A_MONTH*; *y* in *A_YEAR*;
w in *A_WEEKDAY*;

the following relationships hold

SUM(dt, 0) = dt
DISTANCE(dt, dt) = 0
*SUM(dt*1, *DISTANCE(dt*1, *dt*2) + *i*) = *SUM(dt*2, *i*)
*DISTANCE(dt*1, *SUM(dt*2, *i*)) = *i* + *DISTANCE(dt*1, *dt*2)
DAY (DATE(d, m, y)) = d
MONTH (DATE(d, m, y)) = m
YEAR (DATE(d, m, y)) = y
WEEKDAY(F_DATE(w, m, y)) = w
*WEEKDAY(SUM(dt*1,1))
   = **if** *WEEKDAY(dt*1) = *sat*
      then *sun*
      else *succ(WEEKDAY(dt*1))
$0 \leq DISTANCE(DATE(1, m, y), F\_DATE(w, m, y)) \leq 6$

In later chapters we will study these types of relationships in greater depth. Here we leave their interpretation to the reader's intuition.

Some of these properties reflect the nature of the calendar.

We shall now add equations that describe the properties of the Gregorian Calendar. Suppose that *t* is a triple "day, month, year" and *next(t)* and *prev(t)* are the triples that, by the rules of the calendar, follow and precede *t*, respectively. With these (virtual) functions we define:

SUM(DATE(t), n)
   = *SUM(DATE(next(t)), n−1)*
   = *SUM(DATE(prev(t)), n + 1)*.

Further, we have to tie the days of the week to dates; thus we define

WEEKDAY(DATE(1,1,1982)) = fri.

The proper handling of error conditions ...

We also observe that not all triples *t* are valid descriptions of dates. Clearly, the function *DATE(d, m, y)* should not be defined for certain value combinations of *d*, *m*, and *y*. For example, *DATE*(31, 2, *y*) is not a valid date in any year while *DATE*(29, 2, *y*) is all right for some values of *y* but not for others. We should give *DATE* applied to invalid triples (*d*, *m*, *y*) a special value (e.g. *error*) and require that the functions that take dates as arguments return an error value if they are applied to *error*. The relations given are therefore too simple and not quite correct. We can repair them by means of the virtual function "valid" (also based on the actual calendar) which is true if applied to a valid triple (d, m, y) and false otherwise. With this we obtain for example

$$DAY\ (DATE(d, m, y))$$
$$= \textbf{if}\ valid(d, m, y)$$
$$\textbf{then}\ d\ \textbf{else}\ error.$$

... is important!

Handling all error conditions correctly is extremely important and should not be taken lightly. Our (weak) excuse for first giving an incorrect set of specifications is that we do not want to overwhelm the reader with too much information but give him a chance to comprehend the principles involved.

The primitives are correct if they satisfy all the simple properties listed above.

It turns out that an implementation of our primitives is correct if it guarantees all of our (corrected) relationships. This means that the above relationships specify the properties of the primitives sufficiently completely for our purposes. This is a very important fact since this description of the primitives is totally independent of *how* the primitives are programmed. Thus, the separation of the levels of concern is perfect! *What* the primitive operations are supposed to do is described (i) by the specification of their syntax, expressed, for example, by Pascal function headings and (ii) by the specification of their semantics (that is, their meaning) by relationships that define how the operations interact with each other.

We now give a first definition of abstract data types.

Definition:

An *abstract data type* is a system consisting of three constituents:

1. Some sets of objects (given, for example, as Pascal types),
2. A set of syntactic descriptions of (the primitive) functions,
3. A semantic description. That is, a sufficiently complete set of relationships that specify how the functions interact with each other. The technical term for these relationships is (*algebraic*) *axioms*.

For a full understanding and analysis of abstract data types we shall need some basic facts from discrete mathematics. In the next chapter we are going to review these facts.

EXERCISES

E1.1   Give a well-structured (multi-level) description of

how to bake a cake, how to mow a lawn, how to pitch a tent, or how to repair a flat bicycle tire.

The problem is to identify (i) different activities that must be performed in order to complete the task and (ii) the levels of concern of these activities.

E1.2   Specify

function *next*(*t*:*Triple*):*Triple*;

which computes the triple that follows *t* by the rules of the Gregorian calendar, where

Type
Triple = **record**
         day:1..31;
         month:1..12;
         year:*Integer*
     end.

Note that this function cannot actually be programmed in this form since Pascal does not permit functions to compute records. This problem is usually circumvented by implementing instead

procedure *nxt*(*var t*:*Triple*)

where *nxt*(*t*) changes *t* to *next*(*t*).

E1.3   Choose a suitable representation for dates and program the functions *distance, sum, day, month, year,* and *date.*

Mathematical Background

2.1 PROPOSITIONS

The theory concerned with manipulating truth values of assertions ...

Assertions stated in a natural language such as English can be so complex that they are hard to understand and difficult to classify as true or false even if their parts can be analysed and classified easily. Consider, for example, the statement

> If the sun is a star and the earth is flat or (if) the moon is made of green cheese or astronomy is not a science then black holes may exist and the space between stars is filled with beer.

We might quickly conclude that this statement cannot be true because it contains so many false assertions, such as "the moon is made of green cheese" or "the space between stars is filled with beer". But we must be careful. Statements that contain incorrect assertions may be true nevertheless. For example:

> It is not true that the earth is flat.

"The earth is flat" is an incorrect assertion but prefixed with the phrase "It is not true that ...", the combined statement is true. Also consider the assertion

> If the moon is made of green cheese then it (the moon) is edible.

... as arithmetic manipulates numbers is called mathematical logic.

It appears that the task of deciding whether an assertion is true or false is nontrivial. Fortunately, the discipline of *mathematical logic*, gives us a systematic method for manipulating assertions. This method, called the *propositional calculus*, deals with assertions as arithmetic deals with numbers. We shall now study this method.

Propositions are either true or false.

Statements that can be classified as either true or false, *T* or *F* for short, are called *propositions*.

Examples:

> Snow is white.

The moon is made out of green cheese.

$3 > 5$

$99 + 26 = 125$.

Given a proposition *A* (for example, let "*A*" stand for "snow is black") we can form a new proposition by constructing:

'*it is not true that A*'.

We usually say simply 'not *A*' and write ¬*A*. Common sense tells us that

>   **if** *A* (is true) **then** ¬*A* is false

and

>   **if** ¬*A* (is true) **then** *A* is false

The symbol "¬" is called the (unary) operator of negation.

There are several other important operators that allow us to derive new propositions from given ones. All of these are binary operators, that is, they combine two propositions (operands) to form a new one.

For example, the operator "and" may be used to construct the new proposition

>   *A* and *B*

from the proposition *A* and the proposition *B*.

Again, relying on the common usage of the word "and" we conclude that

>   *A* and *B*

is true if both *A* and *B* are true, and false otherwise. Another operator is "implies" as in

>   *A* implies *B*

We also write "*A* ⇒ *B*" or "if *A* then *B*". The proposition

>   if *A* then *B*

is considered true unless *A* is true and *B* is false. Thus the statement

>   if the moon is made out of green cheese,
>   then men have 13 legs

is a correct statement. This does not seem to make much sense. However, someone who claims this can hardly be called a liar! The following example will make this even clearer:

>   If I win in the lottery, then I will buy a Rolls Royce.

This statement cannot be considered false unless, in spite of winning in the lottery, I fail to buy the car.

Yet another operator is "or". Here, however, common usage does not give us the criterion to decide under what circumstances

A or *B*

Since intuition is
not always reliable, ...

should be considered true. Consider the following two sentences: (1) If I win in the lottery or if I get a substantial raise in salary, then I shall buy a new car. (2) If you add one to *or* subtract one from an odd number, you will obtain an even number.

The operator "or" is used differently in these sentences. The difference becomes apparent if we assume that both operands of the "or" are simultaneously true. For the first sentence, this means that I win in the lottery and get a substantial raise; clearly, I would buy a car in this case, too. In the second sentence, however, adding and subtracting one from an odd number leads to the same odd number and not to an even one. Thus, the term "or" may refer to different operators and we need to examine the context in order to decide which one is meant. The "or" of the first sentence is called the *inclusive or* or simply *or*, while that of the second sentence is called the *exclusive or*, frequently denoted by *xor*. Sometimes the context may not even be sufficient to decide which operator is meant. If, for example, prospective parents say that they would be happy having a girl or a boy, it is not clear if they would like twins as well.

... precise definitions
are needed and
accomplished by truth
tables.

For a mathematical theory, uncertainty of this kind is intolerable. We therefore detach the meaning of the logical operators from our linguistic intuition and define it precisely by means of tables. These tables are called (defining) truth tables. We obtain for the operators "¬", "and", "⇒", and "or":

A	¬*A*
F	T
T	F

A	*B*	*A* and *B*
F	F	F
F	T	F
T	F	F
T	T	T

A	*B*	*A* or *B*
F	F	F
F	T	T
T	F	T
T	T	T

A	*B*	*A* ⇒ *B*
F	F	T
F	T	T
T	F	F
T	T	T

A fifth important operator is that of equivalence denoted by ⇔, or by "if and only if" or "iff" for short. *A* ⇔ *B* is true exactly if *A* and *B* are both true or both false.

A	B	A ⇔ B
F	F	T
F	T	F
T	F	F
T	T	T

From now on, we shall stop arguing linguistically about the meaning of operators and depend on the truth tables.

An exampleWith these precisely defined operators, we shall now go back to our original example and see whether it represents a true or false assertion. First we need to agree about the truth values of the assertions from which the whole statement is built:

1. The sun is a star: *T*
2. The earth is flat: *F*
3. The moon is made out of green cheese: *F*
4. Astronomy is a science: *T*
5. Black holes exist: ?
6. The space between stars is filled with beer: *F*

The whole statement now reads

$$((T \text{ and } F) \text{ or } F \text{ or} \neg T) \Rightarrow (? \text{ and } F)$$

Using the truth tables we replace (*T* and *F*) by *F* and $\neg T$ by *F* to give:

$$(F \text{ or } F \text{ or } F) \Rightarrow (? \text{ and } F)$$

Since both (*T* and *F*) and (*F* and *F*) are false, the term (? and *F*) is false. Thus,

$$(F \text{ or } F \text{ or } F) \Rightarrow F$$

Now "or" is a binary operator; thus, in order to evaluate the first part we must decide whether we want to interpret (*F* or *F* or *F*) as meaning (*F* or (*F* or *F*)) or as ((*F* or *F*) or *F*). Fortunately, we find that both interpretations evaluate to *false*. Thus we obtain

$$F \Rightarrow F$$

which, by the definition of "$\Rightarrow$", is true.

There are sixteen different binary operators, ...In addition to the four binary operations defined above, there are twelve more. The complete set of all sixteen binary operations between truth values is given by the following (combined) truth table:

A	B				and				$\Leftrightarrow$				$\Rightarrow$		or	
F	*F*	*F*	*T*	*F*	*F*	*F*	*T*	*T*	*T*	*F*	*F*	*F*	*T*	*T*	*T*	*F*	*T*
F	*T*	*F*	*F*	*T*	*F*	*F*	*T*	*F*	*F*	*T*	*T*	*F*	*T*	*T*	*F*	*T*	*T*
T	*F*	*F*	*F*	*F*	*T*	*F*	*F*	*T*	*F*	*T*	*F*	*T*	*T*	*F*	*T*	*T*	*T*
T	*T*	*F*	*F*	*F*	*F*	*T*	*F*	*F*	*T*	*F*	*T*	*T*	*F*	*T*	*T*	*T*	*T*

... but all can be expressed in terms of "and", "or", and "not".Each of these operations can easily be expressed by a combination of "and", "or", and "$\neg$". For example, the third column (*F T F F*) can be represented by the expression ($\neg A$ and *B*), and "$\Rightarrow$" by ($\neg A$ or *B*).

Parentheses are avoided by precedence rules.We shall see below that only "and" and "$\neg$" (or "or" and "$\neg$") are needed to represent all other operations. But first let us introduce a notational simplification that reduces the number of necessary parentheses:

(1) $\neg A$ is to be interpreted as ($\neg A$),
(2)   Subject to rule (1),
     "*A* and *B*" is to be interpreted as (*A* and *B*).

For example,

$$\neg A \text{ and } B \text{ or } C \text{ and } \neg A$$

is to be understood as

$$((\neg A) \text{ and } B) \text{ or } (C \text{ and } (\neg A)).$$

Simple rules for the manipulation of logical expressions. Complex propositions formed from simple ones by means of operators are frequently called *logical expressions* or simply *expressions* or *formulas*. There are a number of simple relationships that can easily be inferred from the truth tables. These relationships are very important since they are universally used for the transformation of (logical) expressions. The reader is advised to prove their correctness from the truth tables and to commit them to memory.

$$\neg(\neg A) \quad \Leftrightarrow \quad A \tag{2.1}$$
$$A \text{ or } \neg A \quad \Leftrightarrow \quad T \tag{2.2}$$
$$A \text{ and } \neg A \Leftrightarrow \quad F \tag{2.3}$$

{*idempotent law*}
$$A \text{ or } A \quad \Leftrightarrow \quad A \text{ and } A \quad \Leftrightarrow \quad A \tag{2.4}$$

{*commutative laws*}
$$A \text{ and } B \quad \Leftrightarrow \quad B \text{ and } A \tag{2.5}$$
$$A \text{ or } B \quad \Leftrightarrow \quad B \text{ or } A \tag{2.6}$$
$$(A \Leftrightarrow B) \quad \Leftrightarrow \quad (B \Leftrightarrow A) \tag{2.7}$$

{*associative laws*}
$$A \text{ and } (B \text{ and } C) \quad \Leftrightarrow \quad (A \text{ and } B) \text{ and } C \tag{2.8}$$
$$A \text{ or } (B \text{ or } C) \quad \Leftrightarrow \quad (A \text{ or } B) \text{ or } C \tag{2.9}$$

{*absorption laws*}
$$A \text{ and } B \text{ or } A \quad \Leftrightarrow \quad A \tag{2.10}$$
$$(A \text{ or } B) \text{ and } A \quad \Leftrightarrow \quad A \tag{2.11}$$

$$(A \Leftrightarrow B) \quad \Leftrightarrow \quad (\neg A \Leftrightarrow \neg B) \tag{2.12}$$
$$(A \Rightarrow B) \quad \Leftrightarrow \quad (\neg B \Rightarrow \neg A) \tag{2.13}$$

Tautologies are always true. These relationships are true independently of the truth values of the constituent propositions A, B, and C. Expressions with this property are called *tautologies*.

de Morgan's Law We shall now prove an important pair of tautologies, commonly referred to as *de Morgan's Law*.

$$\neg(A \text{ or } B) \quad \Leftrightarrow \quad \neg A \text{ and } \neg B$$
$$\neg(A \text{ and } B) \quad \Leftrightarrow \quad \neg A \text{ or } \neg B$$

We derive the first result using the defining truth tables:

A	B	$\neg A$	$\neg B$	A or B	$\neg(A$ or $B)$	$\Leftrightarrow$	$(\neg A$ and $\neg B)$
F	F	T	T	F	T	T	T
F	T	T	F	T	F	T	F
T	F	F	T	T	F	T	F
T	T	F	F	T	F	T	F

Now, if for all values of A and B

$$\neg(A \text{ or } B) \Leftrightarrow (\neg A \text{ and } \neg B),$$

then, by exchanging the sides and by substituting C for $\neg A$ and D for $\neg B$, we obtain

$$(C \text{ and } D) \Leftrightarrow \neg(\neg C \text{ or } \neg D)$$

and, by negating both sides,

$$\neg(C \text{ and D}) \Leftrightarrow (\neg C \text{ or } \neg D).$$

"and" and "not" ("or" and "not") are sufficient, and ...

Earlier we pointed out that "and" and "$\neg$" are sufficient to represent all other operators. We shall now prove this using de Morgan's Law.

Proof: Since "and", "or", and "$\neg$" are sufficient, we need only show that "or" can be expressed in terms of "and" and "$\neg$":

$$\neg(A \text{ or } B) \Leftrightarrow (\neg A \text{ and } \neg B) \quad \{de \text{ } Morgan's \text{ } Law\}$$
$$(A \text{ or } B) \Leftrightarrow \neg(\neg A \text{ and } \neg B) \quad \{negate \text{ } both \text{ } sides\}. \square$$

... the operator "nor" is sufficient by itself.

It turns out that the operator "nor", defined by

$$A \text{ nor } B \Leftrightarrow \neg(A \text{ or } B),$$

is sufficient by itself for representing all other operators. We leave the proof of this result to the reader as an exercise.

Equivalence is mutual implication.

Many theorems have the form

(*something is true*) iff (*something else is true*).

The proof of such a theorem is frequently simpler if it is split into two proofs exploiting the rule

$$(A \text{ iff } B) \text{ iff } (A \Rightarrow B) \text{ and } (B \Rightarrow A)$$

(prove this using the truth tables!). In order to show that $(A \Rightarrow B)$ we need not worry about what happens if A is false since $(F \Rightarrow B)$ is always true. We only need to make sure that B is always true if A is true.

Two examples

(1)   As an example consider the following proof of de Morgan's Law:

$$\neg(A \text{ or } B) \text{ iff } (\neg A \text{ and } \neg B).$$

We shall show that

$$\neg(A \text{ or } B) \Rightarrow (\neg A \text{ and } \neg B)$$

and that

$$(\neg A \text{ and } \neg B) \Rightarrow \neg(A \text{ or } B).$$

First we determine the values of A and B for which the expression $\neg(A \text{ or } B)$ is true:

$$\neg(A \text{ or } B) \Leftrightarrow T.$$

Thus $(A \text{ or } B) \Leftrightarrow F$.

Now, $(A \text{ or } B) \Leftrightarrow F$ is possible only if A and B are both false. Therefore, we obtain for the right hand side of the implication

$$(\neg F \text{ and } \neg F) \Leftrightarrow T.$$

Similarly,

$$(\neg A \text{ and } \neg B) \Leftrightarrow T$$

requires

$$\neg A \Leftrightarrow T \text{ and } \neg B \Leftrightarrow T;$$

thus

$$A \Leftrightarrow F \text{ and } B \Leftrightarrow F.$$

Therefore we obtain for the right-hand side of

$$(\neg A \text{ and } \neg B) \Rightarrow \neg(A \text{ or } B)$$
$$\neg(F \text{ or } F) \Leftrightarrow T. \ \square$$

(2)   In order to see that this method of splitting proofs works equally well for theorems dealing with other types of objects, for example, numbers, we shall now prove that: The product of two integer numbers x and y is odd if and only if x is odd and y is odd.

We rewrite the theorem to make it look more like a logical expression:

$$(x * y \text{ is odd}) \text{ iff } (x \text{ is odd}) \text{ and } (y \text{ is odd})$$

Proof:
(i)

$$(x \text{ is odd}) \text{ and } (y \text{ is odd}) \Rightarrow (x * y \text{ is odd})$$
$$(x \text{ is odd}) \text{ means } x = 2*i + 1 \text{ for some } i,$$

and

$$(y \text{ is odd}) \text{ means } y = 2*j + 1 \text{ for some } j.$$

Thus,

$$x * y = 4*i*j + 2*i + 2*j + 1$$
$$= 2*(2*i*j + i + j) + 1,$$

which is odd.

(ii)

$$(x * y \text{ is odd}) \Rightarrow (x \text{ is odd}) \text{ and } (y \text{ is odd})$$

that is,

$$((x * y) = 2*k + 1) \Rightarrow$$
$$(x = 2*i + 1) \text{ and } (y = 2*j + 1)$$

At first sight, this seems to be difficult to establish. However, if we agree that $(x \text{ is odd}) \Leftrightarrow \neg (x \text{ is even})$ and that $(x \text{ is even}) \Leftrightarrow (x = 2*i, \text{ for some } i)$, then we can transform the above expression into one that is easy to verify. We use the rule 2.13 and write.

$$\neg (x \text{ is odd and } y \text{ is odd}) \Rightarrow \neg (x * y \text{ is odd})$$

Hence, by de Morgan's Law,

$$\neg (x \text{ is odd}) \text{ or} \neg (y \text{ is odd}) \Rightarrow (x * y \text{ is even})$$

or

$$(x \text{ is even}) \text{ or } (y \text{ is even}) \Rightarrow (x * y \text{ is even})$$

Now suppose that $x = 2*i$ (or $y = 2*j$). Then

$$x * y = 2*(i * y) \text{ or } x * y = 2*(x * j), \text{ which are even.} \quad \square$$

2.2   SETS

An object is rarely of interest just by itself. Most objects become interesting when they are viewed as members of a class or a set. For example, it is unthinkable that there be only a single number, a single letter, word, name, sentence or color. Hence, it does not come as a surprise that the concept of a set is of fundamental importance.

In set theory,
set and *element* are
primitive notions.

       The basic notions of set theory are *sets* and *elements*. Intuitively, we think of a set as a collection of elements (also called *members* or *points*). This is not a (technical) definition of the concept *set*. Such a definition would have to describe sets in terms of more elementary concepts. Clearly, the term "collection" is not any simpler than the term *set*. Since there are no simpler (mathematical) concepts that can be used to explain the concept of a set, *set* is taken as an elementary ("primitive") concept that neither can nor need be defined. The same is true for the term *element*.

       The elements of a set can be any kind of objects, real or imaginary. Obviously, the assertion "x is a member of X", formally written as

$$x \in X \text{ or } x \text{ in } X,$$

is a proposition; it can be either true or false.

A set is defined by
defining its members.

While we cannot define the concept 'set', we can and must precisely define specific sets that we want to use as mathematical objects. For the purpose of this book we consider a specific set X to be defined if, for any object x, the proposition $x \in X$ is defined.

We can define finite sets by listing their members. Customarily, the list is enclosed in braces. For example,

$$X = \{0, 2, 4, 8\}$$

indicates that '0 in X' is taken to be true while '1 in X' and '12 in X' are taken to be false. An alternative way of defining sets specifies a condition that depends on an object as a parameter. An object x is considered to be a member of the set if and only if the condition is true for x. With this method, the above set of even numbers between zero and eight may be specified as follows:

$$X = \{x \mid x \text{ is an even number and } 0 \leq x < 10\}$$

Here X is said to be the set of objects x where x is an even number and greater than or equal to zero and less than ten. With this method, we can also define sets with infinitely many members (infinite sets, for short). For example,

$$X = \{x \mid x \text{ is an even number}\}.$$

Two sets are equal
if they have the same
members.

Two sets are equal if they have the same elements. Formally, we define equality by the expression

$$(X = Y) \text{ iff (for all } x, (x \text{ in } X) \Leftrightarrow (x \text{ in } Y))$$

This definition looks rather obvious and simple. But it has some important consequences as the following examples demonstrate:

$$\{1, 2, 3\} = \{3, 1, 2\}$$

(the order in which elements are listed does not matter),

$$\{1, 2, 3\} = \{1, 1, 2, 3, 3, 1\} = \{1, 2, 2, 3\}$$

(listing the same element repeatedly does not alter the set). The reader is encouraged to apply the definition of equality to the last example in order to understand that it is the definition of equality that ensures that only distinct elements matter.

2.2.1   Operators on sets

From two given sets, a
new set can be formed
by set union ...

There are a number of operators that permit the construction of new sets from given ones. One of these operators is *set union*. The union of two sets X and Y contains all members of X and of Y; formally

$$X \cup Y = \{x \mid (x \text{ in } X) \text{ or } (x \text{ in } Y)\}$$

... and intersection.

The *intersection* of two sets contains only those elements that are members of both X and Y; formally

$$X \cap Y = \{x \mid (x \text{ in } X) \text{ and } (x \text{ in } Y)\}$$

A set may include another set as a subset.

We say that a set Y is a *subset* of a set X if all elements of Y are also elements of X; formally

$$Y \subseteq X \text{ iff for all } x, (x \text{ in } Y) \Rightarrow (x \text{ in } X).$$

The empty set is a subset of every set.

A special set is the set that does not contain any elements. This is called the *empty set* and is denoted by $\{\}$ or $\emptyset$. The proposition

$$x \text{ in } \{\}$$

is false for all values of x. The empty set is a subset of every set. Notice that this follows formally from the definition of a subset:

$$\{\} \subseteq X \text{ iff for all } x, (x \text{ in } \{\}) \Rightarrow (x \text{ in } X)$$

Since $(x \text{ in } \{\})$ is false for all values of x, the implication is always true independently of whether $(x \text{ in } X)$ is true or false.

The powerset is the set of all subsets of a set.

Sometimes we need to specify the set of all subsets of some given set U. This set is called the *powerset* of U and is denoted by $P(U)$. For example,

$$P(\{1,2,3\}) = \{\{1,2,3\}, \{1,2\}, \{1,3\}, \{2,3\}, \{1\}, \{2\}, \{3\}, \{\} \}.$$

A proper subset of a set X is not equal to X nor is it empty.
Equality is proved by mutual set inclusion.

A set Y is called a *proper subset* of X if it is a subset different from X and is not empty.

Earlier we pointed out that the equivalence of two logical expressions can be proved by showing mutual implication. Similarly, the equality of two sets can be demonstrated by showing mutual inclusion. Formally,

$$X = Y \text{ iff } X \subseteq Y \text{ and } Y \subseteq X.$$

A universal set contains all objects of interest.

Frequently, we limit the members of sets that we wish to consider by first defining a universal set U. For example, when investigating integer numbers we might restrict our objects to the integers or, in the context of programming languages, we may restrict our objects to character strings that can be formed from some given set of characters. All other sets must then be subsets of the set U.

Complementation is a unary set operator.

If a universal set exists we can define the *complement* of a set X, denoted by $\neg X$, as the set of all elements in U that are not in X. Thus,

$$\neg X = \{x \mid x \text{ in } U \text{ and} \neg (x \text{ in } X)\}$$

2.2.2 Ordered pairs

Ordered pairs ...

We have seen that two sets are equal if they have the same elements. From this we concluded that an element does not occupy a special position in the set; that is, the order of the elements does not matter. Consequently, it does not make sense to ask, for example, for the "first member" of a set. Now we consider ordered pairs, denoted by (a,b), which are constructs of two elements where the order matters. This is expressed by the definition of equality for ordered pairs:

$$(a,b) = (a',b') \text{ iff } a = a' \text{ and } b = b'$$

Here it makes good sense to call "a" the first and "b" the second member of the pair (a,b). A common example of ordered pairs are the pairs of coordinates used to specify points in a plane. Clearly, (2,5) specifies a different point from (5,2).

... are the members of the cartesian product.

Frequently, we wish to specify the set of all ordered pairs formed from given sets A and B such that the first element of each pair is taken from A and the second from B. This set is called the *cartesian product* of A and B; it is defined as

$$A \times B = \{(a,b) \mid a \in A \text{ and } b \in B\}$$

For example, the points in a plane form the set

$$R \times R \text{ where } R \text{ is the set of all real numbers.}$$

If, in $A \times B$, the set A has n and the set B has m elements, respectively, then the number of elements (ordered pairs) in $A \times B$ is $n*m$.

n-tuples are a generalization of ordered pairs.

It is useful to extend the concept of the "ordered pair" to ordered triples, quadruples, and, in general, to so-called n-tuples.

We obtain triples from ordered pairs $(a,(b,c))$ if we do not care about the inner parentheses and consider the ordered pairs $(a,(b,c))$ and $((a,b),c)$ to be equivalent. Thus, we might as well write (a,b,c) instead. Consequently, the cartesian products

$$A \times (B \times C) \text{ and } (A \times B) \times C$$

produce the same set of ordered triples; thus we consider the cartesian product to be associative, that is to say, we consider

$$A \times (B \times C), (A \times B) \times C, \text{ and } A \times B \times C$$

to be equivalent. Quadruples are derived analogously from pairs of the form $(a,(b,(c,d)))$.

2.2.3   Sets, n-tuples and Pascal

In Pascal, sets occur as types and as objects.

In Pascal, sets occur in two fundamentally different forms:

(1) as data types, and
(2) as data objects.

Types are built-in, such
as integer or real, or
are ...
(1) A data type represents the set of objects considered to be members of the type. For example *integer* denotes the set of those integer numbers that are available to the user. The definition of this subset is not a part of the Pascal language but depends on the particular implementation. We say that the Pascal type *integer* approximates the set of integer numbers.

Similarly, *real* denotes an (implementation dependent) subset of the real numbers.

Although, in Pascal, the terms *integer* and *real* refer to approximations of the sets of integer and real numbers, we shall use these words as names for the complete sets unless we refer specifically to a programming context.

Other simple types are *char* and *boolean*.

... user-defined.
Pascal also permits us to define new types as finite sets of identifiers, for example,

type *grade* = (*pass*, *fail*)

With enumeration
types, the user not only
defines a set ...
The identifiers *pass* and *fail* are the constants of the type.

NOTE: Worries about whether the identifiers *are* the constants of the type or whether they *denote* the constants are unwarranted. If a Pascal manual tells us that the identifiers, indeed, *were* the constants of the type, we had no way of disproving this claim. Since there is a different identifier for every constant and vice versa (such a relationship is called a "bijection" as we shall learn in 2.3.2), the identification of identifiers with constants is legitimate.

Thus, *grade* = (*pass*, *fail*) seems to correspond to the mathematical definition

$$grade = \{ pass, fail \}$$

However, there is a difference. While {*pass*, *fail*} and {*fail*, *pass*} are equivalent,

$$grade = (pass, fail) \text{ and } grade = (fail, pass)$$

are not. The reason is that the definition

$$grade = (pass, fail)$$

... but also an ordering.
defines not only the set {*pass*, *fail*} but also an ordering of the objects *pass* and *fail*. This ordering affects certain relational operators, for example, "<", which can be read as *precedes* (in the definition). Thus, for the type (*pass*,*fail*) the expression

$$pass < fail$$

is **true**, whereas for the type (*fail*,*pass*) it is **false**. More generally,

type $T1 = (a_1, a_2, ..., a_n)$

and

type $T2 = (b_1, b_2, ..., b_n)$

where the sequence of the b_i is a permutation of the sequence of the a_i, define the same sets but they define different orderings among the elements of the sets.

The **record** definition is Pascal's version of the cartesian product.

Pascal also provides a way to specify a type as the cartesian product of two or more sets. This is accomplished by the **record** construct: for example,

type *point* = **record** x: *real*; y:*real* **end**

corresponds to the mathematical definition

point = *real* $\times$ *real*

with the additional property that, in each actual pair, the first component (x-coordinate) can be accessed by the identifier x and the second by y.

Set objects are subsets of user-defined universal sets.

(2) Objects that are sets occur as members of so-called *set types*. A set type is constructed from a *base type*. The base type furnishes the universal set of which all members of the set type are subsets. In other words, the type is the powerset of the base type.

Two examples

For example, the set type

type $s123$ = **set of** $1..3$

specifies the set $\{1,2,3\}$ as the base type of $s123$. The members of the type $s123$ are the elements of the powerset P($\{1,2,3\}$).

Consider also

type *tone* = (c,d,e,f,g,a,b,cc);
    chord = **set of** *tone*

All subsets of the type *tone* may be used as objects, may be assigned to variables, and may be combined using set operators. For example,

var *HARMONY, CACOPHONY*: *chord*;

    HARMONY := $[e,a,cc]$;
    CACOPHONY := $[e,f,b,cc]$;
    HARMONY := *HARMONY* $*$ *CACOPHONY* { $*$ *is intersection*};
    if *a* **in** *HARMONY*
        then *writeln*('*intersection does not work*');

Here the Pascal notation $[e,a,cc]$ corresponds exactly to the mathematical notation $\{e,a,cc\}$: the order of the elements does not matter.

2.3 **FUNCTIONS**

A function associates points of its domain with points of its codomain.

A function expresses a relationship between two sets, called the domain and the codomain. It associates with each element of the domain exactly one element of the codomain. We indicate that a function *"f"* has domain *A* and codomain *B* by

$$f: A \rightarrow B$$

Examples:

sin: *real* → *real*
trunc: *real* → *integer*
chr: 1..128 → *char*

Functions may have more complex domains and/or codomains. Consider the function that gives the distance between two points in the Euclidean plane:

distance: *point* × *point* → *real*.

2.3.1   Revisited: levels of concern

We said earlier that a point in the Euclidean plane is itself represented by an ordered pair of real numbers. Should we therefore not define the distance function by

distance: (*real* × *real*) × (*real* × *real*) → *real* ?

Objects and their representations should not needlessly be identified.

Indeed, we might. But let us take this opportunity to stray a little from our present subject and think about our basic theme: levels of concern. Why do levels of concern enter into the definition of the distance function? Because by (*real* × *real*), we refer to a representation of points (as pairs of numbers) and not simply to points. Such a (casual) identification of an object with its representation is justified only if there is exactly one possible representation. If there are several representations, then we must carefully ponder which one to choose; however, the actual choice does not concern us while we are thinking about the objects represented. These details only add unwanted complexity to the problem. Hence, the actual representation of objects should be considered elsewhere.

It is obvious that the representation of points is not unique. Besides cartesian coordinates, there are, for example, oblique coordinates, polar coordinates, rectilinear coordinates and curvilinear coordinates (the definitions of these types of coordinates are found in any college text book on coordinate geometry). On the other hand, the concept of the distance between two points is clearly independent of the way in which the points are represented. The distance that I measure with a ruler between two points on a map, for example, depends on where the points are, not on *how* I tell where the points are! Good, you may think, but if I visualize the distance function as determined by an algorithm, the representation of the points must be known because the method for computing the distance depends upon it. This is, of course, true. But, while the algorithm for computing the distance depends on the method of representation, the outcome depends only on the (position of the) points, and when we are worried about distances we neither need to know nor wish to be bothered with how that distance is computed or how the points are specified; the two concerns are on different levels.

Points in a plane can be represented by more than two numbers ...

While we are on the subject, we may discuss briefly whether points in a plane are always specified by two real numbers. We may be led to this conclusion since all coordinate systems listed above require two numbers for the definition of a point. But consider the following specification; suppose that at the margin of a map of some district you find the description: "On highway 16, one mile north of the junction of highway 16 and 29, there is a plaque commemorating the battle *XYZ*".

... or by single real numbers.

So, some descriptional methods seem to need more than two numbers, but is it possible to specify a point by only one real number? Yes, indeed! Here is one of many possible ways: let *ABC.DEFGXXX...* represent the *x*-coordinate and *a.bcedxxx...* the *y*-coordinate of a point. The single number,

A0B0Ca.DbEcFeGdXxXxXx...

constructed by interleaving the digits of the two coordinates uniquely specifies the point. If we wish to specify points in any of the four quadrants, we simply need to prefix the representation of the number with 1, 2, 3, or 4 depending upon which quadrant is appropriate.

2.3.2   The four simple classes of functions

We now return to our discussion of functions. There are two important properties that a function may or may not have: A function may be *surjective* and/or *injective*. These two properties may be used to group functions into four natural classes, since some functions have both properties, some have either one or the other, and some have neither.

A surjective function ...

Surjections   While we know that a function must be defined for each value of its domain, we do not know, in general, whether *every* value of the codomain is "used", that is, whether each of its values is associated with some domain value. If this is the case, then we call the function surjective. Figure 2.1 shows two examples of surjective functions.

NOTE: While in Western languages text is scanned from left to right, the procession from argument (domain value) to function symbol to image (codomain value) in conventional mathematical notation goes from right to left. In order to have our figures coincide with this mathematical convention, we draw the domain to the right of the codomain having the arrows that describe the mapping go from right to left. As a result, a function *f* that is the right (left) inverse of a function *g* occurs to the right (left) of *g* in both the formal notation and the figure.

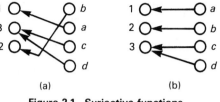

(a)   (b)

Figure 2.1   Surjective functions

The two functions in the figure are in fact equal. Version (b) has been produced from (a) by permutating the order of the elements in the domain and codomain. Since this order, as we know, is immaterial, we may as well choose the one in which the arrows go straight, namely (b).

... has a right inverse, ...   If a function f is surjective, then we can find another function g whose effect is 'undone' by f. More precisely,

> For a function $\quad\quad\quad\quad\quad$ $f: A \rightarrow B$
> there is (at least) one function $\;$ $g: B \rightarrow A$
> such that for all y in B $\quad\quad$ $y = f(g(y))$
> iff f is surjective.

Figure 2.2 illustrates this fact.

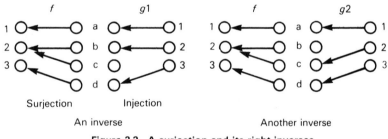

Surjection   Injection

An inverse   Another inverse

Figure 2.2   A surjection and its right inverses

The functions $g1$ and $g2$ are called right inverse functions or simply *right inverses* of f.

... an injective function has a left inverse.   *Injections*   There is no rule that forbids the association of the same value in the codomain with several values of the domain. For example, $y = x*x$ associates the y-value (codomain value) of 1 with the domain values 1 and −1. Functions that always associate *different* values of their codomain with *different* values of their domain are called injective. The functions $g1$ and $g2$ in Figure 2.2 are examples of injections. Injective functions have *left inverses*:

> For a function $\quad\quad\quad\quad\quad$ $f: A \rightarrow B$
> there is (at least) one function $\;$ $g: B \rightarrow A$
> such that for all x in A $\quad\quad$ $x = g(f(x))$
> iff f is injective.

Consequently, the right inverse of a surjective function must be injective and the left inverse of an injective function must be surjective. In other words, if

$$h1(h2(x)) = x, \text{ for all } x,$$

then $h1$ is surjective and $h2$ is injective.

This may seem a little confusing and difficult but the basic idea is very simple (some say disappointingly simple). Contemplate Figure 2.2 again for a moment to convince yourself.

Obviously, functions that are both surjective and injective have both a left and a right inverse. Not quite so obviously, the left inverse and the right inverse are the same function; this function is called an *inverse*. If g is the inverse of an injective and surjective function f, then, clearly, f is also the inverse of g.

A function that is both surjective and injective is called bijective.

Functions that are both surjective and injective are called bijective. Figure 2.3 illustrates a bijective function and its inverse.

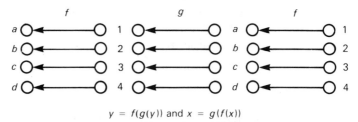

$$y = f(g(y)) \text{ and } x = g(f(x))$$

Figure 2.3   A bijective function and its inverse

Examples

As examples of bijections consider the conversion from decimal numerals to binary numerals or the table that associates characters with Morse codes.

Many modern computers encode characters as strings of eight bits. Since there are fewer than 256 (2^8) legal key combinations for most (ASCII) keyboards, the function (fk) that associates key strokes with binary codes cannot be a bijection. Similarly, the association (fp) between these binary codes and the graphic symbols displayed at the terminal or on the printer cannot be a bijection either. We may expect that the first function is an injection and the second a surjection. If we further assume that the printer can display exactly those symbols that can be specified on the keyboard, then there is a bijection between the legal key strokes and the graphic symbols, and fp is the left inverse of fk.

These concepts are important because they help us to organize our thoughts by providing names for simple but important relationships. For example, we can easily see that we need an injection from a set A to a set B if we want to use the set B to represent the elements of set A. If the function that associates elements from A with those from B is not injective, then we lose information and cannot always recover the element in A from the one in B. These problems occur frequently. Consider, for example, a representation of points in a plane by (single) real numbers, or a representation of dates by integers!

2.3.3   Selectors and field identifiers

Selectors map
n-tuples to their
components.

There is a group of functions that is associated with *n*-tuples, whose members are called *selectors*. Selectors map *n*-tuples to their components; hence, there are *n* different selectors associated with each type of *n*-tuple. For pairs, they are frequently called *first* and *secnd*; for *n*-tuples in general, they may be called $s_1, s_2, ..., s_n$, where the subscript determines the position of the selected value in the tuple. Thus we have for pairs

$$first: \ U \times U \rightarrow U, \text{ with } first \ ((a,b)) = a,$$
$$secnd: U \times U \rightarrow U, \text{ with } secnd((a,b)) = b,$$
$$s_i : U \times U \times ... \times U \rightarrow U \ \{n \text{ factors and } 0 < i \leq n\}$$
$$\text{with } s_i((a_1, ..., a_i, ..., a_n)) = a_i$$

Pascal's notation
for selectors differs
from the mathematical
notation.

While mathematicians commonly use selectors with the functional notation given above, as in

$$first(P) \text{ or } s_3(T),$$

where *P* is an ordered pair and *T* some tuple with more than two elements, their use in Pascal is different. Recall that in Pascal a tuple is defined by means of the record construct, for example

$TUPL = $ **record** *a:type1; ...; z:type9* **end**.

Now, with

var *R:TUPL*,

we access the components of *R* by

R.a, ..., R.z   rather than by
a(R), ..., z(R)

Selectors, such as *a ... z* in our example, are called *field identifiers* in Pascal.

2.3.4   Predicates and quantifiers

Predicates ...

Functions having the codomain {*true, false*} are frequently called *predicates*. An example is the set-membership function

in: elements $\times$ *sets* $\rightarrow$ {*true, false*}.

The definition of the domain in this example is rather vague and is therefore often not very useful. For the set of all elements, anything would qualify, and for the set of all sets, any set would qualify. However, with a universal set U from which all other sets are constructed as subsets, we may write

in: $U \times P(U) \rightarrow \{true, false\}$.

This, now, is a perfectly precise definition (recall that $P(U)$, the powerset of U, is the set of all subsets of U).

The *in*-predicate is usually written as an infix operator (see section 2.2 on sets):

instead of "$in(x, X)$" we write "x in X".

As additional examples, consider

greater: $int \times int \rightarrow \{true, false\}$

or

$S: int \rightarrow \{true, false\}$

with

$$S(n) \Leftrightarrow (\sum_{i=1}^{n} (i) = n(n+1)/2).$$

Clearly, a predicate applied to some argument is a proposition that can be treated using the methods of the propositional calculus.

Frequently, we are interested in expressions of the form

for all n in *integer*, $n \geq 0 \Rightarrow SQRT(n*n) = n$

or

for some n in *integer*, $3*n = -6$.

... and quantifiers.

The phrases "for all" and "for some" are mathematical operators called *quantifiers*. A more modern notation, which we will adopt in this book, separates the quantifier from the predicate by a period rather than by a comma. The scope of a quantifier is the complete expression to its right unless parentheses are used to override this rule. The following two examples illustrate these conventions

for all x in *real*. $x*x \geq 0$,
(for some n in N. $a*n > 0$) $\Rightarrow$ ($a = 0$).

If quantifiers are used with finite sets, such as $\{1,2,3\}$, they can be replaced by simple logical expressions involving "and" and "or" operators. For example,

for all n in $\{1,2,3\}$. $n*n < 10$

can be written as

$(1*1 < 10)$ and $(2*2 < 10)$ and $(3*3 < 10)$,

or

for some n in $\{1,3,5\}$. $(n-3) = 2$

becomes

$(1-3 = 2)$ or $(3-3 = 2)$ or $(5-3 = 2)$.

Because of the relationship of "for all" with "and" and "for some" with "or", it is not very surprising that there is a generalization of de Morgan's Law for quantifiers which holds for all predicates Q:

(for all x in X. $Q(x)$) iff $\neg$(for some x in X. $\neg Q(x)$)

and

(for some x in X. $Q(x)$) iff $\neg$(for all x in X. $\neg Q(x)$).

For our purposes, the above rules for predicates and quantifiers are sufficient. However, there are many more; the discipline that deals with predicates and quantifiers in depth is called the *predicate calculus*.

2.4 NATURAL NUMBERS AND MATHEMATICAL INDUCTION

In this section, we shall discuss the natural numbers, which we interpret to be the non-negative integer numbers. One of our goals is to find a precise definition that describes the fundamental properties of these numbers.

There is hardly another mathematical concept for which we have as good an intuitive understanding as for the natural numbers. We know that the activity of counting is inseparably linked with them, that addition is based on counting and multiplication on addition. Why then should we bother and try to find a mathematical definition for what the natural numbers are? Would that not be an idle exercise in pedantry rather than something of practical use? By no means!

2.4.1 Nature and purpose of formal definitions

Formal definitions detach mathematical concepts ...

We divide our justification into two parts. The first, (a), addresses the general question of what mathematical definitions are and why we need them, and the second, (b), explains why we wish to deal with the natural numbers in particular.

... from the pitfalls of our intuition.

(a) A simple example of a mathematical definition is the truth table for, say, the "and" operator. It replaces our intuition of what the operator does by simple statements that can be recorded in a table and applied mechanically.

Intuition supplies ideas that are verified by formal proofs.

By introducing these statements or rules, we do not abandon intuitive reasoning altogether. This would be a mistake since our intuition frequently shows us ways or results at a glance whereas a formal derivation would be so tedious and boring that we might give up before reaching our goal. Unfortunately, the products of these shortcuts must be treated with great caution, for experience teaches that they are rather unreliable. This is where formal methods come to the rescue. After having developed a good intuitive idea of the method or result, we go back and try to verify our informal thoughts by means of a formal derivation. If this derivation establishes the truth of an assertion, it is called a *formal proof.*

Summarizing, we state that a mathematical definition of an object condenses our understanding of the object into a number of simple assertions. Frequently, these assertions are called *axioms* or *postulates.* Proofs involving the object do not refer to our intuitive understanding of the object but only to these assertions, that is, to the (mathematical) definition of the object.

It is obvious that the assertions must capture completely our understanding of the object. Otherwise, later proofs may say something about the object defined but not about the object we had in mind. However, there can never be a proof that a definition is correct in this sense. No scientific method can incorporate a mind-reading facility! But there are criteria that a definition must meet in order to define something (an empty and, thus, useless definition is, for example, "a coin is a flat object shaped like a circular square"). These criteria are:

Consistency

Definitions must be consistent ...

A definition must be consistent. That is, it must not contain a contradiction. For example, if the truth table for "and" should contain the line "*true* and *false is true*" as well as "*true* and *false is false*", then the definition would clearly be inconsistent.

Completeness

... and should be as complete as necessary.

The second property that we expect of a definition is that it should describe the object *completely.* This means that all properties that the object has should either be mentioned in the definition or be derivable from the definition. It turns out that, for many objects, complete definitions are impossible. Hence we must be content with something less. In any particular case we specify what we expect from the definition, and we call the definition *sufficiently complete* if it meets our expectations.

Reasoning with natural numbers is often needed, ...

(b) There are two reasons why we are particularly concerned with the natural numbers.

(i) The natural numbers occur frequently in computer science. Consequently, we must be able to reason about them. In particular, we often meet statements of the form "for all natural numbers, *XYZ* is true". To verify such a statement we need to use one of the assertions (axioms) that make up the definition of the natural numbers: the axiom of mathematical induction.

... and the natural
numbers is a simple
system to study.

(ii) The definition of the natural numbers is simpler than the sort of definitions that we will need later for the specification of data types. Thus we choose the natural numbers as an example in order to study the development and use of axiomatic definitions.

2.4.2   An axiomatic definition of the natural numbers

Let us now try to find axioms that describe the natural numbers.

The set of the
natural numbers ...

First we observe that the natural numbers form a set. It is also clear that we cannot define this set simply by enumerating all of its elements; that would take too much paper. Further, numbers have more interesting properties than merely that they form a set! Our intuition of natural numbers is not founded on a knowledge of all of the numbers but on the confidence that, given any number, we can find the next one. It is important that, for a given number, there is exactly *one* next number. Otherwise counting would not be what it is. We therefore begin by stating that there is a specific number, namely zero, in the set of natural numbers, and that, given any number, we can find *the* next number. The latter simply implies that there is a function from natural numbers to natural numbers which, when applied to a number, gives the successor of that number.

... contains zero and, for
each of its members, a
successor.

We shall summarize these remarks as propositions using the notation introduced earlier:

Let N be the set of all natural numbers.

$$0 \text{ in } N \tag{1}$$
$$SUCC: N \rightarrow N \tag{2}$$

This is certainly not enough to constitute a definition of the natural numbers. We can easily find many functions that do not have the properties that we feel $SUCC$ should have. Just consider the function where $SUCC(0) = 0$! This seems to be easy to correct. We observe that the sequence of natural numbers begins with zero; hence zero cannot be the successor of any number. We state

Zero is not a successor,
and ...

$$\text{for all } n \text{ in } N. \neg (SUCC(n) = 0) \tag{3}$$

This axiom, unfortunately, still does not prevent, for example, the possibility that $SUCC(1) = 1$, a false proposition! We obviously want "one" to be the successor of "zero" and of nothing else. Perhaps it suffices to state, that every number is the successor of not more than one other number. We can state this by requiring that $SUCC$ be an injection. Thus, we change (2) to read

... the successor
function is an injection.

$$\text{there is an injection } SUCC: N \rightarrow N. \tag{2a}$$

Now it seems to work. N contains 0, $SUCC(0)$, $SUCC(SUCC(0))$, and so forth. Note that with every new application of $SUCC$ we get a new element since all "old" elements except zero are already successors of other numbers. Remember that, since $SUCC$ is an injection, a number can be the successor of at most one number, and (by axiom 3) zero cannot be a successor of any number.

But look at Figure 2.4! Although our axioms seem to ensure that, starting with zero, we reach a new number with every application of *SUCC*, there are elements in the set shown that we will never encounter by way of the successor function if we start with zero, no matter how often we apply it. Clearly, we need additional restrictions on *SUCC*.

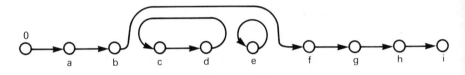

Figure 2.4   A set described by axioms (1) — (3)

All numbers can
be reached from zero
by repeated use of the
successor function.

We can solve this last problem with one more axiom. This axiom, which basically states that every natural number can be reached by a repeated application of *SUCC* beginning with zero, is most important. It is called the axiom of mathematical induction and may be stated as follows:

This is the basis
of mathematical
induction

for all $A \subseteq N$.
$$((0 \text{ in } A) \text{ and}$$
$$\text{for all } n \text{ in } N. (n \text{ in } A \Rightarrow SUCC(n) \text{ in } A)) \Rightarrow (A = N) \qquad (4)$$

In other words, suppose that a subset A of N contains (*i*) 0 and (*ii*) for each of its members it also contains a successor, then A contains all natural numbers. This axiom guarantees, that the self-contained islands as, for example, the elements *c*, *d*, and *e* in Figure 2.4 do not exist.

Because of its importance, we must spend a little more time with the formal version of axiom (4) in order to make sure that we understand it as well as the other three axioms. Consider a set A that (*i*) contains 0 and (*ii*) for which the assertion

if n in A then $SUCC(n)$ in A

is true for all values of n in N. Note in particular, that no claim is made that n or $SUCC(n)$ is, in fact, in A!

Why do these two conditions imply that all natural numbers are in A? Well, the first condition asserts that 0 is in A. The second condition, since it is true for all n in N, says, for example, that "if 0 is in A then $SUCC(0)$ is in A". Hence, since 0 is, in fact, in A, $SUCC(0)$, *i.e.* 1, is in A. Furthermore, since it is true for all n, the second condition states "if $SUCC(0)$ is in A, then $SUCC(SUCC(0))$ is in A", and so on.

If we wish to use this axiom for proving that some set contains all natural numbers, we need to show that

(i)   0 is in the set

(this part of the proof is called "establishing the *base case*").

(ii) n in the set implies $SUCC(n)$ in the set

(this is called the *inductive step*).

Since implication is false only if its left side is true but its right side is false, the second part is always established by assuming that the left side is true and proving, under this assumption, that the right side is true as well. The assumption that the left hand side is true is called the *induction hypothesis*. We shall discuss examples of this proof method very shortly.

The four postulates for the natural numbers were formulated by the Italian mathematician Peano (pronounced Pay-ahno) in the 1880s.

We list them once more together for reference.

The set N of the natural numbers is defined as follows:

0 in N (1)

There is an injection $SUCC: N \to N$ (2)

For all n in N. $\neg(SUCC(n) = 0)$ (3)

For all sets $A \subseteq N$.   (4)

$\quad$ ((0 in A) and

$\qquad$ for all n in N. $(n$ in $A \Rightarrow SUCC(n)$ in $A)) \Rightarrow (A = N)$

SUCC(a) = a'. We may add here that instead of writing $SUCC(a)$ we will, in general, write a'. Thus, the first three natural numbers are 0, 0', 0''. We are not too concerned about the proper names of numbers. We may use "one, two, three", or 1, 2, 3 or I, II, III, or "eins, zwei, drei", or 0', 0'', 0'''. (Each of these denotations uniquely refers to the numbers 1, 2, 3, and that is all that matters.)

In the following discussion, we will pretend that axioms (1) – (4) constitute our complete knowledge of the natural numbers. We will not use any previous experience that we may have concerning addition, multiplication or any other operation since we want to derive all (well-known) facts from these four axioms. We begin by defining the operator of addition.

Addition is based on SUCC. For all natural numbers a and b,

$$a + 0 = a, \tag{5}$$

and

$$a + b' = (a + b)'. \tag{6}$$

If this definition is supposed to describe addition, then it should be possible to determine the value of, for example 4 + 3, that is in our notation,

$\quad 0'''' + 0'''$

By (6)

$\quad 0'''' + 0''' \quad = (0'''' + 0'')'$

$\qquad\qquad\qquad = ((0'''' + 0')')'$

$\qquad\qquad\qquad = (((0'''' + 0)')')'$

and by (5)
$$= (((0''''')')')'$$

We then remove the parentheses and obtain $0'''''''$.

$SUCC(a) = a + 1$

With addition defined, we can, using our axioms, derive that

$$SUCC(a) = a + 1 \text{ or } a' = a + 0'$$
$$a + 0' = (a + 0)' \quad \text{by (6)}$$
$$= (a)' \qquad \text{by (5)}$$
$$= a'$$

Proving that addition is commutative ...

We now tackle a more challenging problem. We wish to show that

for all a, b in $N.\ a + b = b + a$ (t1)

We consider this problem because we want to give an example of a rigorous proof and demonstrate the use of mathematical induction. We use induction by constructing the set of all numbers b, for which our theorem holds using an arbitrary number for a. First we show that 0 is in that set. Thus we claim

$$a + 0 = 0 + a$$

This reduces easily, by (5), to

$$a = 0 + a$$

... appears to be nontrivial if ...

But what can we do with this? Not much with what we currently know. This might seem difficult to accept. Although we know that $a + 0 = a$, we hesitate to conclude that $0 + a = a$ also. Clearly, we cannot seriously doubt that $0 + a = a$. Why then do we act as if we did?

... we stick to the rules of the game.

The reason is that we are playing a game, and the rules of the game are given by the axioms (1) – (6). In this game, a move consists of stating a new assertion, and such a move is only legal if it can be justified by any or all of the rules (1) – (6).

As long as the assertions are simple and familiar, we may feel like fools who worry, without cause, about the truth of the obvious. But we should look at these simple problems as a training ground whose purpose it is to make us comfortable with the technique. The time will come when we face statements (such as "this program computes *XYZ*") whose correctness is not obvious at all, and our present play is a preparation for the work that we will have to do then.

Less irritated and more playful, we return to the previous question of what we can do with the statement

$$a = 0 + a$$

The only thing that we can do, is to look at this as a new theorem that needs to be proved first. Formally it reads,

for all a in $N.\ a = 0 + a$ (t2)

We therefore decide to try the induction axiom again, this time collecting into a set A all values of "a" for which (t2) is true. Thus,

a in A iff $a = 0 + a$

We need to show that

$0 = 0 + 0$ {0 in A} $\qquad$ (i)

and,

for all n in N, $\qquad$ (ii)
$n = 0 + n \Rightarrow n' = 0 + n'$ {n in $A \Rightarrow n'$ in A}.

To test whether 0 is in the set, we note that

$0 = 0 + 0 = 0$ by (5)

So, (i) is true, 0 is in the set. Now we need to show (derive from the axioms) that for all values of n

$(n = 0 + n) \Rightarrow (n' = 0 + n')$.

But this is not difficult:

$n = 0 + n$
$\Rightarrow n' = (0 + n)'$ {*succ of both sides, by* (2)}
and $n' = (0 + n)' \Rightarrow n' = 0 + n'$ {*by* (6)}

Since implication is transitive, that is to say, since

if $(a \Rightarrow b)$ and $(b \Rightarrow c)$ then $(a \Rightarrow c)$

we may conclude from the above sequence of implications that

$(n = 0 + n) \Rightarrow (n' = 0 + n')$,

which establishes (ii). Let us return now to theorem (t1). So far we have established the base case

$a + 0 = 0 + a$.

It remains to be shown that

$(a + b) = (b + a) \Rightarrow (a + b') = (b' + a)$.

Following the now familiar pattern, we obtain

$(a + b) = (b + a)$ {*induction hypothesis*}
$\Rightarrow (a + b)' = (b + a)'$ {*succ on both sides*}
and $(a + b)' = (b + d)' \Rightarrow a + b' = b + a'$ {*by* (6)}

Again we seem to be stuck. In order to show that

$a + b' = b + a' \Rightarrow a + b' = b' + a$

we need a result that does not follow directly from the axioms, namely

$b + a' = b' + a$.

As before, we take this as a new theorem that needs to be proved. Again we need induction (*over a*) to prove our point:

Base case:
$$b + 0' = b' + 0$$

We show this by inferring that P is true when (*true* $\Rightarrow$ P) is true.

$$
\begin{aligned}
(b)' &= (b)' \quad \{obviously\ true\} \\
\Rightarrow (b + 0)' &= (b)' + 0 \ \{by\ a = a + 0\ with\ a = b\ on\ the\ left\ and \\
&\qquad\qquad\qquad\qquad\qquad a = (b)'\ on\ the\ right\} \\
\text{and } (b + 0)' &= (b)' + 0 \Rightarrow b + 0' = b' + 0 \ \{by\ (6)\}
\end{aligned}
$$

Induction Hypothesis:
$$b + a' = b' + a$$

Inductive Step:
$$
\begin{aligned}
b + a' &= b' + a \\
\Rightarrow (b + a')' &= (b' + a)' \\
\text{and } (b + a)' &= (b' + a)' \Rightarrow b + a'' = b' + a' \\
\text{and } b + a'' &= b' + a' \Rightarrow b + (a')' = b' + (a'). \ \square
\end{aligned}
$$

Definition of multiplication.

While we do not intend to derive all of the arithmetic operators from our axioms, we add the definition of multiplication as one further example of such a derivation.

$$a * 0 = 0 \tag{7}$$
$$a * b' = a * b + a \tag{8}$$

Note that addition, which has been already defined, may now be used.

A generalization of the induction principle.

It frequently happens that we want to prove theorems not for all natural numbers but for, say, all even numbers or all natural numbers greater than three. For these cases the following lemma, which generalizes the induction principle, is very convenient.

Suppose we are given a set M of objects and a surjection f that maps the natural numbers onto the set M. Consider, for example, the functions

$$\mathbf{f}(n) = 2*n \quad \text{or} \quad \mathbf{g}(n) = n + 1.$$

The function **f** associates a natural number with every even number, and **g** does the same with every integer greater than zero.

Lemma:
 Let $\mathbf{f}:N \rightarrow M$ be a surjection, then
 all sets B for which
 $\mathbf{f}(0)$ in B and
 $\mathbf{f}(n)$ in B implies $\mathbf{f}(n')$ in B
 contain all members of M.

This follows directly from the induction principle. We construct a subset A of N with the property that **f** maps A onto B. Now, if $A = N$, then $B = M$ since

f is a surjection. We put 0 into A since $\mathbf{f}(0)$ is in B. Further, if, for some n, $\mathbf{f}(n)$ is in B, then we put both n and n' into A because $\mathbf{f}(n)$ in B implies $\mathbf{f}(n')$ in B. Hence, by induction, A contains all members of N, and, consequently, B contains all members of M.

As a consequence of this theorem, we may use any natural number (not only zero) as the basis of induction and we may use induction for any convenient set as long as we can demonstrate that the required surjection exists.

Two informal proofs, and ...

We conclude this section with two more proofs by induction. Both of these proofs are called informal, since they contain common sense arguments. The theorems are concerned with bit strings and permutations. If we wanted to make the proofs formal, we would need to give mathematical definitions for these objects. This would allow us to replace the common sense arguments by references to axioms.

We also assume now that we may use all arithmetic operators.

(i) ***Theorem:*** there are 2^n bit strings of length n.

Base case: n = 1

We begin induction with 1 since the case $n = 0$ is of no interest. A bit string of length 1 contains either a '0' or a '1'; hence there are $2 = 2^1$ strings, and the base case is established.

Using the induction hypothesis that there are 2^n bit strings of length n, we construct all bit strings of length $n+1$ by prefixing all strings of length n with a zero, which gives 2^n strings of length $n+1$, and with a one, which gives again 2^n (different) strings of length $n+1$. We thus obtain $2*(2^n)$, that is, $2^{(n+1)}$ strings. $\square$

(ii) ***Theorem:*** There are $n!$ many permutations of n different objects.

Again, since permuting no objects does not make much sense we start with 1 and observe that there is only 1 permutation. Since $1! = 1$, the base case is established.

Now suppose there are $n!$ many permutations for n objects and add a different $n+1$st object in all possible ways to all of the $n!$ permutations. There are clearly $n+1$ places where the new object can be put among the given n objects: in front of each object, giving n places, and behind the last one. Hence we obtain $n!*(n+1)$ many permutations of $n+1$ objects. The observation that $n!*(n+1) = (n+1)!$ completes the proof. $\square$

... one proof that fails.

We conclude the discussion of inductive proofs with an example that shows how such a proof may fail if the theorem is not true. We shall attempt to prove that

for all $n \geq 1$, $2*n = 2^n$
Base case: $n = 1 \Rightarrow 2*1 = 2^1 = 2$
Induction hypothesis: for all $n \geq i \geq 1$, $2*i = 2^i$

Induction step ($i = n+1$):
$$2*(n+1) = 2*n + 2$$
$$= 2^n + 2 \quad \{by\ the\ hypothesis\}$$
$$= 2^{n+1} \quad \{if\ the\ proof\ succeeds\}$$

But, $2^n + 2 = 2^{n+1}$ only for $n = 1$, and so the proof fails. $\square$

2.5   COMPLEXITY MEASURES

The actual time needed by a computation ...

Frequently, we wish to assess the efficiency of programs, that is, we want to discover whether computing time and storage space is being used economically. This problem can be divided into two parts: assessing the efficiency of the algorithm and assessing the quality of the implementation. Here we will be concerned with the efficiency of the algorithm since improving an implementation, sometimes called code optimization, is straightforward and, to a great extent, is performed automatically by many compilers. In order to evaluate the quality of an algorithm we need a measure of efficiency that permits us to compare it with others. In the quest for such a measure, we confront two problems, which we shall explain in the context of estimating the time efficiency of a simple search algorithm. The problems that we are going to encounter are: (i) that it is rather difficult, if not impossible, to associate an actual time value with the period of execution of an algorithm; and (ii) that the time needed to complete a task using a particular algorithm seems to depend (usually) on the *size* of the problem being solved, that is, on some value derived from the number and/or size of the input data.

... depends on the computer and the language, ...

The actual time needed for a computation depends not only on the algorithm but especially on the computer on which an implementation of the algorithm is run. To some extent, it also depends on the programming language used to express the algorithm. Thus, if we wish to compare algorithms by comparing actual time values, we need to agree on a computer and a language before we start.

... as well as on the size of the problem.

To see how the time needed for a computation depends on (the size of) the input, consider a program that searches in a table of numbers for a particular value. Suppose that these numbers are not stored in any particular order. Thus a search program has to scan the table looking at every entry for the number being sought until a match occurs or the end of the table is reached. If the number required is in the table, then we might find it quickly if it is close to the beginning of the table or less so if it occurs near the end. However, if we had to perform similar searches frequently, we would expect to search, on the average, half of the table before finding a match. Each search for a number that is not in the table would cause a search through all n elements. In any event, we know that in the worst case we have to look at n elements. Since the time for looking at an element and advancing to the next one does not depend on n, the time for finding an element increases in proportion with the number n of elements. There may be some additional time spent at the beginning and at the end of the algorithm (for initialization and completion), but, if n is large, this time may be ignored as being insignificant. We conclude that, for large values of n, the time needed by our search program is asymptotically proportional to n.

The measures of time and space complexity are intrinsic to algorithms.

The latter property is intrinsic to the algorithm. It depends neither on a particular method of implementation nor on the speed of the computer on which the program is run. Hence, it is an excellent measure of the efficiency of the algorithm. We call it the *time complexity* of the algorithm and note that, for our example, the time complexity is asymptotically proportional to n or simply "the complexity is order n", written as $O(n)$. The term "asymptotical" expresses the notion that the assertion is only approximately true and it becomes more accurate as n grows. A similar measure can be derived for the utilization of storage space; this is called the *space complexity* of the algorithm.

The binary search is very fast.

We clarify the concept of complexity by means of another example. Suppose again that we wish to search for a number in a table. This time, however, we assume that the numbers are stored in ascending order. We can now improve our algorithm by proceeding as follows: first we examine the number at the center. We may be lucky and find our target immediately but, even if we do not, we know that the number must be in the first half of the list if it is smaller than the number at the center and in the second half if it is greater. For our next step we follow the same strategy: we examine the center element of the half in which we know the number will be found. With each step we exclude about half of the elements that we have had to consider. We find the complexity of the algorithm by observing that we certainly will have found the number after k steps if

$$(1/2)^k * n \leq 1$$

Hence

$$n \leq 2^k$$

and

$$k \geq \log_2(n)$$

This algorithm is called a *binary search*, and its time complexity is $O(\log(n))$. Since the base of the logarithm contributes only a constant factor, it is immaterial for the order value.

There is an immense difference between $O(n)$ and $O(\log(n))$.

To make us appreciate the difference between $O(n)$ and $O(\log(n))$ the following story may help. Suppose that on your trip around the world you arrive one day in New Crackpot, North Pacific, and you remember that a friend had moved there some time ago. It turns out that New Crackpot is a large city of about 13 million people. Hence the obvious way to find someone whose address one does not know is to look him up in a telephone book. You find a telephone booth with a directory but, to your dismay, you realize that in New Crackpot names are listed not in alphabetical order but on a first come first served basis. As far as you can see, they are in random order.

Guessing that there are about 6 million entries in the directory and remembering from the book on data types and data structures that you have to go through a process of $O(n)$ for looking up the name, you make a rough calculation: reading a name takes perhaps a second and there are about 100 000 seconds in a day (86 400 to be exact, but 100 000 is easier to remember and to use, and it is good enough for a quick estimate). Working day and night, you would need sixty days to check all of the names while, with some luck, you may find your friend's name in half that time.

In comparison, if the names were in alphabetical order, you could do what amounts to a binary search and be finished in

$$\log_2(6\ 000\ 000) < 23 \text{ steps.}$$

Even if a single step takes much longer than before, you would be done in just a few minutes!

Definition of "order" and ...   We generalize the ideas about "order" by saying that a function $f(n)$ that is monotone (the value of $f(n)$ never decreases as n grows) is $O(h(n))$ if

there is a $c > 0$ and an $n_0 \geq 1$
    such that for all $n \geq n_0$, $c * f(n) \leq h(n)$.

Note that the order function only provides an upper bound for the function approximated. Thus, it makes sense to claim, "the time complexity of algorithm *xyz* is $O(n*n)$, it may even be $O(n*\log(n))$, but it is certainly not $O(n)$".

... some simple rules of computation.   The following rules are useful for computing the order of functions:

$c * f(n)$	is $O(f(n))$	(2.1)
$f(n) + k$	is $O(f(n))$	(2.2)
$f(n) + g(n)$	is if $O(f(n)) \geq O(g(n))$ then $O(f(n))$ else $O(g(n))$	(2.3)
$\sum_{i=1}^{n} g(i)$	is $O(n*h(n))$ if $g(n)$ is $O(h(n))$	(2.4)

An example   In order to gain some practice in estimating complexities, let us compute the time complexity of the following sorting method.

Sort a table: find the smallest item in the table and switch it with the top element; then repeat the process starting with the second element and so forth.

Finding the smallest element is $O(n)$. This has to be repeated for all but the last element in the table. We obtain by rule (2.4) and (2.2) that the complete algorithm is $O(n*n)$.

EXERCISES

E2.1   Express all of the sixteen different binary boolean operators using "not", "and", and "or".

E2.2   Show that all boolean operators can be expressed using the operator "nor", defined by

a nor $b \Leftrightarrow \neg (a$ or $b)$.

E2.3   From the following expression, eliminate all occurrences of the operator "implies"($\Rightarrow$); that is, rewrite the expression using only "not", "and", and "or".

$((\text{not } a \text{ or } b) \text{ and } (a \text{ or } c)) \Rightarrow (a \Rightarrow b)$

Is this expression a tautology?

E2.4   For each of the following expressions determine whether it is
always true (*i.e. a tautology*),
never true (*i.e. unsatisfiable*), or
sometimes true (*satisfiable*).

In the last case give values for the variables a, b, and c for which the expression is true as well as values for which it is false.

$a \vee b \Rightarrow a \wedge b$	(1)
$a \wedge b \Rightarrow a \vee b$	(2)
$a \wedge b \wedge \neg c \Leftrightarrow (a \vee b) \wedge c$	(3)

E2.5   For the sets

$A = \{1,2,5,8,15\}$ and $B = \{1,3,5,7,9,11\}$

determine $A \cup B$, $A \cap B$, P(A), P(B), and $A \times B$. Prove that neither $A \subseteq B$ nor $B \subseteq A$.

E2.6   Consider the following sets A and B of character strings formed from members of the set $C = \{a, b\}$:
    Construct A by putting the string containing only a into the set; then, for each string y already in the set, add the concatenated string formed from an element $c \in C$ joined to the front of y (below denoted by *concat(c,y)*).
    Construct B similarly, however, start the set with both a and b, and, instead of strings *concat(c,y)*, add strings *concat(y,c)*.
    Are the sets equal? Is $B \subseteq A$ or $A \subseteq B$? Prove your answer!

E2.7   Consider the functions defined by the following Pascal functions and determine for each of them whether it is injective, surjective, bijective, or none of these; construct an appropriate inverse for those functions that have one.

Type *Subrng* $= 0 \mathrel{..} 9$

function *WHAT_1(x:Integer):Subrng*;
    begin *WHAT_1* $:= x \text{ MOD } 10$ **end**;

function *WHAT_2(x:Integer):Integer*;
    begin *WHAT_2* $= x * x * x$ **end**;

```
      function WHAT_3(x:Subrng):Subrng;
           begin WHAT_3 := (3*x + 5) MOD 10 end;
      function WHAT_4(x:Integer):Integer;
           begin WHAT_4 := x * x end;
```

E2.8   Classify the selector functions for n-tuples. Are they surjective, injective, bijective, or none of these?

E2.9   Determine the negation of the following expressions:

For all $x . x \in N \Rightarrow 10*x < 10\,000;$ (1)
For all x . for some $y . x \in N \Rightarrow (y < x)$ (2)

E2.10   From Peano's axioms prove that

addition is associative $\{a + (b + c) = (a + b) + c\}$;
multiplication is both commutative and associative.

E2.11   Prove the following theorem by mathematical induction.

If a loaf of bread is sliced in the usual way, then there will be $n + 1$ slices after n cuts.

E2.12   In Greek mythology, the Hydra was a serpent with several heads that was very difficult to kill. When one of its heads was cut off by the strike of a sword then immediately three heads grew at its place. It took Hercules, who was supposed to slay the monster, quite a number of strikes until he realized that cutting off heads was not the proper way to proceed.
        How many heads do you think the Hydra had after 5 (after n) of Hercules's strikes if the original number was 9 as the legend asserts? Prove your answer by induction!

E2.13   The powerset P(A) where $A = \{a_1, \ldots, a_n\}$ *has* 2^n members. Prove this assertion by induction!

E2.14   For the differentiation of polynomials, we use the simple rule that

$$d(x^n)/dx = n*x^{(n-1)}.$$

Prove this rule by induction using the product rule!

E2.15   Prove by induction that the binary search will succeed in k steps if the size of the table does not exceed

$$n = 2^k - 1$$

entries and if the required item may not be in the table. Show that at most $(k-1)$ steps are needed if it is known that the item is indeed in the table.

E2.16   Design an algorithm that eliminates multiple entries from a table by replacing all but one of each group of equal entries with a special null entry. Compute the time complexity of your algorithm!

3 Recursive Programs and Recursive Definitions

Recursion is a most elegant concept.

A program or definition is called "recursive" if it refers to itself directly or indirectly. The use of recursion frequently provides very elegant solutions to intricate problems. Therefore, it is worthwhile to acquire the skill of devising recursive algorithms and definitions. Both recursive definitions and programs are used extensively for defining, implementing, and manipulating complex data objects. Hence, it is useful to deal with these issues first, before resuming the study of data types and data structures. Our objective is to show that recursion is not at all obscure or confusing but a most natural means for defining processes and objects.

3.1 THE TOWER OF HANOI

A naive computer solution to the puzzle ...

The Tower of Hanoi is an old puzzle that has become a classic example of a problem with a very elegant solution in form of a recursive algorithm. As a toy, the puzzle consists of a board with three vertical pegs and a number of disks of different sizes with central holes which allow them to be stacked onto any of the pegs (see Figure 3.1). In the initial configuration of the puzzle, all disks are stacked on one peg, the largest disk on the bottom and the other disks on top of it in decreasing size such that each disk rests on one that is larger. It is the object of the puzzle to move this tower one disk at a time to

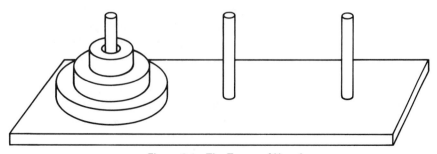

Figure 3.1 The Tower of Hanoi

another peg in such a way that in any intermediate configuration a disk rests on the bottom (on the board) or on a larger disk. To this end the third peg may be used freely for parking disks temporarily. In the final configuration, all disks are stacked on the target peg again in decreasing size from the bottom to the top.

... (composed with some given subprograms) ...

For the algorithmic solution we assume that certain elementary operations for puzzle configurations are provided so that we do not need to worry about the internal representation of the puzzle. These operations are based on the following Pascal types:

> *Puzzle {all puzzle configurations suitably represented}*;
> *Peg* = 1..3;
> *Integer {total number of disks}*.

The operations are

> **function** *NEW_TOWER* (*number_of_disks:Integer*;
> 　　　*first_peg:Peg*):*Puzzle*;
> **procedure** *MOVE_DISK*(*var P:Puzzle; peg*1,*peg*2:*Peg*);
> **procedure** *DRAW_TOWER*(*P:Puzzle*);
> **function** *OTHER_PEG*(*peg 1,peg*2:*Peg*):*Peg*.

NEW_TOWER creates an initial configuration with *number_of_disks* many disks on *first_peg*. *MOVE_DISK* changes the configuration *P* of the puzzle by moving one disk from *peg*1 to *peg*2; it is undefined if *peg*1 is empty. *DRAW_TOWER* prints a picture of the given configuration. *OTHER_PEG* computes the reference to the third peg if two different pegs are supplied. This function could be easily replaced by the expression "6 −*peg*1 − *peg*2" but it seems that *OTHER_PEG* is more descriptive than an expression that happens to compute its associated number. When programming the solution of the puzzle we want to be sure *that* we can get "the other peg" when we need it, but we are not concerned with *how* this is accomplished. *OTHER_PEG* is not defined if *peg*1 and *peg*2 are equal.

... simply enumerates the proper sequence of moves.

Now suppose that we want to write a program that moves a tower of exactly three disks from a given peg (*peg*1) to a second peg (*peg*2). This program could be written as shown in Figure 3.2.

```
procedure MOVE_3(var P:Puzzle; peg1,peg2:Peg);
    begin
        MOVE_DISK(P, peg1, peg2);
        MOVE_DISK(P, peg1, OTHER_PEG(peg1,peg2));
        MOVE_DISK(P, peg2, OTHER_PEG(peg1,peg2));
        MOVE_DISK(P, peg1, peg2);
        MOVE_DISK(P, OTHER_PEG(peg1,peg2), peg1);
        MOVE_DISK(P, OTHER_PEG(peg1,peg2), peg2);
        MOVE_DISK(P, peg1, peg2)
    end.
```

Figure 3.2 This program moves exactly 3 disks

With the number of
disks, *n*, as a
parameter, ...

This program is too specialized to be interesting. We therefore restate the problem in a little more general form: Write a program that moves *up to* three disks from *peg*1 to *peg*2. This program should be evocable by

$$MOVE\_UP\_TO\_3(pz1,\ n,\ p1,\ p2);$$

where $1 \leq n \leq 3$.

Following the above approach we produce the solution in Figure 3.3.

procedure *MOVE_UP_TO_3* (var *P*:*Puzzle*; *k*:*Integer*;
$\qquad\qquad\qquad\qquad$ *peg*1,*peg*2:*Peg*);
$\quad$**begin**
$\quad$ **if** $(0 < k)$ **and** $(k < 4)$
$\quad$ **then**
$\qquad$ **case** *k* **of**
$\qquad$ 1: *MOVE_DISK*(*P*, *peg*1, *peg*2);
$\qquad$ 2: **begin**
$\qquad\qquad$ *MOVE_DISK*(*P*, *peg*1, *OTHER_PEG*(*peg*1,*peg*2));
$\qquad\qquad$ *MOVE_DISK*(*P*, *peg*1, *peg*2);
$\qquad\qquad$ *MOVE_DISK*(*P*, *OTHER_PEG*(*peg*1,*peg*2), *peg*2)
$\qquad\qquad$ **end**;
$\qquad$ 3: **begin**
$\qquad\qquad$ *MOVE_DISK*(*P*, *peg*1, *peg*2);
$\qquad\qquad$ *MOVE_DISK*(*P*, *peg*1, *OTHER_PEG*(*peg*1,*peg*2));
$\qquad\qquad$ *MOVE_DISK*(*P*, *peg*2, *OTHER_PEG*(*peg*1,*peg*2));
$\qquad\qquad$ *MOVE_DISK*(*P*, *peg*1, *peg*2);
$\qquad\qquad$ *MOVE_DISK*(*P*, *OTHER_PEG*(*peg*1,*peg*2), *peg*1);
$\qquad\qquad$ *MOVE_DISK*(*P*, *OTHER_PEG*(*peg*1,*peg*2), *peg*2);
$\qquad\qquad$ *MOVE_DISK*(*P*, *peg*1, *peg*2)
$\qquad\qquad$ **end**
$\qquad$ **end**
$\quad$ **else** *ERROR*('*can only move* 1 *to* 3 *disks*')
$\qquad\qquad\qquad$ {*ERROR displays message and terminates procedure*};
$\quad$**end.**

Figure 3.3 This program moves up to three disks

... the size of the
program grows
exponentially with the
bound on *n*.

This solution, though correct, is rather unsatisfactory since a generalization to higher numbers of disks is very expensive. The number of *MOVE_ DISK* instructions grows exponentially with the number of disks!

Better, but not yet
general, is a solution
built stepwise ...

Searching for a better way we observe that we could move a tower of up to *n* disks easily if we had a library program (similar to *MOVE_DISK*) that could move up to *n*–1 disks. We would move first the top *n*–1 disks to the other peg using the library routine, then the bottom disk to *peg*2, and finally the tower of *n*–1 disks from the other peg to *peg*2 again with the library routine. Assuming that such a program requires a tower to have at least one disk a program that moves, say five disks is shown in Figure 3.4.

... using a sequence
of *MOVE* programs.

Since there is no essential difference between a program that can move five disks and one that can move four, the library procedure *MOVE_4* can be programmed the same way as *MOVE_5* except that it should call another program *MOVE_3*. In turn *MOVE_3* would call *MOVE_2*, *MOVE_2* *MOVE_1*, and *MOVE_1* would never get to the else part of its conditional statement. Thus a *MOVE_0* is not needed.

```
procedure MOVE_5(var P:Puzzle; k:Integer; peg1,peg2:Peg);
begin
    if k = 1
        then MOVE_DISK(P, peg1, peg2)
        else begin {here k is at least 2}
            MOVE_4(P, k-1, peg1, OTHER_PEG(peg1,peg2));
            MOVE_DISK(P, peg1, peg2);
            MOVE_4(P, k-1, OTHER_PEG(peg1,peg2), peg2)
        end
end.
```

Figure 3.4   With a library function that moves four disks, we can easily move five

The size of the complete program now grows proportionally with the bound on *n*.

With this solution, the number of statements needed for a program that can move *n* disks increases only linearly with *n*, which is quite an improvement over the previous solution.

However, we still have not found a program that can solve the puzzle for arbitrarily many disks, that is to say, any program constructed in the fashion described above is limited to puzzles of up to a given maximal size.

The general solution is a program that calls itself!

The general solution is based on the following observation. All programs *MOVE_n* are very similar to each other except that each one calls the one with the next lower value for *n*. What would happen, we may ask, if, in *MOVE_5*, we do not call *MOVE_4* but *MOVE_5* itself! We may argue that *MOVE_5*, since it can move (if correct) up to five disks, can, consequently, move at least four. So it should work! Replacing *MOVE_4* by *MOVE_5* has another consequence: Since *MOVE_4* is not called any longer, *MOVE_3* (which was only called by *MOVE_4*) and, in turn, *MOVE_2* and *MOVE_1* are never called. Also, if we do the same with, say, *MOVE_27*, then *MOVE_26*, *MOVE_25*, etc. are not called either! So it seems that we have finally found the general program that we were looking for, except we do not know yet whether it is going to work.

A program called by itself ...

In order to analyze what happens when a program calls itself we need to know precisely what happens when programs call subprograms. The rules that govern subprogram calls are different for different programming languages. Pascal's rules, which are a simplified version of rules found in PL/I and ALGOL60, can be derived from the following simple model. We may assume that, when a subprogram is called, a new copy of its text is created which is then interpreted independently of any other copy of the program that may currently be around. When this program in turn calls another one, then its text and all intermediate results remain unaltered until control returns, with the exception that the values of variables that are global, or are passed to the subprogram ''by reference'', may change by the actions of the subprogram. Finally, when a subprogram returns control, its text and all intermediate results are abandoned.

... behaves as if it were called by another program.

Consequently, a program called by itself behaves exactly as if it were called by some other program.

NOTE: In order to accomplish the behavior described, copies of the program text need not actually be made. It suffices to provide each invocation of a program with separate storage space for those nonglobal locations that are altered when the program is executed. Instructions, which are read but never modified, need not be copied.

With this as a premise we will now analyze the program *MOVE* shown in Figure 3.5.

A recursive program is analyzed by inductive reasoning.

A program that calls itself (directly or indirectly) is called *recursive*. In order to understand what it does, it is very advantageous to use inductive reasoning. The idea is to prove by induction that the program does what it is expected to do.

Consider the recursive procedure below. We expect that *MOVE*

```
procedure MOVE(var P:Puzzle; k:Integer; peg1,peg2:Peg);
        begin
            if k = 1
                then MOVE_DISK(P, peg1, peg2)
                else begin
                    MOVE(P, k-1, peg1, OTHER_PEG(peg1,peg2));
                    MOVE_DISK(P, peg1, peg2);
                    MOVE(P, k-1, OTHER_PEG(peg1,peg2), peg2)
                    end
        end.
```

Figure 3.5 This recursive program can move an arbitrary number of disks

changes the value of the configuration *P* by moving the top *k* disks from *peg*1 to *peg*2 obeying the rules of the puzzle. We prove this by induction over *k*.

Base case: ($k = 1$) Tracing the first three lines of the program shows that the program works correctly for $k = 1$.

Induction hypothesis: We assume that *MOVE*, invoked with $k = n-1$, properly moves $n-1$ disks from *peg*1 to *peg*2 ($n > 1$).

Induction step: Now we trace *MOVE* for $k = n$ with $n > 1$ and find that

(i) *MOVE* is applied to the configuration *P* for $k-1$ (that is $n-1$) disks with the pegs *peg*1 and *OTHER_PEG*(*peg*1,*peg*2). Since the number of disks to be moved is $n-1$ and since we know that *MOVE* called by itself behaves as if it were called from some other program, the induction hypothesis is applicable, that is to say, we may assume that $n-1$ disks are properly moved from *peg*1 to the third peg. There is one complication, however. The induction hypothesis (*n*–1 disks are properly moved) is based on the assumption that the board does not contain any disks besides the *n*–1 that make up the tower. Here we have *n* disks on the board. Fortunately, the disk that does not participate in the operation is larger than any of those moved, thus any of the latter may legally be placed on top of it.

(ii) *MOVE_DISK* moves the *n*th disk from *peg*1 to *peg*2 and thus puts this disk to its final destination.

(iii) Again by the induction hypothesis, *MOVE* now properly moves the *n*–1 disks from the third peg to *peg*2 on top of the bottom disk.

Thus the assumption that *MOVE* works correctly for *n*–1 disks leads to the conclusion that it works for *n* disks as well. This completes our argument. □

Though not formal, this inductive argument is much better than tracing!

It must be pointed out that this inductive argument is not a proof of correctness in the strict sense. It is about as reliable as tracing a nonrecursive program that does not have loops. It is meant to make tracing a recursive program feasible and make it unnecessary to follow the execution several levels into the sequence of recursive calls. There is no harm in following every action of one or two recursive programs, but *only* to see recursion in action and to become comfortable with the concept and *not* to understand, verify or debug a particular recursive program.

In order to understand recursive programs always use inductive reasoning

It is for this reason that the method of inductive proofs must be thoroughly understood. This method is by no means esoteric or of only theoretical interest but is a most powerful practical tool which should be used by every competent programmer.

The only multi-level trace of a recursive program in this book.

Having said this we will now (and only once) give a complete trace of a recursive program (Figure 3.7); we will trace the execution of *MOVE* for three disks. Figure 3.6 shows the eight configurations that occur when three disks are moved. Since *MOVE* changes the puzzle, we write into each call both the initial and the resulting configuration. For example, the call *MOVE*(*P*1→*P*4, 2, 1, 3) indicates that *MOVE* is supposed to move two disks from peg 1 to peg 3 transforming configuration *P*1 to configuration *P*4.

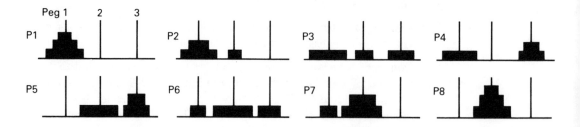

Figure 3.6   The Configurations of the Puzzle

$MOVE(P1 \rightarrow P8, 3, 1, 2)$ {*the process to be traced*}
 begin
   if 3 = 1 **then** . . . {*not executed since condition false*}
     else begin
       $MOVE(P1 \rightarrow P4, 2, 1, 3)$ {*traced next*}
         begin
           if 2 = 1 **then** . . .{*not executed*}
             else begin
               $MOVE(P1 \rightarrow P2, 1, 1, 2)$
                 begin
                   if 1 = 1
                       then $MOVE\_DISK(P1 \rightarrow P2, 1, 2)$
                       else begin {*not done*} **end**
                   end;
               $MOVE\_DISK(P2 \rightarrow P3, 1, 3)$;
               $MOVE(P3 \rightarrow P4, 1, 2, 3)$
                 begin
                   if 1 = 1
                       then $MOVE\_DISK(P3 \rightarrow P4, 2 , 3)$
                       else begin {*not done*} **end**
                 end
             end {$P1 \rightarrow P4$};
       $MOVE\_DISK(P4 \rightarrow P5, 1, 2)$;
       $MOVE(P5 \rightarrow P8, 2, 3, 2)$
         begin
           if 2 = 1 **then** . . . {*not done*}
             else begin
               $MOVE(P5 \rightarrow P6, 1, 3, 1)$
                 begin
                   if 1 = 1
                       then $MOVE\_DISK(P5 \rightarrow P6, 1, 2)$
                       else begin {*not done*} **end**
                   end;
               $MOVE\_DISK(P6 \rightarrow P7, 3, 2)$;
               $MOVE(P7 \rightarrow P8, 1, 1, 2)$
                 begin
                   if 1 = 1
                       then $MOVE\_DISK(P7 \rightarrow P8, 2, 3)$
                       else begin {*not done*} **end**
                 end
             end
         end {$P5 \rightarrow P8$}
 end.

Figure 3.7   The trace of a recursive program

The text of the *MOVE* program can be shortened ...

There is another version of the procedure *MOVE* with an even shorter text that can handle values $k \geq 0$ (instead of $k \geq 1$):

```
procedure MOVE(var P:Puzzle; k:Integer; peg1,peg2:Peg);
  begin
    if k > 0
      then begin
        MOVE(P, k-1, peg1, OTHER_PEG(peg1,peg2));
        MOVE_DISK(P, peg1, peg2);
        MOVE(P, k-1, OTHER_PEG(peg1,peg2), peg2)
      end
  end;
```

... at the expense of an increase in execution time.

Here, the base case is $k = 0$. Although it is textually shorter, this program will run more slowly than the first one, because it evokes many additional calls of *MOVE* of the form $MOVE(P, 0, p1, p2)$, which do not advance the state of the puzzle.

3.2   SORTING

From the definition of sorting ...

As a second example of a recursive algorithm we consider a simple program that sorts a table. First we would like to define what a sorted table is. Why do we bother to do this? Is it not clear to anyone what sorting means? Well, yes. But if we want to prove that an algorithm reorders a table so that it is correctly sorted (say in ascending order), we need a definition more precise than our intuition.

Definition: A finite (sub)table $E[m] \ldots E[n]$ is *sorted*, if

for all $i, j. \ m \leq i \leq j \leq n$ implies $E[i] \leq E[j]$.

From this definition it follows directly that (i) a table with only one element is trivially sorted, and (ii) no element is smaller than the first.

... a method for sorting can be derived.

Also, if we remove the first element from the sorted table, the remaining table still seems to be sorted, unless it is empty. It should therefore be possible to sort a table by moving the smallest element to the front and (!) sorting the rest. Figure 3.8 shows a Pascal program based on this idea. The purpose of the program is to sort the elements of the table E for the index

```
procedure SORT(var E: table; lo,hi:integer);

    {table is a suitable Pascal array type;
    SORT sorts, in ascending order, the part of E
    which starts at lo and ends at hi}

var i_min,i: integer;
    temp: item {table = array[...] of item} ;
begin
    if lo < hi
        then begin
            i_min: = lo;
            for i: =  lo+1 to hi do
                if E[i_min] > E[i] then i_min: = i;
            temp     : = E[lo];
            E[lo]    : = E[i_min];
            E[i_min] : = temp;
            SORT(E, lo+1, hi)
        end
    end;
```

Figure 3.8   A recursive sort program

range from *lo* to *hi*. For example, calling *SORT(E*, 1,25) should sort the first twenty-five elements of *E*. Tracing this program shows that nothing is changed if *lo* = *hi*, that is, if there is only one element in the range to be sorted. If there are at least two elements (*lo<hi*), then the first element and the smallest element are exchanged so that the smallest element is moved to *E[lo]*. Thereafter, *SORT* is applied to the range *lo* + 1 to *hi*, which encompasses all but the first element of the original range.

Here the proof of correctness must show two things: In order to show that this program works correctly, we have to establish two things. First, we must show that the range from *lo* to *hi* is in sorted order when the execution is completed. Secondly, we must show that the final table is a permutation of the original table. In other words, we must show that elements have neither been added nor deleted.

(i) that the resulting table is sorted, ...1. Proof by induction over hi–lo that the range *E[lo]* to *E[hi]* is sorted after the execution of *SORT*.

Base case: *hi–lo* = 0. The range between *lo* and *hi* is clearly in sorted order if *lo* = *hi*, because there is only one element in the range and a set of one element is trivially sorted.

Induction hypothesis: *SORT* works correctly for the range *hi–lo* = *k*–1.

Induction step: SORT, applied to range $hi-lo = k$, will move the smallest element of the range to $E[lo]$. Thus:

> $lo = i\_min$ implies
> for all i with $i\_min \leq i \leq hi$. $E[i\_min] \leq E[i]$

and, by the induction hypothesis,

> $lo < i\_min \leq hi$ implies
> for all i with $i\_min \leq i \leq hi$. $E[i\_min] \leq E[i]$.

Since $(A$ implies $C)$ and $(B$ implies $C)$

> if and only if
>> $(A$ or $B)$ implies C

and since

> $(lo = i\_min)$ or $(lo < i\_min \leq hi)$

is equivalent to

> $(lo \leq i\_min \leq hi)$,

we obtain

> $lo \leq i\_min \leq hi$ implies
> for all i with $i\_min \leq i \leq hi$. $E[i\_min] \leq E[i]$.

Thus, the range for $hi-lo = k$ is sorted.

(ii) that the resulting table is a permutation of the original table.

2. Proof by induction over $hi-lo$ that *SORT* does not add elements to or delete elements from the sequence $E[lo]$ to $E[hi\_min]$.

The proof that *SORT* does not add items to or remove items from the sequence sorted follows a similar inductive pattern. If $lo = hi$, nothing is changed at all, so nothing is added or deleted. Now suppose that the recursive call (*SORT* applied to the index range $lo + 1$ to hi) does not add or delete items. Then, since searching for the minimum and exchanging it with the first item in the sequence does not add or delete any item, *SORT* applied to the index range lo to hi will not add or delete items but will result in a permutation of the elements in this sequence. $\square$

3.3   RECURSIVE DEFINITIONS

Recursive definitions are very important. Three examples follow.

While recursive programs define processes, recursive definitions usually define sets of objects. This method of definition is very important in the field of computer science and it will be used frequently in the remainder of this book. Here we give three examples.

(i) identifiers in
programming
languages, ...

1. The set of all identifiers of a programming language such as Pascal may be specified by the following definition:

An identifier is either a single letter or it is an identifier followed by a letter or a digit.

Therefore, the following are examples of identifiers:

T, T3, TO, T34, T3M, TO4, TOM, ...

The definition can be made more explicit by saying that the set of valid identifiers is constructed as follows:

All strings consisting of single letters are in the set. If some item x is in the set, then so are the items $x\ell$ and xd where ℓ is any letter and d any digit. These, are the only items in the set. □

(ii) a sorted
sequence, ...

2. A sorted sequence may be defined as follows:

A sequence is sorted if it consists of only one element or if the smallest element has the lowest index and the remainder of the sequence is sorted. Again, we may use the more explicit definition that states how the set of all sorted sequences is constructed;

Place into the set all sequences that contain only one element. If x is in the set, then add all sequences ax to the set where a is an item less than or equal to any item in x. □

(iii) the Fibonacci
numbers.

3. The definition of the famous Fibonacci numbers $F(i)$, which constitute a sequence of integers, states that:

$$F(0) = 0, F(1) = 1,$$
$$F(n) = F(n-1) + F(n-2) \text{ for } n \geq 2. \square$$

Here, we find that

$$F(2) = F(1) + F(0) = 1,$$
$$F(3) = F(2) + F(1) = 2,$$
$$F(4) = F(3) + F(2) = 3,$$
$$F(5) = F(4) + F(3) = 5, ...$$

Fibonacci numbers occur frequently in discrete mathematics. There is even a scientific journal called *Fibonacci Quarterly* that deals with applications and properties of Fibonacci numbers. We will also encounter them again later in Exercise T9.2.

EXERCISES

E3.1   You are given a table of integer numbers. Write a recursive program that finds a given number in the table and returns the subscript of the first occurrence of this number (returning a zero if the number is not in the table). The header of the program is

> **function** *FIND*(*x:Integer; tbl:Table*):*Integer;*

with the definitions

> **const** *length* = 50;
> **type** *Table* = **array**[1..*length*] **of** *Integer.*

Prove by induction that your program works correctly.

NOTE: This is strictly an exercise. In practice, since an iterative solution for *FIND* (one that uses a loop instead of recursion) is similarly simple and clear, one would avoid the recursive solution in order to escape the computational overhead that is added by the common implementation of recursion.

E3.2   Give a recursive definition of a valid arithmetic expression in Pascal built with constants and variables, the operators + ,–,*,/, and parentheses.

Hint: Begin with the statement that ''an arithmetic expression is a constant or a variable, or ...''

4 Abstract Data Types

We shall now discuss the various aspects of data types using the paradigm of stacks. Stacks are especially important in the context of translating and executing computer programs. Yet it is not their usefulness or importance, but their simplicity, that makes them an excellent example for abstract data types. Using stacks as our paradigm, we shall explore all major facets of abstract data types, addressing issues of both specification and implementation. In this chapter we wish to make three major points:

(i) making specifications precise is desirable and possible;
(ii) there are many different ways of implementing a program or a data type, and a good programmer is ready to consider novel and unusual ideas; and
(iii) the correctness of an implementation should be proved (more or less formally).

4.1 SPECIFICATION

Specifications are necessary ...

Many programmers take for granted that the specification of programs takes much less time and effort than writing programs. This seems to be a reasonable assumption. In fact, it is a very necessary assumption since, otherwise, division of labor which is essential for programming large projects would be quite impossible. Large projects must be broken down into many parts, and each part must be defined precisely and unambiguously. Then each definition can be given to a different programmer for implementation. Clearly, if the specification of a program took as long as its implementation, the analyst who writes the specifications would write the final programs instead and save his employer the expense of the programming team.

... but often inadequate...

Unfortunately, programmers often discover that specifications, clear and accurate at first sight, prove to be incomplete or, worse, can be interpreted in different ways where the "obvious" interpretation turns out not to be the one intended. If the point of ambiguity is a subtle one, the mistake may appear only under rare circumstances and escape discovery by testing. Imagine the consequences of such a faulty program being part of a large system used for manned space flight missions or air-traffic control operations!

... if written in English ...

Many ambiguities and imprecisions occur because specifications are stated as English narratives. Specifications stated in a natural language not only tend to be imprecise but are often incomplete, and completeness is rather difficult to check. No method is known that reliably decides for any English paragraph whether it addresses every case relevant for the task at hand.

... instead of a mathematical notation.

It is therefore desirable to express specifications using a notation with the precision of a programming language or the language of mathematics, so that specifications can be systematically debugged or, better still, *proved* to be sound and complete. In short, specifications (which describe what needs to be done) should be as precise and correct as programs (which describe how to do it).

Data types are specified by axioms.

In this book we are concerned mainly with the specification of *groups* of programs that realize the operations required on data types. In the following sections, we study how to specify data types by axioms and how to use these specifications both for the application and implementation of types.

4.1.1   Specification of Data Types

For stacks we define NIL_STACK and PUSH, ...

A stack is used to store items such as numbers, characters, records, or even files. The simplest stack is the empty stack denoted by *NIL_STACK*. From a given stack *s*, a new stack may be constructed by "pushing" an item onto it.

NOTE: Often, stacks are viewed as *objects* that, like physical stacks, are *modified* by the PUSH operation in such a way that the original stack "becomes" the updated stack with the new version replacing the old one.

In contrast, we shall, for the moment, view a stack as a *value* from which a new stack is computed by *PUSH*. The difference is that we view *PUSH* as a function that takes a stack and an item and returns a stack; it does *not* change the original one. Thus, if we write

$$t := PUSH(x, s)$$

we end up with *two* stacks, the original stack *s* and the new stack *t*. Later we shall discuss the implications of viewing stacks as (mutable) objects.

This new stack is computed by the function PUSH that takes a stack *s* (the original stack) and an item *x* as arguments. A stack is usually dedicated to the storage of one sort of item, for example, integer numbers.

ISMT_STACK, ...

We need three additional functions for the manipulation of stacks. First, we need a function for checking whether a stack is empty; we call this function *ISMT_STACK*. It takes a stack and returns **true** or **false** as a result. We expect that

$$ISMT\_STACK(NIL\_STACK) = \textbf{true}$$

and that

$$ISMT\_STACK(PUSH(x, s)) = \textbf{false}.$$

TOP, ...

Secondly, we need a function that computes the value last added to the stack by *PUSH*. This function, called *TOP*, takes a stack and returns an item. Hence,

$$TOP(PUSH(x, s)) = x.$$

... and POP.

Finally, we need an operation that removes an item from the top of the stack. This function, called *POP*, takes a stack and returns a stack. *POP* undoes the last application of *PUSH*. Hence,

$$POP(PUSH(x, s)) = s.$$

Since there is no element last added to an empty stack, it does not make sense to apply *TOP* or *POP* to *NIL_STACK*. *TOP* or *POP* applied to *NIL_STACK* cause an exceptional condition, an error. This error is similar to the one triggered by an attempt to read beyond the end of a file and it can be prevented in a similar way by testing a stack for exhaustion before attempting to read its top element or to pop it. We assume that the error handling mechanism of the operating system is invoked by such an event and that control never returns to the point from which *TOP* or *POP* was invoked. Consequently, no value is actually computed in this case. However, it is convenient for our specification mechanism to pretend that control does return and that a special value, *error*, is computed. Thus we specify

$$TOP(NIL\_STACK) = error,$$

and

$$POP(NIL\_STACK) = error.$$

The element *error* is an item common to all possible sets of items. But since *error* does not actually occur as a proper value, it does not need to be given an actual value.

The stack-functions are *strict*.

Now, if *error* becomes the parameter of another function as, for example, in

$$\begin{aligned} &ISMT\_STACK(POP(NIL\_STACK)) \\ &= ISMT\_STACK(error), \end{aligned}$$

then the value of this other function is also *error*. Clearly, if control never returns from

$$POP(NIL\_STACK)$$

it cannot return from

$$ISMT\_STACK(POP(NIL\_STACK)).$$

Functions, that return *error* if any of their arguments have the value *error* are called *strict*. We assume that all stack functions are strict.

Specification
= sets
    + syntax
        + axioms.

Below, we give a complete axiomatic specification of the data type *stack*. Such an axiomatic specification consists of three parts.

(i) A collection of sets. We may think of these sets as Pascal types. Sets will be denoted by words that begin with capital letters. One of the sets is distinguished and is called the *carrier set* of the type. In our example, this is the set of all stacks. In specifications, carrier sets will be underlined. The other sets are called *auxiliary sets*; these are assumed to be defined elsewhere. The particular Pascal type definition of the carrier set depends on the implementation of the type and is therefore not a part of the specification. It is the main virtue of this method of specification that it is completely independent of the implementation technique used.

(ii) Rules which define the syntax for the primitive operations of the type and which, at the same time, introduce their names. We will state these rules as Pascal function headings.

(iii) Logical expressions (predicates) that are true under certain general conditions. We give these predicates as Pascal expressions of the type Boolean. The predicates, called axioms, depend on parameters given as single-letter identifiers. The identifiers represent members of sets specified in the first few lines of the axiom portion of a specification. We now give the formal specification of the data type Stack.

Type *Stack*
Sets *{Pascal types}*: <u>*Stack,*</u> *Item, Boolean*
Syntax:
> **function** *NIL_STACK*:*Stack*;
>> *{NIL_STACK is actually just a constant, but the only way to define a constant with a user defined type in PASCAL is by way of a function without parameters}*
>
> **function** *ISMT_STACK*(*s*:*Stack*):*Boolean*;
> **function** *TOP*(*s*:*Stack*):*Item;*
> **function** *POP*(*s*:*Stack*):*Stack;*
> **function** *PUSH*(*x*:*Item*; *s*:*Stack*): *Stack;*

Axioms: The functions *ISMT_STACK*, *TOP*, *POP*, and *PUSH* are strict and
> for all *x* in (*Item* − {*error*}) and
>> *s* in (*Stack* − {*error*}),

the following expressions yield **true**:

$$ISMT\_STACK(NIL\_STACK) \tag{4.1}$$

$$\textbf{not } ISMT\_STACK(PUSH(x, s)) \tag{4.2}$$

$$TOP(PUSH(x, s)) = x \tag{4.3}$$

$$POP(PUSH(x, s)) = s \tag{4.4}$$

$$TOP(NIL\_STACK) = error \tag{4.5}$$

$$POP(NIL\_STACK) = error \tag{4.6}$$

end {*Type Stack*}.

The following example shows how these axioms are used to analyze programs. Consider the sequence of statements below:

$$s := NIL\_STACK; \hspace{3cm} \{1\}$$
$$s := PUSH(3, PUSH(4, s)); \hspace{2cm} \{2\}$$
$$x := TOP(s); t := POP(s); \hspace{2cm} \{3\}$$
$$y := TOP(t). \hspace{3.5cm} \{4\}$$

We claim that, after the execution of this sequence, the value of x is 3 and the value of y is 4 . Formally, we show this as follows:

In line {2}, s is assigned the value

$$PUSH(3, PUSH(4, NIL\_STACK)).$$

Hence x, assigned the value $TOP(s)$ in line {3}, becomes

$$TOP(PUSH(3, PUSH(...))) = 3 \; \{axiom \; (4.3)\}.$$

Further, y is assigned the value of

$$
\begin{aligned}
&TOP(t) \\
=\; &TOP(POP(s)) \\
=\; &TOP(POP(PUSH(3, PUSH(4, ...)))) \\
=\; &TOP(PUSH(4, ...)) \hspace{2cm} \{axiom \; (4.4)\} \\
=\; &4 \hspace{4.5cm} \{axiom \; (4.3)\} \; . \; \Box
\end{aligned}
$$

4.1.2 Completeness of Specifications

Specifications must not only be precise ...

For a person who accepts our convention of sets and knows Pascal, the specification of stacks given above is precise and unambiguous. Therefore, this specification can be used both as a set of instructions for implementers and as directions to users; and it makes all further communication between these two groups unnecessary if, and this is essential, it is sufficiently complete.

... but also sufficiently complete

If it is not (sufficiently) complete, then there are cases where (i) the user cannot predict, from the specification, how the various functions behave and, conversely, (ii) the implementer is not clearly told how certain parts of the functions are to be programmed. For example, if axiom (4.6) were missing, then neither the user nor the implementer would know what to expect from or what to do with $POP(NIL\_STACK)$. But how can we know whether our specification is complete? How can we be sure that we do not need yet another axiom to cover some other special case?

That specifications are
complete ...
In order to answer this question we first need to understand better what completeness actually is. From the above example, we may infer that a specification is sufficiently complete if the user (or implementer) never faces a situation where the outcome of an operation is uncertain. Let us concentrate on the *user* of stacks. With the primitive operations the user constructs stacks by pushing elements onto, and popping elements off, stacks already in existence. Now, by means of the specification, the user must be able to predict the outcome of *ISMT_STACK* and *TOP* for all stacks that he could possibly construct with *PUSH*, *POP*, and *NIL_STACK* (there are no other ways of constructing stacks), provided that he always knows the values of the "items" that he uses with *PUSH*.

... can be proved.
The argument that our definition is sufficiently complete is, therefore, best divided into two parts:

(1)   the identification of the set of all stacks that a user can construct;
(2)   the demonstration that *TOP* or *ISMT_STACK* applied to any of these stacks gives a defined value.

(1) Intuition tells us that all stacks can be constructed only using *NIL_STACK* and *PUSH*, and that the use of *POP* does not lead to any stacks that could not be constructed without *POP*. It is important to understand that stacks have this property because we *want* them to have it, and not because of some formal mathematical reason. It is a common sense property of stacks as we think of them intuitively. In fact, given a picture of a specific stack (Figure 4.1), we can construct the unique expression which defines this stack and vice versa. Thus there is a bijection between the set of all stacks and the set of all

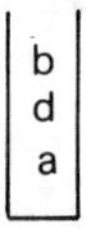

$$\begin{array}{|c|} \hline b \\ d \\ a \\ \hline \end{array} \quad PUSH(b, PUSH(d, PUSH(a, NIL\_STACK)))$$

Figure 4.1   A Stack Model and the Corresponding Reduced Stack Expression

expressions that define stacks using *NIL_STACK* and *PUSH*. Hence we can safely talk, for example, about the stack

   PUSH(a, PUSH(b, NIL_STACK))

since there can be no doubt about what we mean.

Mathematics enters into the problem when we try to make sure that our specification of stacks (the set of axioms) expresses this property.

All stacks are
of the form *NIL_STACK*
or *PUSH(x, s)*, ...
The following definition of the *reduced form* of stack expressions helps us to state precisely what we need to prove.

> *Definition:* A stack expression is in "reduced form" (it is a *reduced expression*) if it is either the expression *NIL_STACK* or an expression of the form *PUSH(i, s)* where *i* denotes some item and *s* is a reduced stack expression.

Lemma: By using the axioms, all expressions that compute a stack can either be reduced or have the value *error*.

Proof: Because of the syntactic properties of *NIL_STACK*, *PUSH*, and *POP*, expressions that compute stacks have the form

NIL_STACK or *PUSH(i, s)* or *POP(s)*

where *i* is in Item and *s* is another constructible stack. For the following inductive argument it is convenient to refer to the length of an expression. We say that an expression is of length 1 if it is the expression "*NIL_STACK*". We say that an expression is of length *n* > 1 if it is of the form *PUSH(i, s)* or *POP(s)* and *s* is an expression of length *n* − 1. For example, the expression

PUSH(3, POP(PUSH(5,PUSH(1,NIL_STACK))))

has length 5, while

PUSH(TOP(PUSH(3,NIL_STACK)), NIL_STACK)

has the length of 2, since the subexpression

TOP(PUSH(3,NIL_STACK))

does not contribute to the length of the (outer) expression.

We now prove the lemma by induction over *n*, the length of an expression.

Base case: By definition, *NIL_STACK*, the only expression of length 1, is in reduced form.

Induction hypothesis: Suppose that all expressions *s* which are not longer than n ≥ 1 can be reduced either to *PUSH(x,s′)* (where *s′* is reduced) or to *NIL_STACK* or evaluate to *error*.

Inductive step: Suppose *s* is of length *n*.

(a) Then *PUSH(x,s)* can be reduced by the reduction of *s* or evaluates to *error* if *s* evaluates to *error;*

(b) for *POP(s)* we obtain error if *s* reduces to *NIL_STACK* or, if *s* has the value *error*, or by axiom 4.4, we obtain *s′* if *s* reduces to *PUSH(x,s′)*. □

... and all expressions can be analyzed with the given axioms.

Thus, all stack expressions can be transformed to reduced form unless they have the value *error*.

(2) Now we can easily prove the following

Theorem: The axiom set of the primitive functions of the data type Stack is sufficiently complete.

Proof: We must simply show that all possible results computed by *ISMT_STACK* and *TOP* are determined by an axiom. By the above lemma we may assume that all stacks are given by reduced expressions.

ISMT_STACK(error)	= *error* {strictness},	(1)
ISMT_STACK(NIL_STACK)	= **true** {axiom(4.1)},	(2)

$$
\begin{array}{llll}
ISMT\_STACK(PUSH(i,s)) & = \textbf{false} & \{\text{axiom}(4.2)\}, & (3) \\
TOP(error) & = error & \{\text{strictness}\}, & (4) \\
TOP(NIL\_STACK) & = error & \{\text{axiom}(4.5)\}, & (5) \\
TOP(PUSH(i,s)) & = i & \{\text{axiom}(4.3)\}, & (6)
\end{array}
$$

4.2   IMPLEMENTATION

Finding the best possible implementation ...

There are many different ways by which we can implement stacks. Which one we should choose depends on pragmatic considerations concerned with efficiency (both of speed and storage utilization) and with specified limitations. For example, if we know that we will never need to stack more than some small number k of items at any one time, we might take advantage of this and limit stacks to k entries in order to improve storage or time efficiency. On the other hand, if we need several stacks or similar devices and if we cannot predict how many items are stored in any particular one, we might choose a more general implementation method that uses some additional bookkeeping space in order to achieve a better overall space efficiency.

... requires both a good sense for the natural and an open mind for the unusual.

Since the behavior of a "stack" corresponds closely with our knowledge of physical stacks, the implementation methods that come to mind will most likely imitate the stacking process. This is not necessarily bad; in fact it may turn out that the method best suited for our purpose is one that imitates stacking. However, we must practice looking beyond the seemingly natural if we want to find the most appropriate solution to a programming problem.

We shall discuss four different methods of stack implementation. These are implementations based on

(i)   a scalar (enumerated) type;
(ii)   integer numbers;
(iii)   arrays;
(iv)   the axioms themselves (in a direct way).

We shall begin with a method that does not imitate stacking at all. Although this method is rarely used in practice because of its obvious limitations, it will help us to make an important point about abstract data types: the objects of a type (in our example the members of the set "Stack") may be viewed as *atomic values*, that is, values that are merely code words whose further analysis does not reveal anything about the properties of the stacks they represent.

NOTE: The term "atomic" originally meant "indivisible". Therefore, strictly speaking, in a binary computer only bits are atomic. However, it is useful to extend this term to objects whose internal structure does not reflect their purpose so that no relationship can be found between the objects and their use or meaning other than by a tabular definition. As an example, consider the old teletype character set where the bit patterns of the characters did not even reflect the alphabetic or numeric ordering of the letters or digits, respectively.

4.2.1   Size-restricted (Bounded) Objects

For a bounded
stack ...

The implementation that we are about to discuss is manageable only if we put two rather severe restrictions on the stacks that we permit to be constructed:

(1) no more than three items are permitted on a stack at any one time;
(2) the items to be stacked are restricted to the set of boolean values **true** and **false**.

... an operation is
needed that can check
whether the stack is
full.

Because of the size restriction we need one additional operation that tests whether the stack is full. Furthermore, for the specification of this operation we need an operation that permits the computation of the current size of a stack. This operation, needed only for the specification of the test for overflow, is not one of the primitives known to the user. Such an operation is called *hidden*, and it is not, nor does it need to be, implemented.

We define

function *SIZE(s:Stack):Integer*; {*hidden*}
function *ISFL_STACK(s:Stack):Boolean*;

and the additional axioms

$SIZE(NIL\_STACK)$	$= 0$	(4.7)
$SIZE(PUSH(x, s))$	$= SIZE(s) + 1$	(4.8)
$ISFL\_STACK(s)$	$= (SIZE(s) = 3).$	(4.9)

4.2.2   Implementation Based on a Scalar Type

If an implementation
is based on a set
without internal
structure, operations
must be specified by
tables, ...

We now give the implementation of our stack functions.

Type *Stack* $= (a,b,c,d,e,f,g,h,i,j,k,l,m,n,p)$;

We insist that

NIL_STACK always returns "*a*",

and specify the remaining primitive functions by the tables in Figure 4.2.

s	PUSH(x,s) x: true	false	POP(s)	TOP(s)	ISMT_STACK(s)	ISFL_STACK(s)
a	b	c	error	error	true	false
b	d	f	a	true	false	false
c	e	g	a	false	false	false
d	h	l	b	true	false	false
e	i	m	c	true	false	false
f	j	n	b	false	false	false
g	k	p	c	false	false	false
h	error	error	d	true	false	true
i	error	error	e	true	false	true
j	error	error	f	true	false	true
k	error	error	g	true	false	true
l	error	error	d	false	false	true
m	error	error	e	false	false	true
n	error	error	f	false	false	true
p	error	error	g	false	false	true

Figure 4.2   Implementation of stacks based on an enumerated type

Thus, according to this table, we have, for example,

$PUSH(\textbf{true}, a) = b,$

$PUSH(\textbf{false}, f) = n,$

and

$TOP(f) = \textbf{false}.$

... verified line
by line, and ...

Clearly, the elements of the set "Stack" have no internal structure that has been exploited for this implementation. The only innate structure of such a scalar type is its ordering, but that has no bearing on the correctness of the implementation; the implementation remains correct even if we permute arbitrarily the ordering of the objects "$a,b,...$" in the type declaration.

Another example may help to illustrate how our implementation works.

$TOP(POP(PUSH(\textbf{true}, PUSH(\textit{false}, NIL\_STACK)))),$

gives

$TOP(POP(PUSH(\textbf{true}, PUSH(\textbf{false}, a))))$ *{by property of NIL_STACK}*

$= TOP(POP(PUSH(\textit{true}, c)))$ *{by the first line of the table}*

$= TOP(POP(e))$ *{by the third line}*

$= TOP(c)$ *{by the fifth line}*

$= \textbf{false}.$

The reader is encouraged to verify that the functions defined by the tables satisfy all of the axioms. This is done by systematically evaluating the axioms for all possible table entries.

... implemented by
arrays.

The actual coding of these functions in Pascal amounts to implementing the tables by arrays. This seems simple enough and we would not bother discussing it any further if it were not for the problem of the error conditions. Our first attempt at coding the functions starts with the definition of arrays for *PUSH*, *POP*, *TOP*, *ISMT_STACK* and *ISFL_STACK* as follows:

> **var** *PUSH:* **array** [*Boolean, Stack*]   **of** *Stack;*
> *POP:* **array** [*Stack*]   **of** *Stack;*
> *TOP:* **array** [*Stack*]   **of** *Boolean;*
> *ISMT_STACK:* **array** [*Stack*]   **of** *Boolean;*
> *ISFL_STACK:* **array** [*Stack*]   **of** *Boolean;*

and initialize

$PUSH~[\textit{true}, a] := b; PUSH~[\textit{false}, a] := c;$ etc.

Error messages ...

This works fine until we reach *PUSH* [*true, h*]. But *PUSH* [*true, h*] should yield *error*, that is, the attempt to compute it should lead to an error condition intercepted by the operating system (recall that *error* is not an actual value but the indication that control does not return to the point of invocation). If the compiler generates code that checks array bounds during execution, we could solve the problem by declaring

> **var** *PUSH:* **array** [*Boolean, a..g*]   **of** *Stack;*
>   *POP:*   **array** [*b..p*]   **of** *Stack;*
>   *TOP:*   **array** [*b..p*]   **of** *Boolean.*

... produced at the wrong level are cryptic.

To be sure, this solves our problem, but it is a less than perfect solution since it causes cryptic messages in the case of an error. Instead of the simple message *stack overflow* or *POP(NIL_STACK) = error* we are given the bewildering comment *subscript out of range*. The problem is that the message is not generated at the proper level. In order to correct this we have to program actual functions (not just array references) that test explicitly for overflow etc., issue the proper message and return to the system. Unfortunately, basic Pascal does not have a statement that permits the transfer of control to the system from any but the main level. Therefore, we have to transfer control from the level where the problem is detected to the outermost (main) level using a **goto**. This is not a very nice solution since it forces us to refer to a global label from the inside of a procedure or function. As an alternative, many implementations offer a *HALT* procedure that allows the termination of execution at any level. With this we could write, for example

> **function** *PUSH(x:Boolean; s:Stack):Stack;*
>
>   {*since we now use the name PUSH for the function, we rename the array as PUSH_ARRAY*}
>
>   **begin**
>   **if** *PUSH_ARRAY* [*x, s*] = *a* { *we use "a" to signal the error condition; recall that "a" is the empty stack, an impossible result of PUSH*}
>   **then begin**
>   *writeln*('*stack overflow*');
>   *HALT*
>   **end**
>   **else** *PUSH:= PUSH_ARRAY* [*x, s*]
>   **end.**

Returning explicit error codes encourages poor programming style.

Finally, we might ask why we should not introduce a real error code that we return to the calling program instead of transferring control to the operating system. If we wanted to do this, we would need a separate error code for each different set of values because Pascal does not allow intersecting type sets. But that is a minor point. The important reason for not having actual error codes is the following: programs should be written in such a way that run-time errors are prevented, that is to say, a program that causes a run-time error should be considered incorrect. For example, before popping a stack we should test whether the stack is empty, if that is a possibility. If we do return an actual error code from a program that has detected an error condition, we tempt the programmer to intercept the error *after* it has occurred rather than encourage him to prevent it beforehand. Also if, in the excitement of writing a masterpiece, the programmer has forgotten to test for errors both before and after they could occur, finding this mistake may be complicated if the program does not stop immediately upon finding an error. Returning an error code, the program would stumble along for a while until finally some secondary error would cause its termination. But at that time, control would have passed the point where the trouble originated, and the programmer might have great difficulty in backtracking to find the source of the error.

We now resume our discussion of implementation alternatives. Since the set defined as the scalar Pascal type $(a,b,...)$ does not have any structure of its own (apart from its ordering), we have no choice but to specify the stack functions by tables. *ISMT_STACK* is an exception, because it is false everywhere except at the value "*a*". Thus we could have written

> **function** *ISMT_STACK(s:Stack):Boolean;*
> > **begin**
> > > *ISMT_STACK*: = $(s = a)$
> > **end.**

4.2.3   Implementation Based on Integer Numbers

If implementations are based on sets with rich internal structure, ...

For our second implementation, we choose a set with a much richer internal structure: the integer numbers. By exploiting the operations of addition, multiplication, integer division, and the *MOD* operation (which computes the remainder of a division) we can obtain a rather simple implementation that does not require explicit tables for the functions.

We observe that with $a,b,c \geq 0$, $a*b + c \leq MAXINT$, and $c < b$ where *MAXINT* is the largest Pascal integer,

$$(a*b + c)\, DIV\, b = a \tag{4.10}$$

and

$$(a*b + c)\, MOD\, b = c \tag{4.11}$$

Suppose now that we want to implement a stack for the items 0..9. We decide to represent the empty stack by the number 1, the stack *PUSH(4,NIL_STACK)* by 14, the stack *PUSH(7, PUSH(4,NIL_STACK))* by 147 and so on. The following implementation accomplishes this:

> **const** *base* = 10; *limit* = 1000000000;
> **Type** *Stack* = *Integer; Item* = 0..9;

> **function** *NIL_STACK:Stack;*
> > **begin** *NIL_STACK* : = 1 **end;**

> **function** *ISMT_STACK(s:Stack):Boolean;*
> > **begin** *ISMT_STACK* := $(s = 1)$ **end;**

```
function PUSH(x:Item; s:Stack):Stack;
     begin
          if s < limit
               then PUSH := s*base + x
               else begin
                         writeln('stack overflow');
                         HALT
                    end
          end;

function POP(s:Stack):Stack
     begin
          if s = 1
               then begin
                         writeln('never pop an empty stack');
                         HALT
                    end
               else POP := s DIV base
          end;

function TOP(s:Stack):Item;
begin
     if s = 1
          then begin
                    writeln('TOP(NIL_STACK) not defined');
                    HALT
               end
          else TOP := s MOD base
     end;

function ISFL_STACK(s:Stack):Boolean;
     begin ISFL_STACK := (s >=limit) end.
```

With the base of 10, the example is particularly easy to understand. But the method works, of course, for any base less than *limit*. The value of *limit* is determined by the largest integer number that can be represented in the computer. Determining the formula that relates the cardinality *base* of the set of items, the largest integer *MAXINT* and the value of *limit* to each other is left as an exercise.

... verification amounts to reducing one set of axioms to another.

We conclude the discussion of this second implementation by proving that it is correct. We accomplish this by reducing the stack axioms to (4.10) and (4.11).

First we notice that our functions are strict and that

$$POP(NIL\_STACK) = POP(1) = error$$

and

$$TOP(NIL\_STACK) = TOP(1) = error$$

Now consider, for example, the axiom

$$TOP(PUSH(z, stk)) = z.$$

If $stk < limit$, then $PUSH(z, stk) = stk*base + z$.
Thus, we must show that

$$TOP(stk*base + z) = z.$$

Since

$$stk*base + z > 1 \ (base > 1 \text{ and } stk \geq 1),$$
$$TOP(stk*base + z) = (stk*base + z) \ MOD \ base$$
$$= z \ \{by \ 4.11\}. \ \square$$

Since (4.10) and (4.11) relate the basic operations of "+", "*", "DIV", and "MOD" to each other, we may interpret these as axioms for the integer operations. Thus, proving the correctness of this implementation amounts to showing that the programs for *PUSH* etc. satisfy the stack axioms, provided that the axioms for the integer operations are satisfied.

The reader may enjoy verifying that the other stack axioms are met also.

With a small modification of our packaging procedure, we can achieve a slightly denser representation for our stacks. We accomplish this by choosing 0 (zero) for *NIL_STACK*, and write

$$PUSH := s*base + x + 1,$$
$$POP \ \ := (s - 1) \ DIV \ base, \text{ and}$$
$$TOP \ \ := (s - 1) \ MOD \ base.$$

An explanation of why this version works is left as an exercise.

4.2.4   Implementation Based on Arrays

Restrictions of the previous methods ...

The implementation based on integer numbers still does not give us the general stack that we would like to have, in fact, it imposes severe restrictions on both the maximal size of a stack and the cardinality of the set of items that can be put onto a stack. The next method removes practically all restrictions but it will confront us with a new problem of a logical nature. Studying this problem will help us to refine our understanding of data objects. The problem is concerned with the seemingly obvious concept of equality. But rather than trying to explain the problem in the abstract at this point, we shall keep the reader in suspense for a few paragraphs and first describe the implementation method itself.

... are caused by the limited storage space allotted to each value.

It seems quite obvious that the limitations of the previous two implementation methods are due to the limited storage space that we have allotted to a stack. A stack represented by a number of the set $0..MAXINT$ cannot be expected to hold more than $MAXINT$. Obviously, we need several storage locations, an array for example, in order to house a stack of larger size for larger items.

Using a separate
array for each value ...

At first sight, it seems most straightforward to use one array for each stack. The array would take over the role previously played by the integer number. Created sufficiently large, it would accommodate any stack. At second glance though, this is not such a good idea. There are two reasons for this, a superficial one and a fundamental one. We shall discuss the fundamental reason first.

... is wasteful ...

A most important consideration is that we wish to remove as many limitations on stacks as possible. In particular, we wish to remove the restriction on the size of the stack, that is to say, we wish to eliminate the necessity for the overflow test. The worry about stack overflow does not seem to belong on the level of concern where the stack is used to solve, say, a language translation problem. There, we would like to take the position that there is practically unlimited stack space. To be sure, we know that the computer has only a finite store but we prefer not to worry about this limitation and are prepared to accept the occasional run-time error message: *problem too large, insufficient memory*. If we wanted to ensure that our programs behaved in this way using one array for each stack, then we would need to make these arrays a little larger than was required for any reasonable problem. Now suppose that we need several stacks and that, unexpectedly, one of these grows very large while others contain only a few items. Then it may happen that our program terminates because of "insufficient memory", although there is still much unused space in many of the arrays (stacks). Clearly, we would much prefer an implementation where one stack could obtain additional space at the expense of others so that we do not run out of storage space unless *all* available locations have actually been used.

... and impractical with
conventional languages.

A more mundane reason for not using one array for each stack is a restriction imposed by the language Pascal (it is also found in FORTRAN, PL/I, and other languages). Function procedures can only return scalar values such as integers, characters etc., but not structured values such as arrays or records. Hence, we could no longer use function procedures for *PUSH* and *POP* if these functions were to return arrays.

In a common array
for all data, stack
values are represented
by indices.

Consequently, rather than have a separate array for each stack, we use a large common array shared by all stacks. Here, a stack is represented by the index of its top element; the name of the array is assumed to be known implicitly to all primitive functions. Since we also need to know where the last (bottom) element of the stack is, we either need a second index or the current size of the stack; or, we must make it possible to test if an entry is the bottom of a stack. Suppose that we decide to adopt the latter solution. We therefore define the elements of the common array by

> **type**
> > *Entry* = **record** *info:Item; bottom:Boolean* **end**

and declare the array itself by

> **var** *space*: **array**[1..*max*] **of** *Entry*

where *max* is an integer constant, suitably chosen.

With the code "0" conveniently chosen for the empty stack, valid stacks are integer numbers between 0 and *max*, hence

type *Stack* = 0..*max*;

The common array is private to the stack primitives.

We consider the array *space* to be an area private to the stack primitives. There is a special variable *av*, also private to these operations, that contains the index of the next unused (available) record in *space*. Initially, *av* is assigned the value 1. Figure 4.3 shows how stacks are stored in the array *space*.

(a)

```
        1  2  3  4  5  6  7  8  9
av: 1 | ?  ?  ?  ?  ?  ?  ?  ?  ? |   space.bottom
      | ?  ?  ?  ?  ?  ?  ?  ?  ? |   space.info
```

(b)   s1 := PUSH('a', NIL_STACK)
        s1: 1

```
        1  2  3  4  5  6  7  8  9
av: 2 | T  ?  ?  ?  ?  ?  ?  ?  ? |   space.bottom
      | a  ?  ?  ?  ?  ?  ?  ?  ? |   space.info
```

(c)   s2 := PUSH('b', s1); s3 := PUSH('c', s2)
        s1: 1   s2: 2   s3: 4

```
        1  2  3  4  5  6  7  8  9
av: 4 | T  F  T  F  F  T  ?  ?  ? |   space.bottom
      | a  b  a  c  b  a  ?  ?  ? |   space.info
```

(d)   s1 := POP(s3)
        s1: 5   s2: 2   s3: 4

```
        1  2  3  4  5  6  7  8  9
av: 7 | T  F  T  F  F  T  ?  ?  ? |   space.bottom
      | a  b  a  c  b  a  ?  ?  ? |   space.info
```

(e)   s4 := NIL_STACK; s5 := PUSH('z', s4)
        s1: 5   s2: 2   s3: 4   s4: 0   s5: 7

```
        1  2  3  4  5  6  7  8  9
av: 8 | T  F  T  F  F  T  T  ?  ? |   space.bottom
      | a  b  a  c  b  a  z  ?  ? |   space.info
```

Figure 4.3 Stacks Housed in a Common Array

We see that *PUSH*(*x*, *s*) creates a new stack beginning at *av* by placing the item *x* at that position and by copying *s* to the right of *x*. In contrast, *POP*(*s*) does not need to produce a copy of *s*. We now give the Pascal code for the stack primitives.

```
function NIL_STACK:Stack;
    begin NIL_STACK := 0 end;
```

```
function ISMT_STACK(s:Stack):Boolean;
    begin ISMT_STACK := (s = 0) end;
```

```
function PUSH(x:Item; s:Stack):Stack;
    var s1: Stack;
    procedure ERROR;
        begin
            writeln('insufficient memory;' ,
                'problem too large');
            HALT
            end;
    begin
        if av > max then ERROR;
        space[av].info : = x;
        PUSH : = av;
        if s = 0
            then
                    space[av].bottom : = true
            else begin
                    space[av].bottom : = false; s1 : = s − 1;
                    repeat
                        s1 : = s1 + 1; av : = av + 1;
                        if av > max then ERROR;
                        space[av] : = space[s1]
                        until (space [s1].bottom = true)
                end;
        av : = av + 1
        end;
function POP(s:Stack):Stack;
    begin
        if s = 0
            then begin
                writeln('POP(NIL_STACK) = error');
                HALT
                end
            else
                if space[s].bottom {= true}
                    then POP : = 0
                    else  POP : = s + 1
        end;
function TOP(s:Stack):Item;
    begin
        if s = 0
            then begin
                writeln('TOP(NIL_STACK) = error');
                HALT
                end
            else TOP : = space[s].info
        end.
```

4.2.5 The Substance of an Implementation: the Functions *ABSTR* and *VALID*

Verification, ...

As we try to convince ourselves that these implementations of the operations satisfy the stack axioms, we find that all the axioms except one are easily verified.

NOTE: We cannot give a formal verification since we have not established axioms for all of the Pascal features that we have used; but confidence may be gained by careful tracing, because our programs are rather simple.

... while possible for most axioms, ...

Clearly,

$$ISMT\_STACK(NIL\_STACK) = \textbf{true}$$

and

$$ISMT\_STACK(PUSH(x, s)) \quad = \textbf{false} \ \{av \ is \ never \ 0\}.$$

Also, *TOP(NIL_STACK)* and *POP(NIL_STACK)* yield *error*, and *TOP(PUSH(x, s))* = *x* since *PUSH* deposits *x* at the place whose index it returns.

... causes problems for one ...

However, with

$$POP(PUSH(x, s)) = s$$

we have a problem. Consider, in Figure 4.3(e), the stacks *s1* and *s2*. We find that

$$s1 = POP(s3) \ \{by \ assignment\}$$
$$= POP(PUSH(`c', s2)) \ \{also \ by \ assignment\}$$

Thus, *s1* = *s2* should hold.

... because some values are equivalent but formally NOT equal.

Looking at the stack represented by *s1* we find it is

$$PUSH(`b', PUSH(`a', NIL\_STACK))$$

and we find the same for the stack represented by *s2*. But — and this is rather disturbing — *s1* = 5 and *s2* = 2, and 5 isn't the same as 2! It seems that, while the spirit of the axiom is obeyed, the letter of the rule is violated:

$$POP(PUSH(x, s)) \text{ and } s \text{ are not equal!}$$

In other words the Pascal expression

$$POP(PUSH(x, s)) = s$$

has the value **false** and not **true**. We cannot disregard this problem if we are serious about our pledge to provide specifications as precise and rigorous as programs. Let us state the problem once more: While the stacks represented by *s1* and *s2* are equal, the values that represent them are different.

Remember that we did not have this problem for any of the previous two implementations. So what exactly causes this problem here? What is the fundamental difference between this and the previous two implementations?

The reader may spend a few minutes in an effort to pinpoint the problem himself before reading the answer in the next paragraphs.

The fundamental difference between the first two implementations and the third one is the following. Both of the previous implementations provided a one-to-one correspondence between the stacks and the objects used to represent the stacks. In the second implementation, for example, the value

   15472

always represents the stack

   $PUSH(2, PUSH(7, PUSH(4, PUSH(5, NIL\_STACK))))$

Thus, we may conclude that not only equal representations denote equal stacks but also that representations that are different denote stacks that are different.

In our third implementation the association between the representations of stacks (i.e. the indices) and the stacks is not determined once and for all from the beginning by preestablished rules, but is constructed as the computation progresses. The representations do not denote stacks directly, they only tell where the definitions of the stacks denoted can be found. So, the representations actually denote locations, and clearly, two different locations may contain identical definitions.

We may cast these ideas in mathematical terms as follows:

If the mapping from the concrete set to the abstract set is not a bijection ..

For each of the first two implementations, the mapping from representing values (for example, integers) to representable stacks is a bijective function (if all stacks are considered, then the function is only injective, but the set of representable functions is easy to isolate). For the third implementation, however, the mapping function is neither bijective, injective nor surjective.

With a bijective mapping between them, stacks and the integers that represent them can be identified with each other. Since we can recover each from the other, it simply does not matter whether we think of a specific stack as, for example,

   $PUSH(2, PUSH(7, NIL\_STACK)$ or as 172.

... then we must proceed very carefully!

On the other hand, if the mapping is not a bijection, we must carefully distinguish between values and their representations. Our troubles above with the verification of *PUSH* and *POP* occurred precisely because we did not make this distinction. Instead of expecting that the programmed functions *PUSH* and *POP* satisfy the axioms, we may only require that the stacks represented have the correct properties.

ABSTR maps representations to abstract values.

In order to express this thought more concretely, let us denote the function that maps the array subscripts to stacks by *ABSTR*. In addition, programmed functions such as *PUSH*, *POP* etc., compute array subscripts rather than the abstract stacks they denote. Therefore, if there is any risk of confusion, we denote the programmed functions by *PUSHc* and *POPc* and reserve the names *PUSH* and *POP* for the functions defined by the axioms (the suffix "*c*" stands for "*concrete*"). Now we can state precisely what we expect the functions *PUSHc* and *POPc* to compute:

$$ABSTR(POPc(s)) = POP(ABSTR(s)), \tag{4.12}$$

and

$$ABSTR(PUSHc(x,s)) = PUSH(x, ABSTR(s)). \tag{4.13}$$

For the other stack primitives we obtain, analogously:

$$ABSTR(NIL\_STACKc) = NIL\_STACK, \tag{4.14}$$
$$ISMT\_STACKc(s) = ISMT\_STACK(ABSTR(s)), \tag{4.15}$$
$$TOPc(s) = TOP(ABSTR(s)). \tag{4.16}$$

Line (4.12), for example, says that the stack represented by *POPc(s)* is the same as the stack that we obtain if we apply *POP* itself to the stack represented by *s*. With the axiom *POP(PUSH(x,s))* = *s* we obtain by substitution

$$POP(PUSH(x, ABSTR(s))) = ABSTR(s)$$
$$= POP(ABSTR(PUSHc(x,s)))$$
$$= ABSTR(POPc(PUSHc(x,s))) = ABSTR(s)$$

Thus, if we knew the function *ABSTR*, then we could verify *PUSHc* and *POPc*!

Specifying *ABSTR* from the details of the implementation of stacks based on arrays is not very difficult.

(a) Since we represent *NIL_STACK* by 0, *ABSTR* should map 0 to *NIL_STACK*.

(b) If *space*[n] .*bottom* is **true** for some given subscript *n*, then *ABSTR* should map *n* to a stack with just one element, namely, to *PUSH* (*space[n] .info, NIL_STACK*).

(c) Finally, if *space*[n].*bottom* is **false**, then *n* represents a larger stack whose continuation is found in the array at position $n+1$. Thus *ABSTR* should map *n* to *PUSH(space[n].info,ABSTR(n + 1))*.

Thus we have

$ABSTR(n)$
$= $ **if** $n = 0$
    then *NIL_STACK*
    else
        if *space*[n].*bottom*
           then *PUSH(space[n].info, NIL_STACK)*
           else *PUSH(space[n].info, ABSTR(n + 1))*.

We demonstrate how *ABSTR* maps subscripts to stacks by applying it to *s3* of Figure 4.3(c) reproduced here in Figure 4.4.

s3:	4	s1:	1	s2:	2		

1	2	3	4	5	6	7	8	9
T	F	T	F	F	T	?	?	?
a	b	a	c	b	a	?	?	?

bottom
info

Figure 4.4   Stacks of figure 4.3 (c)

Now,

$$ABSTR(s3) =$$
$$ABSTR(4) =$$
    if $4 = 0$
        then *NIL_STACK* {*inactive*}
        else
            if *space*[4].*bottom* {= *T*}
                then *PUSH*(*space*[4].*info*, *NIL_STACK*)
                else *PUSH*(*space*[4].*info*, *ABSTR*(4 + 1))

        = **if** F { = *T*}
           then ... {*inactive*}
           else *PUSH*('c', *ABSTR*(5)).

Evaluating *ABSTR*(5) we derive then

$$ABSTR(s3) = PUSH('c', PUSH('b', ABSTR(6)));$$

finally, since *space*[6].*bottom* is **true**, we obtain

$$ABSTR(s3) =$$
$$PUSH('c', PUSH('b', PUSH('a', NIL\_STACK))).$$

With a little reflection we may convince ourselves that using this definition of *ABSTR* we obtain equality for

$$ABSTR(s) \text{ and } ABSTR(t)$$

whenever the information stored at *s* represents the same stack as the information stored at *t*.

On closer inspection we notice, however, that the function *ABSTR* is not yet completely defined. In particular, we have not yet specified its proper domain. As it stands, the domain of *ABSTR* seems to be the union of the singleton set {0} and the set of possible subscripts for the array *space*. But what is, say, the value of *ABSTR*(25) if the array *space* has been utilized only up to subscript 17 (assuming that 1..*max* with 25 ≤ *max* is the type of the subscripts)? Well, of course, it is undefined!

Now, while we can tolerate a function not being defined everywhere, we certainly want to know for which arguments it is defined; we want to know its actual domain!

The actual domain of ABSTR is defined by the predicate VALID.

In order to specify the actual domain of *ABSTR* for the implementation based on arrays, we need to determine which subscripts are currently valid representations of stacks and which are not. This seems to call for a predicate that, applied to any possible subscript of "*space*", returns the value **true** if this subscript represents a valid stack and **false** if it does not. Let us call this predicate *VALID*. Obviously, since 0 represents *NIL_STACK*, *VALID*(0) is **true**. For subscripts other than 0 we find that *VALID*(n) is **true** only if $0 < n < av$ and $av \le (max + 1)$. Furthermore, we notice that, with $n \ne 0$, *space*[n].*bottom* must be **true** or ($n + 1$) must be a valid argument for *ABSTR* as well. Putting these requirements together we derive the following definition:

> *VALID*(n)
> > **iff** ($n = 0$)
> > **or** ($0 < n < av$) **and** ($av \le max + 1$)
> > > **and** (*space*[n].*bottom* **or** *VALID*($n + 1$)).

Now, what is *VALID* good for?

First, it defines the domain of *ABSTR*. Thus, by computing *VALID*(s) we find out whether the expression *ABSTR*(s) makes sense.

Secondly, *POPc* and *PUSHc*, if correct, ought to compute stack representations in the domain of *ABSTR* if they are given stack representations in this domain; hence

> **if** *VALID*(s),
> > **then** *VALID*(*POPc*(s)) **and** *VALID*(*PUSHc*(x,s)).

In order to avoid any wrong conclusions, we would like to stress: *VALID*(n) only implies that n is in the domain of *ABSTR* and *not* that n is a proper stack. Suppose that *PUSH* does not assign any values to *space*[n].*info* but updates *space*[n].*bottom* properly. In this case *VALID*(n) may be **true** but *ABSTR*(n) would find an undefined "*info*" field and, thus, yield an error rather than a proper abstract stack.

ABSTR and *VALID* help (i) to verify the correctness of an implementation and ...

With *ABSTR* and *VALID* we now have the tools for verifying the correctness of an implementation. Suppose a function *fc* is to represent the abstract function *f* from stacks (and possibly, auxiliary sets) to stacks. Then, for *fc* to be correct, the following must be true:

$$VALID(s) \Rightarrow VALID(fc(s)), \tag{4.17}$$

and

$$VALID(s) \Rightarrow (ABSTR(fc(s)) = f(ABSTR(s))). \tag{4.18}$$

Furthermore, if g is a function from stacks (and, possibly, auxiliary sets) to an auxiliary set, then

$$VALID(s) \Rightarrow (gc(s) = g(ABSTR(s))). \tag{4.19}$$

As an example, we shall now verify the function *POP* for the implementation of stacks by arrays. First we compute *VALID*(*POPc*(s)) assuming *VALID*(s):

type *subrng* $= 0..max;$

function *POPc*(s:*subrng*):*subrng;*
    begin
        if $s = 0$
            then *ERROR*(...)
            else if *space* [s].*bottom*
                then *POP* $:= 0$
                else *POP* $:= s + 1$
    end.

Clearly, if $s = 0$, then *POP* reports an error; thus $VALID(POPc(0))$ is of no concern.

If $0 < s < av$, then, by $VALID(s)$, *space* [s].*bottom* or $VALID(s + 1)$ is **true**. In either case *POPc* returns a valid result, namely 0 or $s+1$, respectively.

Secondly, we show that

$$ABSTR(POPc(s)) = POP(ABSTR(s)).$$

For $ABSTR(POPc(s))$ we obtain

$ABSTR(POPc(s)) =$
    if $s = 0$
        then $ABSTR(error) = error$
            {*for ABSTR is considered strict*}
        else
            if *space* [s].*bottom*
                then $ABSTR(0) =$
                    NIL_STACK
                else $ABSTR(s + 1);$

and for $POP(ABSTR(s))$

$POP(ABSTR(s)) =$
    if $s = 0$
        then $POP(ABSTR(0))$ $=$
            $POP(NIL\_STACK) = error;$
        else
            if *space* [s].*bottom*
                then
                    $POP(PUSH(space$ [s].*info*, $NIL\_STACK)) =$
                    NIL_STACK {*by axiom 4.4*}
                else
                    $POP(PUSH(space$ [s].*info*, $ABSTR(s + 1))) =$
                    $ABSTR(s + 1).$

Now suppose our *POP* operation were programmed incorrectly as follows:

```
function FALSE_POP(s:subrng):subrng;
    begin
        if s = 0
            then ERROR(...)
            else FALSE_POP := s + 1
    end.
```

Here we obtain

$ABSTR(FALSE\_POPc(s)) =$
    if $s = 0$
        then $ABSTR(error)\{= error\}$
        else $ABSTR(s + 1),$

which should be equal to

$POP(ABSTR(s)) =$
    if $s = 0$
        then *error*   *{correct}*
        else
                if *space*$[s].bottom$
                        then NIL_STK $\{\neq ABSTR(s+1)$; *incorrect*$\}$
                        else $ABSTR(s + 1)$ *{correct}* .

Thus trying to establish (4.12) we discovered the error. Not all errors are discovered by this method. Functions sometimes have to perform certain housekeeping activities that do not affect the value returned but that set the stage for the next reference to the function. For example, the code of the function *PUSH* given at the end of section 4.2.4 finally replaces *av* by $(av + 1)$. If we forget to add this command, then $ABSTR(PUSHc(...))$ will still give the correct result, but when invoked the next time *PUSH* will destroy the stack previously created. In order to find errors of this sort we have to establish (4.17), that is, for *PUSH* in particular we have to show that

$$VALID(s) \Rightarrow VALID(PUSH(x,s)).$$

To see how the error of leaving out '$av = av + 1$' reveals itself, consider the expression $PUSH(x,NIL\_STK)$. Since NIL_STK is represented by 0, *PUSH* executes the lines

```
if av > max then error;
space[av].info := x;
PUSH := av;
space[av].bottom := true;
{av := av + 1 we assume was left out}.
```

Now

$VALID(0)$ **{true}** *should imply* $VALID(PUSH(x,s))$
    $= VALID(av),$

however

$$VALID(av) = (av = 0) \qquad\qquad \{always\ false\}$$
$$\mathbf{or}((0 < av) \qquad\qquad \{true\}$$
$$\mathbf{and}\ (av < av) \qquad\qquad \{false\}$$
$$\mathbf{and}\ (av \leq max + 1) \qquad\qquad \{true\}$$

is **false**.

Hence $VALID(PUSH(x,s))$ is not implied by $VALID(s)$, that is to say, the code of *PUSH* must be incorrect.

... (ii) to document the details of an implementation.

Besides their value for program verification, the functions *ABSTR* and *VALID* document the details of an implementation of a data type in a precise and concise way. Therefore, we will call them *implementation descriptors*. It is good practice to define the implementation descriptors before writing the code for the actual primitives of a new type. In fact, for the purpose of documentation, they should be defined even if *ABSTR* is a bijection between the set of valid representations and the set of representable values. For the implementation by integers we obtain, for example:

$ABSTR(n) =$
    if $n = 1$
        then *NIL_STACK*
        else $PUSH(n\ MOD\ base, ABSTR(n\ DIV\ base))$

and

$$VALID(n)\ \mathbf{iff}\ n = 1\ \mathbf{or}\ VALID(n\ DIV\ base).$$

If ABSTR is not a bijection then...

We conclude this section by drawing one additional lesson from our original problem. We noticed that the representations of equal objects are not guaranteed to be equal unless *ABSTR* is a bijection (or at least an injection). Consequently, a comparison of the following kind

        var $s1,s2$: *Stack;*

        .
        .
        .

            if $s1 = s2$
                then ...
                else ...

        .
        .
        .

will not give the desired result because $s1$ and $s2$ may be formally different while the stacks they represent are equal. The deeper reason for this problem is the fact that the Pascal operator "$=$" does not properly implement the comparison of abstract stacks. Denoting by *EQ* the proper comparison function for abstract stacks, we can express this by

for some $s1,s2$.
$$(s1 = s2) \neq EQ(ABSTR(s1), ABSTR(s2)).$$

Thus the comparison for stacks

function $EQ(s1, s2$: Stack):*Boolean*

where

$$EQ(s, t) \text{ iff } ABSTR(s) = ABSTR(t)$$

must be programmed by the implementer.

EQ can be coded as a recursive program as follows:

... the test for
equality must be made
a primitive of the type.

function $EQ(s1,s2$:*Stack*):*Boolean;*
    begin
        if $s1 = s2$
            then $EQ :=$ **true**
            else
                if $(s1 > 0)$ **and** $(s2 > 0)$
                    then $EQ := (TOP(s1) = TOP(s2))$
                          and $EQ(POP(s1), POP(s2))$
                  else $EQ :=$ **false**
    end.

We leave the verification of this program as an exercise for the reader.

With the addition of this equality predicate, the user of our stack primitives may now ignore the fact that these operations compute representations of the abstract stacks instead of the abstract stacks themselves; he may identify *PUSHc* with *PUSH*, *POPc* with *POP*, and so on, but he must never compare two stack values using " $=$ " but using only EQ. We therefore might consider replacing the stack axiom

$$POP(PUSH(x,s)) = s \tag{4.4}$$

by

$$EQ(POP(PUSH(x,s)), s). \tag{4.4a}$$

However, we shall not do this, but instead interpret " $=$ ", if used in axioms, as a relational operator for abstract values and not as the operator provided by Pascal.

In the remainder of this book, we will usually not explicitly distinguish between names for the abstract operations and names for their concrete implementations but trust that the reader appreciating the difference will easily infer from the context which of the two concepts is intended.

4.2.6   Direct Implementation of the Axioms

Direct implementation
of the axioms ...

For the last example, we will implement the stack operations by directly implementing the rules of the axioms. We will store empty stacks as

NIL_STACK and nonempty stacks as *PUSH(x, s)*. Clearly, we do not need to store the word *NILSTACK* or the word *PUSH*, nor do we need to store parentheses or commas. Instead of *PUSH(x, s)* we store the ordered pair *(x,s)* and instead of *NILSTACK* we store some shorter code. Since we want to manipulate many stacks we provide storage space for many ordered pairs by setting up the array

> **var** *space*: *array* [1..*max*] *of Pair*

with *Pair* defined as follows

> **type** *Pair* = *record info:Item*; *stk:Stack* **end**.

As before, we represent a stack by the index of the record that contains it and, as before, we choose "0" as the code for the empty stack. Thus we obtain

> **type** *Stack* = 0 .. *max*.

... is similar to the implementation based on arrays ... Again we assume that the array *space* may be manipulated only by the stack operations and that there is a special variable *av*, initialized to 1, which indicates where in the array space the next available record is.

We first give the implementation descriptors *ABSTR* and *VALID*:

> *ABSTR*(*n*)
> 　　= **if** *n* = 0
> 　　　　**then** *NIL_STACK*
> 　　　　**else** *PUSH*(*space*[*n*].*info*, *ABSTR*(*space*[*n*].*sk*))

> *VALID*(*n*)
> 　　**iff** (*n* = 0) **or** (0 < *n* < *av*) **and** (*av* < *max* + 1)
> 　　　　**and** *VALID*(*space*[*n*].*stk*)

Now, all that *PUSH* has to do is to place its arguments into a new record and return the index of that record, *TOP* and *POP* return the value of the *info* or the *stk* field, respectively, *NIL_STACK* and *ISMT_STACK* are coded in the same way as in the third implementation. Thus, we obtain:

> **function** *PUSH(x:Item*; *s:Stack):Stack;*
> 　　**procedure** *ERROR*;
> 　　　　**begin**
> 　　　　　　*writeln('insufficient memory;'*,
> 　　　　　　　　*'problem too large')*;
> 　　　　　　*HALT*
> 　　　　**end**;
>
> 　　**begin**
> 　　　　**if** *av* > *max*
> 　　　　　　**then** *ERROR*
> 　　　　　　**else begin**
> 　　　　　　　　*space*[*av*].*info* := *x*;
> 　　　　　　　　*space*[*av*].*stk* := *s*;

$$PUSH := av;$$
$$av := av + 1$$
> **end**
end;

function *TOP(s:Stack):Item*;
> **begin**
>> **if** $s = 0$
>>> **then** *begin*
>>>> *writeln('TOP(NIL_STACK) = error')*;
>>>> *HALT*
>>> **end**
>>> **else** *TOP := space[s].info*
> **end**;

function *POP(s:Stack):Stack*;
> **begin**
>> **if** $s = 0$
>>> **then** *begin*
>>>> *writeln('POP(NIL_STACK) = error')*;
>>>> *HALT*
>>> **end**
>>> **else** *POP := space[s].stk*
> **end.**

... but easier to verify, ...

Since this implementation simply duplicates the stack axioms, we can easily verify that the implementation is correct and guarantees them. Nevertheless, it may help our intuitive understanding if we study, by an example the storage structure maintained by this implementation. Figure 4.5 shows what the array looks like after the given code segment is executed.

$s := NIL\_STACK$;
$s1 := PUSH('b', PUSH('a', s))$;
$s2 := PUSH('c', s1)$;
$s3 := PUSH('d', s1)$;
$s4 := PUSH('e', s3)$;
$s3 := PUSH('f', s3)$;
$s1 := POP(s4)$;

	info	stk	
1	a	0	
2	b	1	
3	c	2	← s2
4	d	2	← s1
5	e	4	← s4
6	f	4	← s3
7	?	?	
8	?	?	

Figure 4.5   The Common Array of the Direct Method

Because it is cumbersome to analyze the structure by looking up records from given indices, we draw, instead, a different type of diagram (Figure 4.6). Into a field that contains an index (that is, a stack) we put the tail of an arrow whose head points to the record to which the index belongs. For example, into the *stk* field of record 6 we put the tail of an arrow that points to record 4. Also, since none of our functions ever takes advantage of the actual position of a record in the array (none of the functions does arithmetic with indices) we do not draw the records as an array but as single cells rearranged in such a way that we can follow the arrows easily. Customarily, *NIL_STACK* is denoted by the symbol ⏚.

... and more efficient and elegant.

The most striking property of the structure depicted in Figures 4.5 and 4.6 is the great economy with which space is utilized.

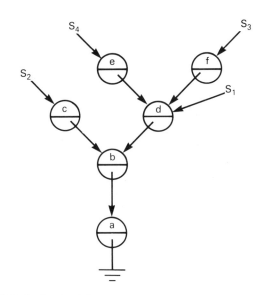

Figure 4.6 The Stacks of Figure 4.5, Represented by an Arrow Diagram

We have four stacks with a total of fourteen entries stored in only six cells. The stacks do not interfere with each other because each cell receives its contents at the time when it is created and these contents are never changed thereafter.

Direct implementation = linked allocation, ...

The principles underlying this direct implementation are used in many ways for the implementation of a great variety of data types. We shall devote the entire Chapter 5 to this method. Since cells are linked together by their indices (addresses) the method is usually called the method of *linked allocation*. It is an important property of this method that it views the indices only as names of cells and *not* as numbers that are subject to arithmetic.

... array based implementation = sequential allocation.

In contrast, the method that exploits the fact that indices are numbers that can be added etc., is called *sequential allocation*. Logically related items are stored at sequential indices.

4.2.7   Array-based Versus Direct Implementation

Despite some
similarities ...

Both methods store the stacks in a common array space and represent the stacks by indices into this array space. Both methods use the same code for the functions *TOP*, *NIL_STACK*, and *ISMT_STACK*.

... the direct method
is usually preferable.

While the array-based method uses simpler records — the second field (bottom) only contains one bit while the second field (stk) of the direct method needs to accommodate an index of the array — the direct method saves a great deal of time and storage space because its *PUSH* operation does not need to copy an entire stack before putting a new element on top.

4.3   VALUES AND MUTABLE OBJECTS

The user should
not pursue storage
economy by the (low-
level) *DISPOSE*
operation ...

Execution of a statement of the form

$$s := POP(s)$$

replaces the original value of *s* by a new one. Therefore, keeping the storage structure of the old one would be wasteful unless, elsewhere in the program, there is a copy of *s*. In order to give the user the option of recycling the storage space, we may be tempted to invent an operation, *DISPOSE*, that recovers the storage space of a cell no longer needed. *DISPOSE* could be used in the following way:

$$t := POP(s); \; DISPOSE(s); \; s := t.$$

The reader will agree that such a salvage operation does not belong in the program that uses stacks; as a storage management function, *DISPOSE* is on a much lower level of concern.

... but by the (high-
level) concept of
mutable objects.

As a more legitimate way of getting the user involved in storage economy, we may consider the treatment of stacks as objects that can be modified rather than as values from which new values can be computed.

Here we have to pause for a moment in order to clarify our terminology. Since we now use the words "object" and "value" to describe properties of our data, we need some other word that refers to the concrete thing that we use to represent an object or a value. We shall call that thing a *datum* (with the plural "data").

Returning to our discussion on objects, we observe that we should use *procedures* rather than functions to modify the objects (the stacks) to compute new ones. Thus we would write

$$POP(s) \quad \text{and} \quad PUSH(x,s) \quad \text{instead of}$$
$$s := POP(s) \quad \text{and} \quad s := \text{PUSH(x,s)}.$$

The procedure *POP*, for example, updates the stack *s* and returns the top cell to some pool of available space (disposes of the top cell).

NOTE: How such a pool of available cells is managed is the subject of Chapter 5; for now, the reader may take it on trust that this can be done.

Common sense tells us that we may only dispose of a cell if it is no longer needed. This is an important principle with a number of consequences. Hence a somewhat stronger formulation is in order.

Be sure never to dispose of a cell still needed.

Fundamental rule for the use of DISPOSE

Never dispose of a cell unless you are absolutely certain that the cell is no longer needed (anywhere in your program).

Does

procedure *POP*(*var s*:*Stack*)

obey this rule if it disposes of the top cell of a stack as we have just described it? Not, if it disposes of the cell accessed by the parameter *s*! Consider the segment *t*1 := *t*2; *POP*(*t*2)! After *POP* returns control, *t*1 still "needs" the cell originally accessed by *t*2.

Since we usually do not know how a program uses a subprogram, we derive the following corollary from the rule above:

Corollary rule for the use of DISPOSE:

Do not dispose of a cell within a subprogram if the cell is accessed by a parameter of this subprogram unless, due to the nature of the subprogram, a violation of the fundamental rule is impossible.

Now we seem to be in a dilemma. On the one hand we want *POP* to salvage the top cell of the stack (that is why we invented the idea of a mutable object in the first place); on the other hand, we are not supposed to dispose of the cell by which the stack is accessed. Obviously, we can only accommodate both demands if we make sure that the top cell of the stack is not also the cell by which the stack is accessed. But accessing the stack by any other cell, such as the bottom cell, does not help: when the stack contains only one item, then there is only one cell and that, for all we care, is on top!

There are two solutions to the problem.

(i) We do not permit the assignment of an object to another variable (as in *t*1 := *t*2, above). As a result, each object would then be associated with exactly one variable; hence, when a variable is assigned a new (stack) value, a cell that becomes superfluous can be deleted since no other variable could possibly have a claim to it. We shall call objects treated in this fashion *mutable objects of the first kind.*

The requirement that assignments may not be used should not be interpreted too literally. It should prohibit different parts of a program from sharing the same objects in arbitrary ways, but it should not interfere with certain local manipulations of objects that are frequently needed. Consider, for example, the following segment involving objects stored in *stck* and *next*:

$$temp := stck; \; stck := next; \; next := temp.$$

Although, temporarily, *temp* and *stck,* later *stck* and *next*, and finally *next* and *temp* refer to the same object, there is no threat to the integrity of these objects since at the end of this short segment *stck* and *next* again refer to different objects (suppose that outside this segment *temp* is never used). In spite of these concessions, objects of the first kind are too restricted for most applications.

(ii) For *mutable objects of the second kind* arbitrary assignments are permitted. This becomes possible by accessing the actual stack indirectly through an extra location (commonly called a head cell). This cell is to represent the stack, but it is not to be part of the stack proper and thus it does not store an item. Its purpose is to ensure that the top cell of the stack is reached from only one place, namely from this special cell. This makes the stack proper a mutable object of the first kind. Note that *POP* no longer needs a variable parameter. The parameter of *POP* now refers to the head cell, which, for a given stack object, always remains the same. Hence arbitrary assignments of objects are now possible. We may even use objects as *items* in other data types without any additional complications.

Mutable objects are *places* not *values*.

Consequently, a datum that represents a mutable stack (object) no longer represents a particular instance (value) of a stack but a location of a stack value or, if you like, a case that contains a stack value. One might say that this is nothing new because both the array implementation and the direct implementation use indices into the array (that is, addresses of places) as representations of a stack. However, this fact is of no concern to the user! The user can treat these data as representations of particular stack values because he can be sure that the same datum represents the same value throughout his entire program. In contrast, with mutable stack objects the same datum always represents the same *container*, but the contents may change from one moment to the next. Control is achieved by ensuring that each stack value (and any of its parts) can be accessed through only one object. Hence, if, due to a modification, a cell is eliminated from a value, this cell can safely be deleted since no other object has a claim to it.

The greater control over the utilization of storage gained by mutable objects is purchased, unfortunately, at the price of a more complex behavior. Consider the example in Figure 4.7 (*s* is some stack object).

$$t := s; \quad x := TOP(t); \quad POP(s); \quad y := TOP(t)$$

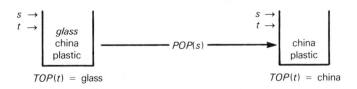

Figure 4.7   Behavior of stack objects

4.3.1 Specification of Mutable Objects

The proper handling
of procedures ...
Since data types of mutable objects use procedures for some of their primitive operations, we are faced with the problem of fitting procedures (which unlike functions do not return values by their names) into expressions that can serve as axioms. Also, "stacks" are now members of the set of all stack containers rather than members of the set of all stacks (stack values).

... is accomplished by
means of an implicit
parameter of type
Store.
Obviously, at any instant, each stack container houses a particular stack unless its contents are undefined. The association between these containers and actual stack values can be viewed as a mapping (a function) from the set of containers to the set of stack values. Given a stack object (container), this mapping, aptly called the *store*, will tell us what is in it.

In order to make the notion of a store more precise, we will raise it to the status of a new abstract data type.

This exercise has a very important purpose: we wish to develop a general method for specifying mutable objects using the definition of the corresponding values. Then, all future data types can be defined as values even if they are meant to be implemented and used as objects. This is of great advantage because value specifications, not being burdened with the complications introduced by the store, are much simpler than the kind of specifications that we would obtain if we tried to define objects directly.

Definition of
conditional
expressions.
Here and later on we shall use one additional facility not available in Pascal: *conditional expressions*. The expression

   if p **then** x **else** y

has the value x if the predicate p is true otherwise it has the value y.

Conditional expressions are merely a convenience; predicates stated with conditional expressions can always be stated without them. For example,

   $z = ($**if** p **then** x **else** $y)$

expresses the same logical relation as

   p **and** $(z = x)$ **or** $\neg p$ **and** $(z = y)$.

Now we give the definition of the abstract data type *Store*:

Type *Store:*

Sets: *Store, Object {Stackobj}, Value {Stack}*

Syntax:

   function *NIL_STORE*: *Store*
        {gives a new store};
   function *ASGN*(*v*:*Value*; *s*:*Object*; *st*:*Store*):*Store*
        {the store returned associates v with s and otherwise behaves as st};
   function *CONT*(*s*:*Object*; *st*:*Store*):*Value*
        {retrieves the content of s according to store st}

Axioms: ASGN and *CONT* are strict and
for all *st* in *Store* – {error},
    s,t in *Object,*
    v in *Value*
$CONT(s, NIL\_STORE) = error;$ (4.20)
$CONT(s, ASGN(v, t, st))$ (4.21)
    = **if** $(s = t)$
        then v **else** $CONT(s, st);$
$ASGN(x, s, ASGN(y, t, st))$ (4.22)
    = **if** $(s = t)$
        then $ASGN(x, s, st)$
        else $ASGN(y, t, ASGN(x, s, st))$
end {*Store*}.

The following lemma will prove useful for later derivations:

Lemma:

$CONT(s,st) \neq error$
implies
$ASGN(CONT(s,st), s, st) = st$ (4.23)

This lemma expresses the commonsense observation that the store is not changed if an object is assigned the value that it already owns. Proving the lemma confirms that the axioms describe this property of the store correctly.

   We prove the lemma by induction over the length of the expression for the store *st*.

Base case: $st = NIL\_STORE$ gives $CONT(s,st)$ the value *error*; hence the premise of the implication is false, and so the lemma is true.

Induction hypothesis: assume that the lemma is correct for expressions *st* no longer than *k*.

Induction step: Consider $ASGN(CONT(s,st'), s, st')$ with

   $st' = ASGN(x, t, st)$ and length$(st) = k$.

Now,

$ASGN(CONT(s,st'), s, st') =$
    $ASGN(CONT(s, ASGN(x,t,st)), s, ASGN(x,t,st)) =$
    if $s = t$
        then $ASGN(x, s, ASGN(x, t, st))$
            $= ASGN(x, t, ASGN(x, t, st))$
            $= ASGN(x, t, st) \{by\ 4.22\}$
        else $ASGN(CONT(s,st), s, ASGN(x,t,st))$
                    $\{by\ 4.21\}$
            $= ASGN(x, t, ASGN(CONT(s,st), s, st))$

$$\{by\ 4.22\}$$
$$= ASGN(x,t,st) \quad \{by\ the\ ind.\ hyp\} \ \square$$

In definitions, parameters of type Store are mentioned explicitly.

Since at any instant there exists only one store, it is not explicitly mentioned in programs, but is considered to be implicit. Hence, instead of $CONT(s,st)$ we would simply write $CONT(s)$, and instead of $st := ASGN(v, s, st)$ we would write $ASGN(v, s)$ interpreting $ASGN$ as a procedure rather than as a function. In our specifications we shall include the store, nevertheless, because doing so permits us to express them as (Pascal-like) expressions similar to the axioms for stack values given earlier.

Now we can define the operations on mutable stack objects in terms of the operations on stack values. Basically, an object operation first retrieves a value using $CONT$, then it refers to the proper value operation to obtain the desired result and, if this is again a stack value, it saves it using $ASGN$. Thus, for every primitive function on values that returns a member of the carrier set, we create a procedure on objects with the same parameters as the function except that parameters of type stack value become parameters of type stack object. If the original function does not have a parameter of type Stack (as *NIL_STACK*) the procedure created is given an additional parameter of type Stack object. For functions on values that return members of auxiliary sets we create functions on objects by again simply replacing parameters of type Stack value by those of type Stack object. For the purpose of specification we give every operation an additional parameter of type Store and we interpret Pascal procedures as functions with the codomain Store. For distinction, we attach the suffix "*o*" and the suffix "*v*" to the names of the object and value functions, respectively:

NIL_STACKo:	$Stackobj \times Store \rightarrow Store$
ISMT_STACKo:	$Stackobj \times Store \rightarrow Boolean$
PUSHo:	$Item \times Stackobj \times Store \rightarrow Store$
POPo:	$Stackobj \times Store \rightarrow Store$
TOPo:	$Stackobj \times Store \rightarrow Item$

For *st* in *Store*, *s* in *Stackobj*, and *x* in *Item*:

NIL_STACKo(*s,st*)	=	$ASGN(NIL\_STACKv,\ s,\ st)$
ISMT_STACKo(*s, st*)	=	$ISMT\_STACKv(CONT(s,st))$
PUSHo(*x,s,st*)	=	$ASGN(PUSHv(x,CONT(s,st)),s,st)$
POPo(*s,st*)	=	$ASGN(POPv(CONT(s,st)),s,st)$
TOPo(*s,st*)	=	$TOP(CONT(s,st)).$

Two examples may illustrate how these specifications are used to analyze program segments. Consider the segment

$$\{store\ st1\}\ PUSH(x,s);\ POP(s).$$

Since $PUSH(x,s)$ provides the store for $POP(s)$, this segment translates to the expression

$$st3 = POPo(s,\ st2)\ with\ st2 = PUSHo(x,\ s,\ st1).$$

Now,

$$st3 = ASGN(POPv(CONT(s,st2), s, st2)),$$

and

$$st2 = ASGN(PUSHv(x, CONT(s,st1)), s, st1).$$

Further,

$$CONT(s, st2)$$
$$= CONT(s, ASGN(PUSHv(x,CONT(s,st1)), s, st1))$$
$$= PUSHv(x,CONT(s,st1)) \{by\ 4.21\},$$

thus

$$st3 = ASGN(POPv(PUSHv(x,CONT(s,st1))), s, st2)$$
$$= ASGN(CONT(s,st1), s, st2) \{by\ axiom\ 4.4\}$$
$$= ASGN(CONT(s,st1), s, ASGN(z, s, st1))$$
$$\quad with\ z = PUSHv(x,CONT(s,st1))$$
$$= ASGN(CONT(s,st1), s, st1) \{by\ 4.22\}$$
$$= st1 \{by\ lemma\ 4.23\}.$$

We see that $POP(s)$ cancels the effect that $PUSH(x,s)$ has on the store, which is reassuring. We also see, that the derivation of this result is of considerable complexity, while the analogous fact for stack values is given as an axiom. As a second example consider

$$\{st1;\}\ PUSH(x,s);\ PUSH(y,t);\ z:=\ TOP(s).$$

$PUSH(x,s)$ gives the store $st2 = PUSHo(x,s,st1)$ to $PUSH(y,t)$, which modifies the store to $st3 = PUSHo(y,t,st2)$. Finally, we have $z = TOPo(s,st3)$.

Now,

$$z = TOPo(s,\ PUSHo(y,t,st2))$$
$$= TOPv(CONT(s,\ ASGN(PUSHv(y,CONT(t,st2)),t,st2)))$$
$$= TOPv(CONT(s,\ st2)) \qquad\qquad \{by\ 4.21\}$$
$$= TOPv(CONT(s,\ PUSHo(x,s,st1)))$$
$$= TOPv(CONT(s,\ ASGN(PUSHv(x,CONT(s,st1))),s,st1))$$
$$= TOPv(PUSHv(x,CONT(s,st1))) \qquad \{by\ 4.21\}$$
$$= x \qquad\qquad\qquad\qquad\qquad \{by\ 4.3\}.$$

Here we see how the axioms ensure that the evaluation of $TOP(s)$ ignores the statement $PUSH(y,t)$, which is irrelevant to the value of $TOP(s)$.

The general rule for specifying objects from values derives in a straightforward way from the specific example of stacks. Without loss of generality we assume that, in procedures on objects, the next to the last parameter refers to the object to be modified, and the last one is of type Store. Let Po be a procedure that modifies an object and Pv the corresponding function on values. Further, let Fo be a function on objects that computes an auxiliary type and Fv be its value counterpart. Now we have

The general rule: specification of mutable objects from the specification of the corresponding values.

$$Po(x0,...,xn,\ s,\ st)$$
$$= ASGN(Pv(y0,...,yn,\ CONT(s,st)),\ s,\ st), \qquad\qquad (4.24)$$

and

$$Fo(x0,...,xn) = Fv(y0,...,yn) \qquad\qquad\qquad\qquad (4.25)$$

where $yi = xi$ if xi is of an auxiliary type, and $yi = CONT(xi, st)$ if xi is of the carrier type. With these rules we may (and shall) always specify our abstract data types as types of values.

4.3.2   Implementation of Mutable Objects

Mutable objects need header fields or head cells.

From our introductory discussion on the subject one might infer that mutable objects are of interest only if implementation by cells is contemplated. This is not true. To be sure, implementation by enumerated types and by integers, while not impossible, is of no great interest. But both linked and sequential implementation methods can profitably be adapted to stack objects. If a stack s is a mutable object, then s represents the place where the object resides. *PUSH* and *POP* no longer change the value of s but the stack accessed through s. As has been pointed out earlier, direct implementation, which depends on cells, must be modified by adding a *head cell*, that is linked to the top of the stack proper and whose index represents the object stack. Figure 4.8 shows the storage structure for such a stack.

ABSTR and *VALID* can also be constructed for mutable objects.

We would, of course, like to have implementation descriptors for mutable objects similar to those for values. From the way objects are specified, we may assume that we need to describe not only the implementation of stacks but also of stores. This would be a correct yet cumbersome path to take. It turns out to be sufficient (and much easier) to describe the implementation of the store operation *CONT* only.

The representation of a store is a mapping from objects to representations of values, thus — a store of representations. Further, since they manipulate representations of values and not the (abstract) values themselves, our procedures use and compute store representations rather than abstract stores. Now we can proceed with the definitions of *ABSTR* and *VALID* for mutable objects.

First we give the definition for the function *ABSTR* as a function from objects and representations of stores to abstract values:

function $ABSTRo(s:Stackobj;\ st:store\_rep):Stack;$

with the relationship

$$ABSTRo(s,st) = ABSTRv(CONTc(s,st)) = CONT(s,st')$$

where st and st' are the concrete and abstract store, respectively, and $CONTc(s,st)$ returns the representation of the value held by s. Simply stated, $ABSTRo(s,st)$ is the current abstract value associated with s. Therefore, for

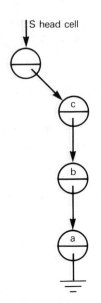

Figure 4.8   A Stack Object with a Head Cell

concrete functions *Foc* on objects and their abstract counterparts *Fv* on values we obtain the relationship

$$ABSTRo(s, Foc(..., s,st))$$
$$= Fv(..., ABSTRo(s,st)),$$

which allows us to verify whether the implementation *Foc* of a primitive operation *Fo* is correct. For example, we have

$$ABSTRo(s, PUSHoc(x,s,st))$$
$$= PUSHv(x, ABSTRo(s,st)).$$

NOTE: As with functions on values, a function *Fo* on objects is represented by a concrete function *Foc* that computes a store representation instead of an abstract store. With the implementation depicted by Figure 4.8, a concrete store is the set of all head cells with their current contents.

Consider the concrete example of Figure 4.8 assuming that, as with direct implementation, cells are housed in the array "space" of pairs where

type *pair* = **record** *info:Item*; *stk:Stack* **end**.

The head cell is also a slot in the array with *stk* referring to the stack value. Thus,

$$CONTc(s, st) = space[s].stk,$$

and hence

$$ABSTRo(s, st)$$
$$= ABSTRv(space[s].stk);$$

$ABSTRv(n) = $ **if** $(n=$o$)$ **then** NIL_STACKv
$\qquad\qquad$ **else** $PUSHv(space[n].info, ABSTRv(space[n].stk))$.

Now let us verify the

$\qquad$ **procedure** $PUSH(x$:$Item$; s:$Stack)$;
$\qquad\qquad$ **var** $temp$: $Stack$;
$\qquad\qquad$ **begin**
$\qquad\qquad\qquad$ **if** $av > max$
$\qquad\qquad\qquad\qquad$ **then** $ERROR$ $(...)$
$\qquad\qquad\qquad\qquad$ **else** begin
$\qquad\qquad\qquad\qquad\qquad$ $temp$: $=$ $space[s].stk$;
$\qquad\qquad\qquad\qquad\qquad$ $space\;[av].info := x$;
$\qquad\qquad\qquad\qquad\qquad$ $space\;[av].stk := temp$;
$\qquad\qquad\qquad\qquad\qquad$ $space\;[s].stk := av$;
$\qquad\qquad\qquad\qquad\qquad$ $av := av + 1$
$\qquad\qquad\qquad\qquad$ **end**
$\qquad\qquad$ **end**

by computing

$ABSTRo(s,PUSHo(x, s, st))$
$= ABSTRv(space[s].stk$ $\{after\ PUSH(x,s)\})$
$= ABSTRv(av–1)$ $\qquad\qquad$ $\{by\ code\ above\}$
$= PUSHv(space[av–1].info,$
$\qquad ABSTRv(space[av–1].stk))$ $\{by\ def.\ of\ ABSTRv\}$
$= PUSHv(x,ABSTRv(temp))$ $\qquad$ $\{by\ code\}$
$= PUSHv(x,ABSTRv(space[s].stk$ $\{before\ PUSH\}))$
$= PUSHv(x,ABSTRo(s, st))$ $\qquad$ $\{by\ def.\ of\ ABSTRo\}$.

The definition of $VALIDo$ is straightforward:

function $VALIDo(s$:$Stackobj$; st:$store\_rep)$:$Boolean$

$VALIDo(s,st)$ **iff** $VALIDv(space[s].stk)$

$VALIDv(n)$ **iff** $(n=0)$
$\qquad$ **or** $(0 < n < av)$ **and** $(av \le max + 1)$
$\qquad\qquad$ **and** $VALIDv(space[n].stk)$.

Here we could reasonably raise the objection that a dispose operation (however it may work) probably requires an allocation scheme that can no longer be based on a simple incrementation of av. As we will discover in Chapter 5, this is quite true. For the time being we will repair this deficiency by assuming two operations for the handling of the available space that replace

$\qquad (av := av + 1)$ $\qquad\qquad\qquad\qquad\qquad\qquad$ $\{in\ PUSH\}$

and

$\qquad (0 < n < av\ and\ av \le max + 1)$ $\qquad\qquad\qquad$ $\{in\ VALIDv\}$

by, respectively,

$ADVANCE(av)$

and **not** $IS\_AVAIL(n)$.

Mutable objects can be
implemented using
sequential allocation. If no more than two stack objects are needed, then sequential allocation (implementation based on arrays) is particularly attractive. The stacks are begun at the two ends of an array and grow towards the middle. Overflow occurs if the tops of the stacks meet. The records of the array need to accommodate the items stacked, but no extra space is needed for marking the bottom because the bottoms coincide with the ends of the array. Figure 4.9 shows both the code of the *PUSH* operation and the storage structure for this method.

The stacks are represented by the numbers 1 and 2. These numbers select the index of the top of the stack and the increment $+1$ or -1 from the arrays *TOPOS* (top position) and *INCR*. The empty stack is denoted by the values 0 and 8 for stacks 1 and 2, respectively. Here the triple

$(TOPOS[i], INCR[i], EMPTY[i])$

represents the stack value housed by the objects.

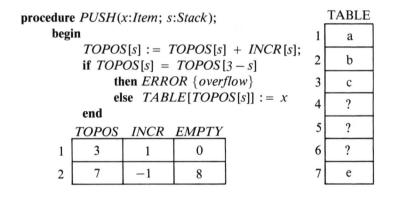

Figure 4.9 Sequential implementation of Stack Objects

Consequently, *ABSTR* has the following form:

$ABSTR(i) = ABSTRv(TOPOS[i], INCR[i], EMPTY[i]),$
$ABSTRv(n, i, e)$
$\quad = \textbf{if } (n = e)$
$\qquad\qquad \textbf{then } NIL\_STACK$
$\qquad\qquad \textbf{else } PUSH(TABLE[n], ABSTRv(n-i, i, e)).$

Writing the code for the other stack operations is left as an exercise.

4.3.3   Dynamic creation of mutable objects

If mutable objects are to be created dynamically, ...

None of the operations specified above for mutable stacks — not even *NIL_STACK* — computes a stack object; therefore, we must assume that the set of stack objects is given from the beginning (as, for example, the set of characters is given *a priori* in most programming languages). *NIL_STACK* does not produce a new stack object but associates an empty stack with a given stack object; in other words, *NIL_STACK* empties a given stack (object).

... then their formal specification requires ...

For the purpose of creating new stack objects on demand, we could introduce the function

$$NEW\_STACK: \rightarrow Stackobj,$$

or we could change *NIL_STACK* into a function that creates a new stack object associated with an empty stack:

$$NIL\_STACK: Store \rightarrow Store \times Stackobj.$$

... the formal specification of the assignment operator.

Both of these methods cause severe complications for our axioms because they force us to incorporate the assignment into the set of primitive operations. With stacks interpreted as values, the expression

$$PUSH(3, NIL\_STACK),$$

makes good sense; its result is a new stack that contains a 3; the expression can be used wherever a stack value is needed. With the object interpretation and *NIL_STACK* as a function

$$PUSH(3, NIL\_STACK)$$

(which is not an expression with a value but a statement) does not make sense since it creates a stack object that is not accessible; we have no name for it! In order to obtain such a name we must write

$$s := NIL\_STACK; PUSH(3, s)$$

Thus, the assignment is now an indispensable part of our system and so is the concept of a variable. The store is no longer only a mapping from stack objects to stacks but also from variables to stack objects, and the assignment is a function that computes a new store, associating a variable with a stack object. Thus

$$assignment: Store \times Variables \times Stackobj \rightarrow Store.$$

One could object to this seemingly unexpected concern about the formal semantics of assignment by pointing out that assignments have been used informally in previous examples. Why then are we suddenly so concerned about their formalization?

Previously we dealt with (i) stack values and (ii) stack objects that could be modified but not created. In both cases we were able to translate code segments into a form that did not contain any assignments. While this translation involved some informal treatment of assignments, the resulting form could be verified formally by means of the given axioms. With the operation *NEW_STACK* or the modified version of *NIL_STACK* this translation is no longer possible unless all occurrences of *NEW_STACK* or *NIL_STACK* are also eliminated from the resulting form.

Formal proofs can be checked mechanically.

Having formal verifications (proofs) for the correctness of programs is very desirable because formal proofs are more likely to be correct; moreover, they can be *checked* mechanically by a computer program (*finding* a proof mechanically is quite a different matter).

Clearly, we cannot claim that we have formally proved some property of a code segment if our derivation contains not only formal rules but also the informal handling of assignments. However, if we can subdivide the proof into a translation part, which is not formal, and a verification part, which is formal, then the formal part may be verified mechanically while the informal, less reliable part, which is now relatively small and well isolated, can be scrutinized separately by hand.

Having made this point, we will, nevertheless, refrain from formalizing the semantics of the assignment because that would go beyond the intended scope of this book. We shall simply remember that allowing mutable objects to be created on demand at run time causes additional complexity for the specification.

Dynamic creation of mutable objects is often necessary.

For very practical reasons we cannot completely avoid this additional complexity since the assumption that our objects exist from the beginning is usually not true. Think of the implementation that uses linked allocation with a head cell. Properly initialized head cells cannot be declared in the same way as ordinary variables that come into existence before our program (or subprocedure) starts running. Therefore we need two versions of the operation *NIL_STACK*.

(i) In *NIL_STACK(s)*, the contents of *s* are undefined if *s* has never been used before. Here, using, for example, the linked implementation depicted in Figure 4.8, we would let *NIL_STACK* place into *s* the index of a newly created head cell which contains the value of an empty stack.

(ii) In *NIL_STACK(s)*, *s* already contains the index to a head cell of some existing stack. In this case, we wish to maintain the head cell (it might be accessed from other variables) and we wish to salvage the space occupied by the stack by returning its cells to a list of available space.

Notice that (4.24) allows for both interpretations. Unfortunately, we cannot perform both operations with one program (unless we add a parameter which tells the program which of the two strategies to follow) since we cannot test which of the cases obtains because, in case (i), the value of *s* is "undefined". Pascal does not permit testing for an undefined variable; in fact, expressions that contain a reference to an undefined variable are invalid. Hence, if we wish to be able to empty an existing stack immediately instead of popping each element separately, then we must provide two operations:

> **procedure** *NEW_STACK(var s:Stack_obj)*

for initialization, and

> **procedure** *NIL_STACK(s:Stack_obj)*

for emptying an already existing stack. We should not use *NEW_STACK(s)* unless *s* is undefined, because applying *NEW_STACK* to an existing stack is both wasteful and a source of logical errors. Consider the following code segments:

> *t := s; NEW_STACK(s).*

We have learned, that the assignment, *t := s*, allows *t* and *s* to refer to the same stack. However, after *NEW_STACK(s)*, *s* and *t* refer to different stacks; *NEW_STACK* does not empty the object accessed by *s* but replaces the current object of *s* (which is also the current object of *t*) by a new empty stack while it does not affect the state of *t*. Thus, after *NEW_STACK(s)*, *s* and *t* refer to different stack objects.

Notice also that *NEW_STACK* is the only stack primitive that has a variable parameter.

4.3.4   Objects or values, which should we choose?

Mutable objects complicate specifications and call for discretion; ...

Viewing stacks (or other data forms) as mutable objects instead of values makes it necessary to introduce the implicit set of stores. The elements of this set are mappings (functions) that associate objects (containers) with their contents. The resulting axioms are more complicated than those used previously for the value interpretation. Allowing the dynamic creation of mutable objects leads to even more complexity. This must be considered a disadvantage of mutable objects, for simple semantic rules promote — and complex rules obstruct — both the correct implementation and use of a data type. Also, the fact that the set of stores does not explicitly appear in programs may be a possible source of error.

... functions with side-effects may add even more complexity.

If we accept these complications (and there may be good reasons to do so), then we may go even one step further and consider functions that change the store besides returning a value. For stacks, an operation *POP_TOP* is often considered convenient. *POP_TOP(s)* removes the top element from the stack s and returns its value. Thus,

> *POP_TOP*: *Stackobj* × *Store*→ *Item* × *Store*

with the specification

> *POP_TOPo(s,st)*
>   = *(TOPv(CONT(s,st)),*
>   *ASGN(POPv(s,CONT(a,st)), s, st)).*

Functions that modify one or more objects in addition to returning a value are said to have a side effect. It is good practice to avoid functions with side effects. Occasionally, as with *POP_TOP*, such a function may perform an operation that many perceive as very natural. Only if the specification of the side effect does not cause additional complications, should a programmer consider the implementation of such a function. In the above example, the crucial step was that from values to objects. Hence, adding *POP_TOP*, which causes little additional complexity, may be judged acceptable.

Deciding between
values and objects
deserves care.

Whether a programmer opts for values or for objects is frequently a matter of habit more than of careful analysis. It should be remembered that all that can be done with the object approach can be done with the value approach as well. Yet sometimes the price that must be paid in terms of storage utilization or time efficiency for a value implementation may be unacceptably high. In a way, the two views may be compared with solving a (mathematics) problem with pen and ink (the value view) or with pencil and eraser (the object view). The first method may require more paper but it definitely has its own elegance and neatness. In fact, there is a breed of programming languages, called *functional* or *applicative* languages, that do not even provide mutable objects; they work exclusively with values.

EXERCISES

Theoretical Exercises

T4.1   Evaluate the following expressions

(1) *TOP(POP(POP(PUSH(3,POP(PUSH(4,PUSH
     (5,(PUSH(6,NIL_STACK)...).*

(2) *ISMT_STCK(POP(POP(PUSH(3,NIL_STACK))))*

For each step cite the axiom which justifies the step.

T4.2   Reduce the following expressions

(1) *PUSH(1,PUSH(2,(POP(POP(PUSH(5,PUSH(4,NIL_STACK)...);*

(2) *PUSH(1,POP(NIL_STACK)).*

T4.3   Consider the function B defined by the following axioms.

$B(NIL\_STACK) = error;$
$B(PUSH(x,s)) =$ **if** $ISMT\_STACK(s)$
   then x **else** $B(s)$.

(1) Evaluate the following expression

$B(PUSH(1,POP(PUSH(2,PUSH(3,NIL\_STACK)))));$

(2) What does the function B do?
What would be a more descriptive name for it?

T4.4 For the implementation of stacks by integers (Section 4.2.3, page 67) determine the relationship between the values *base*, *MAXINT*, and *limit*.

T4.5 For the implementation of stacks by integers (Section 4.2.3), the text provides the proofs that the Pascal programs given satisfy the axioms

$$POP(NIL\_STACK) = error,$$
$$TOP(NIL\_STACK) = error, \text{ and}$$
$$TOP(PUSH(x,s)) = x.$$

Prove that the other stack axioms are satisfied also.

T4.6 At the end of section 4.2.3, a second (denser) representation is suggested. Prove that this implementation is correct as well.

T4.7 Give the implementation descriptors *VALID* and *ABSTR* for the implementation of stacks based on an enumerated type as described in Section 4.2.2 (page 63).

T4.8 Using the relationships (4.17) – (4.19) on page 76, prove that the Pascal functions *PUSH* and *TOP* given for the direct implementation in Section 4.2.6 (page 80-83) are correct.

T4.9 Find the function *VALID* for the implementation of two stacks sharing one array (Section 4.3.2, page 94). Remember that *VALID* should express which stack representations are meaningful. In particular, *VALID* must deal properly with overflow and underflow conditions.

T4.10 Using *VALID* and *ABSTR* verify the correctness of the procedure *PUSH* for the implementation of the two stacks sharing one array (Section 4.3.2, page 94).

Programming Exercises

P4.1 Implement the stack operations for stack objects using the direct method with head cells.

P4.2 Implement two stack objects sharing a common array (Section 4.3.2, page 94) and prove that your implementation is correct.

P4.3 Many programs use stacks to "put things on ice" if something more urgent comes along. The stack discipline, last-in first-out, assures that items are recovered from the stack in their order of urgency.

To see this mechanism in action, write a program that evaluates arithmetic expressions consisting of the binary operators +,–,*, *DIV*, and integer numbers as operands. Assume that the operators are evaluated from left to right (no other priority rules are implied) unless parentheses are used to indicate a different order. The method works roughly as follows:

There are two variables one for the left and one of the right operand, as well as one for a binary operator. As input is read, the first number is assigned to the left operand, then the operator is placed into its variable, and so on. If both operand variables are filled, then the operation is performed and the result becomes the new left operand.

If, instead of a right operand, a left parenthesis is encountered, then both the left operand and the operator are put on the stack, and the variable of the left operand is the next to be filled from the input. If, instead of an operator, a right parenthesis is found, then the current left operand becomes the right one, and the left operand and the operator are recovered from the stack; then the operation is performed yielding a new left operand.

When the end of the expression is found (e.g. in form of a semicolon), then the stack should be empty. If the stack is not empty at this point or if it becomes empty prematurely, then the parentheses do not match.

Work out the remaining details for yourself and write the program with a stack whose items are pairs consisting of an integer number and an operator. Make sure that you can process all character strings and not only valid expressions and allow for the issuing of meaningful error messages for incorrect input strings.

P4.4   Develop an algorithm that uses two stacks to sort a sequence. Implement the algorithm as a procedure with the header

procedure *SORT_STK* (*s*:*Stack*);

Create the second stack within the sort procedure. Besides the two stacks you are allowed one other variable to store an item. Assume that the items are integer numbers.

There are several strategies for sorting sequences with two stacks. One moves the items back and forth between the two stacks making sure that small items get to the top of stack *A* and large items to the top of stack *B*.

Cells

Cells are used for implementing other types.

Cells may be used for the implementation of other data types. We have already met cells informally in the previous chapter for direct and linked implementation of stacks. In this chapter, we shall raise them to the status of a data type and examine this type in greater depth. Three major issues will be addressed:

(i) cells as values,
(ii) cells as mutable objects,
(iii) common programming language support for cells.

We shall again deal with the specification as well as the implementation and the practical use of cells.

The compartments of cells are called *fields*.

In general, cells are aggregates of several compartments, called *fields*. In order to simplify our discussion, we consider only the simplest form of cells sufficient for the implementation of stacks. These are cells with two fields: one for an item and one for another cell. The reader will see for himself that the generalization to cells with more fields is straightforward. We assume that there is one specific cell that does not have any fields at all: the null-cell, called *NIL_CEL*. We need at least five operations:

Cell values need the operations
NIL_CEL,
ISNIL,
CELL,
HD, and *TL*.

> **function** *NIL_CEL* : *Cells*
>   {*creates a null-cell*},
> **function** *ISNIL*(*c*:*Cells*):*Boolean*
>   {*tests for a null-cell*},
> **function** *CELL*(*x*:*Item*; *c*:*Cells*):*Cells*
>   {*creates new cell for an item and a cell*}
> **function** *HD*(*c*:*Cells*):*Item*
>   {*"head", retrieves item field from cell*},
> **function** *TL*(*c*:*Cells*):*Cells*
>   {*"tail", retrieves cell field from cell*}.

In addition,
cell objects need
SET_HD,
SET_TL, and
DELETE.

These operations are sufficient if cells are viewed as values. If we interpret cells as mutable objects, then we need operations for changing the contents of a cell and for deleting a cell. Thus for objects we add the operations

> **procedure** *SET_HD*(*c*:*Cells*; *x*:*Item*),
> **procedure** *SET_TL*(*c*,*d*:*Cells*),
> **procedure** *DELETE*(*c*:*Cells*).

With the data type *Cells*, we can keep the details of memory allocation and packing and unpacking data out of programs that implement primitives of other data types. That is to say, in this chapter we deal once and for all with the different ways of implementing the mathematical concept of an ordered pair or, in general, an *n*-tuple; from the next chapter on we shall take the cell primitives for granted and cease to worry about how they are actually implemented. In order to demonstrate the benefit of this approach, consider the code of the function PUSH for the direct implementation of a stack using the cell primitives. The reader is urged to compare this program with the one given in Section 4.2.6.

> **type** *Stack* = *Cells*;

> **function** *PUSH*(*x*:*Item*; *s*:*Stack*):*Stack;*
>   **begin** *PUSH* : = *CELL*(*x*,*s*) **end**.

Sometimes we will need more than one type of cell for the implementation of other types, and we will take the liberty to invent new names for the additional functions needed. For example, instead of *CELL* we may use the name *PAIR* for the function that creates a cell of a different type, or instead of *HD* and *TL* we may use *FRONT* and *REAR* or *FIRST* and *SECND*.

5.1 SPECIFICATION OF CELLS AS VALUES

The type
of cell values
is very simple.

The specification of the value operations for cells follows the pattern of the stack specification. Thus the following text needs no additional comments.

Type *CELLV*

Sets: *Cellv*, *Item*, *Boolean*

Syntax:

> **function** *NIL_CEL* : *Cellv*;
> **function** *ISNIL*(*c*:*Cellv*):*Boolean*;
> **function** *CELL*(*x*:*Item*; *c*:*Cellv*):*Cellv*;
> **function** *HD*(*c*:*Cellv*):*Item*;
> **function** *TL*(*c*:*Cellv*):*Cellv*;

Axioms:

All functions are strict and

for all *c* in *Cellv* − {*error*} and
     x in *Item* − {*error*}

ISNIL(*NIL_CEL*)	(5.1)
not *ISNIL*(*CELL*(*x, c*))	(5.2)
HD(*NIL_CEL*) = *error*	(5.3)
HD(*CELL*(*x, c*)) = *x*	(5.4)
TL(*NIL_CEL*) = *error*	(5.5)
TL(*CELL*(*x, c*)) = *c*	(5.6)

end {*CELLV*}.

5.2 IMPLEMENTATION OF CELL VALUES

A standard error procedure improves the readability of programs.

Throughout the remainder of this book we shall assume that we can invoke the following error procedure whenever necessary:

procedure *ERROR*(*id*:*Name*; *code*:*Error_code*);
    begin
        writeln('***** *ERROR detected in*' , *id*);
        CAUSE(*code*); *HALT*
    end;

with

type
    Name   = **packed array**[1..9] **of** *char*;
    Error_code = (*overflow, underflow, e_o_file,*
                exhausted, {*others as needed*}).

The procedure *CAUSE* retrieves a meaningful message from a table of error messages subscripted by the Pascal type *Error_code*.

5.2.1   Implementation by integer numbers

The implementation of cells by integers is similar to the implementation of stacks by integers except that, with cells, we pack exactly two pieces of data into one integer number, one of which is itself of type cell. But this seems to be an impossible task: an integer clearly cannot accommodate an item and another integer; there is not enough room for both. We can solve this problem only by finding a representation for cells that takes up much less space than an integer number. The subscript into an array of integers is such a representation. Let

var *space:* **array**[1..*MAXCEL*] **of** *Integer* be the array, where

const *MAXCEL* = 5000   {*some suitable number*};

then *i* is used to represent *space*[*i*]. With *factor* suitably chosen and *c* in *Cellv* (= 0..*MAXCEL*) we obtain

$ABSTR(c) =$
    if $c = 0$
        then *NIL_CEL*
        else *CELL*(*space*[*c*] *DIV factor*,
            ABSTR(*space*[*c*] *MOD factor*)),

and
    $VALID(c)$
        iff ($c = 0$) or ($c < av$ and $av \leq MAXCEL + 1$).

Now, with *av* initialized to 1, the code of cell is:

function *CELL*(*x:Item*; *c:Cellv*):*Cellv;*
    begin
        if $av > MAXCEL$
            then *ERROR*('*CELL*   ', *exhausted*)
            else begin
                CELL := *av*;
                space[*av*] := *x*∗*factor* + *c*;
                av := *av* + 1
            end
    end.

Constructing the code for *HD*, *TL*, etc. is left to the reader as an exercise.

The size of *factor* is determined by the maximal range *MAXCEL*; in fact, *factor* = *MAXCEL* + 1. If we wish to provide an equal range of, say, *R*, for both the *HD* and the *TL* component, we proceed as follows:

$MAXINT = R * factor + R$ where $factor > R$;

With *factor* = $R + 1$ we obtain

$MAXINT = R^2 + 2*R,$

hence

$MAXINT + 1 = R^2 + 2*R + 1 = (R + 1)^2$

thus

$factor = R + 1 = SQRT(MAXINT + 1).$

If no component of a cell is itself a cell of the same kind, then all components may fit into an integer number, and the array space can be saved. Now the body of *CELL*(*x*, *y*) consists of the single statement

$CELL := x * factor + y.$

5.2.2   Direct implementation of the cell axioms

When implementing the cell axioms directly, we represent cells by subscripts into an array of records, each with one field for an item and one for another cell. Thus we need the following definitions:

```
const max = 5000;
type   Cellv = 0..max;
       Pair = record inf:Item; next:Cellv end;
var    av:Cellv; space: array[1..max] of Pair.
```

In order to be valid, a subscript referring to a cell must have been produced by the function *CELL*. In practice this means that the space accessed by the subscript may no longer be a part of the pool of available space. This is the case if its value is less than the current value of *av*. Thus,

$$VALID(c) \text{ iff } 0 \le c < av \textbf{ and } av \le max + 1;$$

and

$$ABSTR(c)$$
$$= \textbf{if } (c = 0)$$
$$\textbf{then } NIL\_CEL$$
$$\textbf{else } CELL(space[c].inf,$$
$$ABSTR(space[c].next));$$

```
procedure INITL;
        {is invoked at the beginning of a program that uses cells}
        begin av := 1 end;
```

```
function NIL_CEL:Cellv;
        begin NIL_CEL := 0 end;
```

```
function ISNIL(c:Cellv):Boolean;
        begin ISNIL := (c = 0) end;
```

```
function CELL(x:Item; c:Cellv):Cellv;

        begin
            if av > max
                then ERROR('CELL      ', exhausted)
                else begin
                    CELL := av;
                    space[av].inf := x; space[av].next := c;
                    av := av + 1
                end
        end;
```

```
function HD(c:Cellv):Item;

        begin
            if c > 0
                then HD := space[c].inf
                else ERROR('hd      ',null_cell)
        end;
```

```
function TL(c:Cellv):Cellv;

   begin
      if c > 0
         then TL := space[c].next
         else ERROR('tl           ',null_cell)
      end.
```

At the time when *CELL* reports that no more cells are available, there will most likely be a considerable number of abandoned cells to which the user has lost access. It would be most desirable if these cells — they are called "garbage" in the colorful jargon of the trade — could now be recovered and reused so that *CELL* would not need to give up for lack of available space. The activity of finding these lost cells, known by the equally colorful term "garbage collection", is a nontrivial process. We shall study this process in depth in Chapter 10. Here we simply observe that without garbage collection the strict value interpretation of data is usually impractical because the "loss of cells" is an inherent feature of this style of programming.

5.2.3 Cells built with Pascal's variant record types

Sometimes we wish to use several different kinds of cells (cells with different types of fields) for the implementation of certain abstract types. As an example, consider a stack storing both characters and integer numbers. Simply creating two arrays of the proper types of records is not a very good solution. First, to identify a record we now need not only a subscript but also some code to select the array. Secondly, with two arrays of available cells, we lose some storage efficiency because the two types of cells do not share a common space. When we run out of one kind of cell we may still have ample room in the other array; yet nevertheless we must terminate the program.

We could use a single array if we decided to work with one universal cell type instead of several specialized types. With a set of fields sufficiently rich, a universal cell can replace any required cell simply by idling unnecessary fields. Yet this solution is still rather wasteful. Clearly, it would be desirable if fields which are never used simultaneously, share the same storage space.

Here Pascal's *variant record types* come to the rescue. With variant records, we can define the cells for the stack of characters and integers as follows:

```
type
      Version = (character, number);
      Vcell   = 0..max;
      Vpair   = record
                     NXT: Vcell;
                     case Version of
```

$$character: (C\_INF: Char\ );$$
$$number: \ (I\_INF: Integer)$$
       end.

Now a variable declared, for example, by

       var $C: Vcell$

can be used as a variable either of the type

       record $NXT: Vcell$; C_INF: *Char* **end**,

or of the type

       record $NXT: Vcell; I\_INF: Integer$ **end**.

We select the first (second) variant by assigning a value to C_INF (I_INF). It is usually necessary to record the current variant in the record so that it can be checked at run time. The field in which the variant is recorded is called a "tag field". In our example this tag field would be of type Version.

     Thus

type $Vcell$ = **record**

                $NXT: Vcell;$
                $SORT: Version$ {*the "tag"*};
                case *Version* **of** ...
                end.

Pascal allows us to abbreviate this definition to

type $Vcell$ = **record**

                $NXT: Vcell;$
                case $SORT: Version$ **of** ...
                end.

There are other rules for variant records, and the reader may consult a good Pascal reference manual (for example, Jensen and Wirth, [JW74]) for further details.

     We complete our example by defining and implementing the variant cell type needed for variant stacks.

Type VARCEL

Sets: $\underline{Varcel}$, *Char, Integer, Ilk* = (*ccel, icel, vacc*)

Syntax:
       function $NIL\_CEL: Varcel;$
       function $KIND(c: Varcel): Ilk;$
       function $CHAR\_CELL(x: Char;\ c: Varcel): Varcel;$
       function $INTR\_CELL(n: Integer;\ c: Varcel): Varcel;$
       function $CHARTR(c: Varcel): Char;$
       function $NUMBER(c: Varcel): Integer;$
       function $NEXT(c: Varcel): Varcel;$

Some axioms:

$$KIND(NIL\_CEL) = vacc$$
$$KIND(CHAR\_CELL(x,c)) = ccel$$
$$KIND(INTR\_CELL(x,c)) = icel$$
$$CHARTR(CHAR\_CELL(x,c)) = x$$
$$CHARTR(INTR\_CELL(x,c)) = error$$
$$NEXT(CHAR\_CELL(x,c)) = c$$

etc.

With the declaration

var *space*: **array**[1..*max*] **of** *Vcell*

we obtain for *ABSTR*

$$ABSTR(n) =$$
if $(n = 0)$
    then *NIL_CEL*
    else if *space*[*n*].*SORT* = *character*
      then *CHAR_CELL*(*space*[*n*].*C_INF*,
        ABSTR (*space*[*n*].*NXT*))
      else *INTR_CELL* (*space*[*n*].*I_INF*,
        ABSTR (*space*[*n*].*NXT*)).

As an example of actual code consider

```
function CHAR_CELL(x:Char; c:Varcel):Varcel;
    begin
        if av = max + 1
            then ERROR(...)
            else
                begin
                    CHAR_CELL := av;
                    space[av].SORT  := character;
                    space[av].C_INF := x       ;
                    space[av].NXT   := c       ;
                    av := av + 1
                end
    end.
```

The reader should have no difficulty in programming the remaining operations.

Clearly, a stack for different types of items must itself provide means for checking the type of the top item as well as two "push" and two "top" operations that add and retrieve items, respectively, according to type. In order to test the top item, we may again introduce an operation that returns one of three values depending on whether the stack is empty or displays a character or an integer.

5.3   CELLS AS MUTABLE OBJECTS

With cell objects,
CELL is a procedure.

While, in general, we may need cell values or cell objects with more than two fields and with a variety of auxiliary sets, we shall, in the following exposition, continue to use cells that have exactly two fields, one for an item and one for another cell.

Cells, then, interpreted as values are ordered pairs that can be created but never modified. These ordered pairs are represented by some kind of index or subscript. Thus, if at some time a program creates, say, the pair $(a,3)$ and lets some index i represent it, then i will represent this same pair throughout the execution of the program.

> NOTE: Take this statement with a grain of salt. To be sure, as long as we keep track of the index i, i will be associated with $(a,3)$. However, once we lose track of the index, that is, once we abandon the pair $(a,3)$, "the system" may reuse the same index — if it can — when we call for the creation of a new cell later.

If cells are interpreted as mutable objects, then the index no longer represents a pair of data but the place where a pair is stored, that is, the record variable associated with the index. Hence, with objects, we have two additional operations, *SET_HD* and *SET_TL*, that permit us to change the components of the pair to which the given index refers.

Cell objects are
very different from
stack objects.

So far, cell objects seem to be rather similar in principle to stack objects, yet there are several important differences concerned with (i) the nature of the values associated with cell objects, (ii) the concept of the null object and (iii) the dynamic creation of objects. We shall deal with these issues next.

(i) One component of the value of a cell object is itself of type *Cells*. Since this component should now refer to a record *variable* instead of a fixed pair of data, it should be a cell object rather than a value. We pointed out earlier that objects as items in data types never cause problems as long as the same datum *always* represents the same object. With stacks we obeyed this rule by creating some sort of a permanent head cell. But giving each cell a permanent headcell is out of the question since it completely defeats the purpose of cell objects: storage economy. Now, since the datum representing a cell — the index to the record of a cell — represents no object once its cell is deleted, we will have to break the above rule. After all, if it was not for the storage economy gained by the *DELETE* operation, we would never use objects in the first place. This, unfortunately, makes cell objects a data type that is inherently unsafe.

A "dangling reference"
is a nasty error!

The kind of error caused by this deficiency of cell objects is called a *dangling reference*. Suppose that *DELETE* is used with a variable c which is later used again with an operation such as *HD*. The cell accessed is no longer part of the user's data structures but is a cell on the list of available space.

What makes such an error particularly annoying is the difficulty of finding it. *HD* (and even *TL*) applied to a deleted cell *c* may yield a reasonable value, and no immediate error may result. Consequently, the program may run for quite a while without displaying any symptoms of illness. Doing (probably) ever more damage as it continues, it will most likely leave us with an untraceable entanglement of cells when it finally terminates.

What is meant by a "safe object type" is most concisely defined using the descriptor *VALIDo*.

NOTE: Recall that

$$VALIDo: obj \times store\text{-}rep \rightarrow Boolean;$$

for the other details of this notation review section 4.3.1.

An object type is called *safe* if, for all operations *Fo* that yield a store when applied to instances *s* of this type.

$$VALIDo(s, Fo(s,...))$$

is guaranteed. Clearly, the type *Cells* is unsafe because *DELETE* produces invalid cells, that is, because

$$VALIDo(c, DELETE(c))$$

is false. If they must be used at all, unsafe types should only be used in the construction of rather small subprograms and for the exclusive purpose of implementing a higher level type that no longer has this deficiency.

(ii) Because cell objects contain other cell objects, we need the concept of a null object; without it we could have only circular or infinite constructs. Notice that, in contrast, the stack object *s* modified by *NIL_STACK(s)* is *not* a null *object*, instead it *contains* the null *value* of type *Stack*. What we need for cells is a distinguished (constant) object *NIL_CELo* without fields that can take the place of a cell.

(iii) Finally, a means for the dynamic creation and (!) deletion of cell objects are an essential part of this type. Recall that the dynamic creation of stack objects, if desired, called for a procedure, *NEW_STACK*, that required a variable parameter. Here *CELL*, creating new cells, needs a variable parameter. *DELETE* could also have a variable parameter and return, say, the null object, but this would merely be an aesthetical consideration that certainly would not solve the dangling reference problem. We shall discuss this issue a little further in the next section on implementation.

Cell objects are not derived from cell values; they need their own specification.

Now, since cell objects are not related to cell values as simply as stack objects are to stack values, we cannot use the rules (4.24) and (4.25) to transform the specification of cell values into that of objects. We have to go back and redesign the type *Cells*. This new specification, again stated first for values, will be different from all others given in this book: the (value) type specified cannot be implemented unless an implementation of the object type already exists (because the values use the objects as an auxiliary set)! Only when the relationships (4.24) and (4.25) are used to derive the corresponding object type, does a complete (recursive) specification of cells emerge.

Type: *CELLS {values underlying mutable cell objects}*

Sets: *Cellval, Item, Boolean, Cellobj*

Syntax:
function *NIL_CELv:Cellval;*
function *IS_NILv* *(c:Cellval) :Boolean;*
function *CELLv*   *(x:Item;*   *b:Cellobj):Cellval;*
function *HDv*   *(c:Cellval) :Item;*
function *TLv*   *(c:Cellval) :Cellobj;*
function *SET_HDv(x:Item;*   *c:Cellval) :Cellval;*
function *SET_TLv (b:Cellobj; c:Cellval) :Cellval;*

Axioms: all functions are strict, and
         for all *c in Cellval− {error}*,
              b, d in Cellobj− {error}, and
              x,y in ITEM− {error}:

$$IS\_NILv(NIL\_CELv) \text{ is true} \tag{5.7}$$
$$\textbf{not } IS\_NILv(CELLv(x,c)) \tag{5.8}$$

$$HDv(NIL\_CELv) = error \tag{5.9}$$
$$TLv(NIL\_CELv) = error \tag{5.10}$$
$$HDv(CELLv(x,b)) = x \tag{5.11}$$
$$TLv(CELLv(x,b)) = b \tag{5.12}$$

$$SET\_HDv(x,NIL\_CELv) = error \tag{5.13}$$
$$SET\_TLv(b,NIL\_CELv) = error \tag{5.14}$$
$$SET\_HDv(x,CELLv(y,b)) = CELLv(x,b) \tag{5.15}$$
$$SET\_TLv(d,CELLv(y,b)) = CELLv(y,d) \tag{5.16}$$

end *{CELLS}*.

Assuming that the auxiliary type of cell objects is defined, it is easy to prove that this specification is sufficiently complete. But cell objects are *not* yet defined, and thus we ought to worry whether the specification obtained by adding rules (4.24) and (4.25) is actually sufficient; in particular, we ought to worry whether the carrier set of cell objects, emerging as a combination of the transformed carrier of the cell values with the auxiliary set of cell objects, is well defined. For the value specification above, the operations that define the carrier set are *NIL_CEL* and *CELL*. With (4.24) and the store value *st*, we can write the corresponding object operations as

     NIL_CELo(c) = ASGN(NIL_CELv, c, st),
and
     CELLo(x, b, c) = ASGN(CELLv(x,b), c, st).

The procedure
NIL_CELo ...

The parameter *c* is variable for both *NIL_CELo* and *CELLo*.

But wait, something seems to be peculiar about the datum brought back by *NIL_CELo*. To be sure, it is not too surprising that this datum cannot be analyzed by functions such as *HD* and *TL*. Consider, for example,

$$HDo(c, NIL\_CELo(c, st))$$
$$= HDv(CONT(c, NIL\_CELo(c, st)))$$
$$= HDv(NIL\_CELv) = error.$$

We are used to this behavior from *NIL_STACKo*, for example. However, *c* after *NIL_CELo(c)* differs from *s* after *NIL_STACKo(s)* in a fundamental way. While *s* can, at least, be modified (for example, by *PUSH(x,s)*), *c* cannot. This is an important point. To appreciate it better, let us pause for a moment and look at a few examples.

On the one hand, consider *s* after the operation

$$PUSHo(x, s, NIL\_STACKo(s, st)).$$

It is, of course, a stack object whose value is the stack with just *x* on it. In contrast

$$SET\_HDo(x, c, NIL\_CELo(c, st))$$

and

$$SET\_TLo(b, c, NIL\_CELo(c, st))$$

are invalid since they create an erroneous store. Finally,

$$CELLo(x, b, c, NIL\_CELo(c, st))$$

replaces the datum of the variable *c* but does not *change* the object represented by the original datum of *c*. The operation *NIL_CELo(c,st)* only affects a subsequent *IS_NILo*; that is, *IS_NILo(c,NIL_CELo(c,st))* yields true for all *c* and *st*.

Consequently, after the segment

$$NIL\_CEL(c); \ NIL\_CEL(d);$$

... always computes
the same value; it
should be made a
constant!

the values of *c* and *d* are indistinguishable in every respect, and the variables *c* and *d* can be used interchangeably as long as their contents are not changed. Therefore, *NIL_CEL* should not create a new object on each occasion that it is called (as *NIL_STACK(s)* does); it should always produce the same one. For this reason, we may as well turn *NIL_CEL* into a constant or, for that matter, into a function without parameters. This constant is, of course, the null cell object discussed earlier.

The carrier set
of cell objects is well
defined.

Now our perennial question concerning the sufficiency of the specification of cell objects comes down to showing that the carrier set given by the set of reduced expressions is well defined. Clearly: (i) *NIL_CEL* (now a constant) is in the set, and (ii) if some object *b* is in the set, then so is the object held by the variable *c* after *CELL* (*x*, *b*, *c*). It remains to be demonstrated that (iii) no other elements are in the set.

Specification
of *DELETE*.

Proving (iii), which amounts to showing that cells computed by *TL*, *SET_HD*, and *SET_TL* can be expressed in the form (i) or (ii), is not very difficult. The proof must be based on (5.7)-(5.16) and (4.20)-(4.25).

The specification of cell objects is still not quite complete; in spite of its repeatedly alleged importance, the procedure *DELETE* has not yet been specified. Properly used, *DELETE* has no logical effect on a program, therefore, its specification only needs to guard against improper usage. One axiom suffices:

$$CONT(c, DELETEo(c, st)) = error. \tag{5.17}$$

5.4 IMPLEMENTATION OF CELL OBJECTS

It is interesting that the descriptors for the usual implementation of cell objects are exactly those for cell values except that the variable *c* is now of type cell object rather than cell value. Because of this we give the code for *CELL*, *SET_HD*, and *SET_TL* without further comment and leave the implementation of the other operations to the reader.

```
procedure CELL(x:Item; d:Cells; var c:Cells);
    begin
        if av > max
            then ERROR(...)
            else begin
                c := av; {instead of CELL := av}
                space[av].inf := x; space[av].next := d;
                av := av + 1
            end
    end;

procedure SET_HD(c:Cells; x:Item);
    begin
        if c > 0
            then space[c].inf := x
            else ERROR('SET_HD     ', null_cell)
    end;

procedure SET_TL(c:Cells; d:Cells);
    begin
        if c > 0
            then space[c].next := d
            else ERROR('SET_TL     ', null cell)
    end.
```

The implementation
of *DELETE* requires
changes in *INITL* and
CELL.

Implementation of the operation *DELETE* is not quite as simple. Of course, the only purpose of *DELETE* is to allow the recycling of a cell that is no longer needed so that it can be reused by a later invocation of *CELL*. With the current version of *CELL* this seems to be impossible since *CELL* expects all unused (available) cells to be located as a contiguous block at and beyond the current value of *av*. *CELL*, therefore, must be changed. The basic idea underlying this change is the conversion of the sequentially allocated list of available cells into a linked list of available cells. This is easily achievable since the two fields of these cells are not used while the cells are part of the available space, awaiting a call by *CELL*. Hence, we can link all available cells together using, for example, the field *next*. The list can be organized as a stack, so that cells are removed from its top by *CELL* and put back onto its top by *DELETE*. The initialization routine *INITL* has to construct the original stack of all available cells. While the programs for *HD*, *TL*, *SET_HD*, and *SET_TL* are not affected, the programs for *INITL*, *CELL*, and *DELETE* now have the following form:

```
procedure INITL;
    var i: Cells;
    begin
        for i := 1 to max – 1
            do space[i].next := i + 1;
        space[max].next := NIL_CEL;
        av := 1
    end;
```

av		inf	next
1	1		2
	2		3
			⋮
			max
max			0

```
procedure CELL(x:Item; d:Cells; var c:Cells);
    begin
        if ISNIL(av)
            then ERROR('CELL      ', exhausted)
            else begin
                c := av; av := space[av].next;
                space[c].inf := x;
                space[c].next := d
            end
    end;

procedure DELETE(c:Cells);
    begin
        space[c].next := av;
        av := c
    end.
```

Because of the changes in *CELL* and *INITL*, *VALID* must be modified. Before, a cell *c* was in use if "$0 \leq c < av$"; now a cell *c* is being used if it is not accessible, directly or indirectly, from *av*. This condition can be expressed by the predicate

$PATH(c,d:Cells):Boolean;$ with
$PATH(c,d)$
    iff **not**$(d = 0)$
        and $((c = d)$ **or** $PATH(space[c].next, d)).$

With this, we obtain

$VALID(c)$ iff $0 \leq c \leq max$
      and not $PATH(av, c).$

The specification and implementation of mutable cells with variants does not pose any additional problems and, thus, does not need to be discussed here.

    In order to combat the dangling-reference problem, we might consider having *DELETE* set its parameter to *NIL_CEL* so that a later use of *c* by *HD*, *TL*, or some other operation would trigger an error. This is reasonable, but it does not solve the problem: first, we would have to make the parameter "*c*" of *DELETE* a "variable parameter", which would prevent us from using statements such as

$DELETE(TL(s));$

and secondly, even if we are prepared to tolerate this inconvenience, this measure would deal with only a fraction of the potential problems. Consider the execution of the segment:

$CELL(a, NIL\_CEL, c1);$
$CELL(b, c1, c2;$
$DELETE(c1);$
$c3 := TL(TL(c2)).$

Then *c3* links right into the available space list although *c1* has not been used after it has been deleted by *DELETE(c1)*.

It is useful to have a cell package with tests for debugging ...

    A more effective method requires both extra time and storage space. It works by providing an extra bit with each cell that is set to one if the cell is on the list of available space and set to zero otherwise. The proper status of this bit is easy to maintain: The bit is cleared in *CELL* and set in *DELETE*. Now all cell operations can test whether the cells given to them as parameters are, indeed, "good" cells, that is, cells not on the list of available space.

    Can we be sure that this measure solves the problem? Consider the following case:

$DELETE(c1);\ CELL(x, y, c2);\ ...$

If the pool of available cells is operated as a stack, then the cell deleted by *DELETE(c1)* will immediately be (re)allocated by *CELL(x, y, c2)*. Hence, if some variable contains a copy of *c1*, then it will now refer to the cell accessed by *c2*! Can you imagine the kind of spooky errors that can result from such an oversight? A (partial) cure is to operate the available space list as a queue rather than as a stack. At least as long as there are many cells still available, there is a good chance that an error occurs before the dangling cell is reused.

This is clearly not a total solution; and this problem should be viewed as yet another piece of evidence that writing simple, logically clear programs that can be proved to be correct is a necessity and not a luxury!

Nevertheless, runtime tests may sometimes detect errors that have escaped our scrutiny; thus dispensing with them entirely would certainly be a mistake. However, if we feel that programs should not be complicated by these extra tests (after all, a program released for production is supposed to be correct, so why should we continue to test its validity?), then we may consider providing two sets of cell primitives. We would use one set which includes these tests for debugging, and the other set, without tests, for production. We might even consider taking out the test for *NIL_CEL* that is included in the current versions of *HD*, *TL* and so on, since, in a correct program, all operations are applied only to proper arguments. In such circumstances runtime errors will never occur.

Removal of tests
for production may not
always be advisable.

Whether this step is to be taken needs to be decided on a case by case basis. The decision ought to depend on our confidence in the correctness of the program and the damage that could occur if the program runs riot.

5.5   COMMON LANGUAGE SUPPORT FOR CELLS

Pascal's procedures
"new" and "dispose"
have the same purpose
as *CELL* and *DELETE*.

Modern programming languages such as Pascal usually provide facilities that perform the functions of *CELL* and *DELETE*. In Pascal, the counterpart of *CELL* is called "new" and that of *DELETE* is called "dispose". The initialization of the available space is automatically performed before any statement of the user's program is executed.

Pascal's cell
objects are called
pointers.

The main difference between our implementation and the one provided by Pascal is that the values which refer to cells are not simply integers (subscripts) but are members of one of a family of new, independent types called *pointer types*. The mechanism works as follows. Suppose that *t* is some type, for example,

   {*type*} *t* = **record** *inf*:*Item; next*:*Cells* **end**.

Then we may create a second type, called "pointer to *t*", by the definition

   {*type*} *Cells* = ↑ *t*.

Since the type *Cells* occurs also in type *t*, Pascal requires that we declare the two types in reverse order:

   type *Cells* = ↑ *t;*

   t = **record** *inf*: *Item*; *next*:*Cells* **end**.

Now, if we want to create a cell of type *t*, we write

   var *c*: *Cells;*
         new(*c*).

The new cell is accessed by $c\uparrow$ (read: the variable to which c points). Thus we may assign values to the fields of the cell by

$$c\uparrow.inf := x;\ c\uparrow.next := s.$$

Pascal's null object is called *nil*.

The special pointer that represents the null-cell is a system constant called **nil**.

In order to become familiar with pointer types, let us use them for the implementation of our cell operations. We follow our previous implementation very closely, changing only the parts that are affected by the use of Pascal's facilities.

type *Cells* $= \uparrow Pair$

> {*Cells, the set of indices of pairs in the previous
> implementation, now becomes the set of pointers to pairs*};

Pair $=$ **record** *inf:Item; next: Cells* **end;**

function *CELL*(*x:Item*; *c:Cells*):*Cells;*
    var *cc:Cells*;
        begin
            new(cc);
            $cc\uparrow.inf := x;\ cc\uparrow.next := c;$
                {*new(cc) allocates a record of type Pair.
                 We refer to this record by $cc\uparrow$;
                 we say $cc\uparrow$ is the record to which
                 cc points*}
            CELL := *cc*
            end;

function *HD*(*c:Cells*):*Item;*
    begin
        if $c <>$ **nil**
            then *HD* := $c\uparrow.inf$
            else *ERROR*(...)
        end;

function *TL*(*c:Cells*):*Cells;*
    begin
        if $c <>$ **nil**
            then *TL* := *c* .*next*
            else *ERROR*(...)
        end.

The operations *SET_HD*, *SET_TL*, and *DELETE* required for cell objects have the following form:

```
procedure SET_HD(c:Cells; x:Item);
    begin
        if c < > nil
            then c↑.inf := x
            else ERROR(...)
    end;

procedure SET_TL(c:Cells; d:Cells);
    begin
        if c < > nil
            then c↑.next := d
            else ERROR(...)
    end;

procedure DELETE(c:Cells);
    begin
        dispose(c)
    end.
```

For cell systems with variant record types the function *new* must be told which type of record it is supposed to create. This is done by way of a second parameter. For example, with

```
type Version = (character, number);
     Cells   = ↑Vpair;
     Vpair = record
                 NXT:Cells;
                 case SORT: Version of
                     character: (C_INF: Char);
                     number:   (I_INF: Integer)
             end,
```

we obtain

```
function CHAR_CELL(x:Char; c:Cells):Cells;
    var cc: Cells;
    begin
        new(cc, character);
        cc↑.SORT := character;
        cc↑.C_INF := x; cc↑.NXT := c;
        CHAR_CELL := cc
    end.
```

There are additional rules that govern the use of variant record types with pointers. For these rules we refer the reader to a good manual on Pascal.

In a production program we would probably not use the functions *CELL* etc. but use *new* etc. as inline code. Here we will continue to use our functions mainly for notational simplicity. In particular, for the formulation of specifications, the consistent use of functional notation such as $HD(x)$ seems to be less confusing than using a second notation, namely $x↑.inf$ or $x↑.hd$.

6 Linear Data Types

Members of linear
types ...

In Chapter 4, we discussed the specification and implementation of abstract data types by the example of the type "stack". Our goal was not so much to explore stacks but to understand the basic concept of "type". In this chapter, our interest is different: here we wish to explore a specific family of types, called *linear types*, assuming that, by now, we understand the concept of "type" sufficiently well.

... have two
distinguished items: the
first item and the last.

Linear types consist of objects that assemble "items" in sequential order. These objects have clearly distinguished first and last, or top and bottom elements. *Stack* is a linear type. *TOP(s)* computes the top element. The bottom element is found by a simple program:

```
function BOTTOM(s:Stack):Item;
    begin
        if ISMT_STACK(s)
            then ERROR  {empty stacks are bottomless}
            else if ISMT_STACK(POP(s))
                then BOTTOM  : =  TOP(s)
                else BOTTOM  : =  BOTTOM(POP(s))
    end.
```

(Notice that this program is completely independent of the implementation of stacks; it is based exclusively on the stack primitives; hence we need not change this program if we switch, for example, from the direct to the array-based implementation.)

Operations for
linear types ...

As we set out to study other linear data types, we remember that data types are determined by their operations. Therefore, it seems reasonable to start by inventing all kinds of operations that could be performed on sequential (linear) objects and arrange them into new types. On the other hand, we might first try to justify new types by looking for areas of applications for linear objects. Yet, with our limited programming experience, we may be better off with the first approach since working with a concept as general as linearity in order to find its serious uses seems to be much harder than playing with it in order to explore its properties. Consequently, we choose to play rather than work.

As a result of our amusement, we can expect to find a sizeable set of operations from which we might be able to extract some subsets that form interesting types. We shall not even try to find immediate uses for all of these types but look at them as an enrichment of our repertoire of objects that we know how to handle. We shall cement the connection between this more theoretical activity and actual programming problems at the end of this chapter by way of a case study that involves several interacting data types.

We shall investigate the operations on linear objects (we shall call them *sequences* from now on) in a systematic fashion by exploring all kinds of functions of one and two arguments. It will become evident that functions of three or more arguments are too numerous to be considered in this fashion. Since they would not display substantially new aspects of the class of linear types, we shall not deal with them here. Let us begin.

... can be constructed in a systematic manner. (margin note)

6.1   SPECIFICATION

6.1.1   Functions on sequences with only one argument

The sets on which our functions operate are

Sequence, Item, Boolean, and (perhaps) *Integer.*

Functions with one argument are of the form
f: sequence → some type. (margin note)

Clearly, the functions that are worth exploring either take a sequence as an argument or compute a sequence as a result, or both. Functions from items to integers, for example, are hardly operations that we would count among the primitives of a type of sequences. With a little more reflection we can also see that the only interesting operation that computes a sequence but does not take a sequence as an argument is the operation *NUL* (which has no argument but computes an empty sequence). We might consider a function *Item*→ Sequence that creates a new sequence with one item, but that does not give us a truly different operation. This does not mean that such an operation may not be justified or useful in a practical project but it would not constitute more than a minor variation of some other type. Thus, we assume that we have the operation

NUL: → Sequence

and the following single argument functional forms

$t1$: *Sequence → Sequence*
$t2$: *Sequence → Item*
$t3$: *Sequence → Boolean*
$t4$: *Sequence → Integer.*

We noted earlier, that a sequence has two distinguished elements, the first one and the last one. Hence, obvious operations of the type

$t1$: *Sequence → Sequence*

are

function *POP_FIRST*(*s*:*Sequence*):*Sequence;*
function *POP_LAST* (*s*:*Sequence*):*Sequence;*
function *ROTATE*(*s*:*Sequence*):*Sequence;*
{*there are two versions: one moves the first element to the rear, the other moves the last element to the front*}.

These seem to be the most important functions of this type. Similarly, we have for the type $t2$

function *FIRST*(*s*:*Sequence*):*Item;* and
function *LAST* (*s*:*Sequence*):*Item;*

For type $t3$ we have

function *ISMT*(*s*:*Sequence*):*Boolean;*

and for type $t4$

function *SIZE*(*s*:*Sequence*):*Integer;*

We can already state the following axioms

For all *s* in Sequence,

ISMT(NUL)	(6.1)
SIZE(NUL) = 0;	(6.2)
SIZE(POP_FIRST(s)) = *SIZE(s)* – 1	(6.3)
SIZE(POP_LAST(s)) = *SIZE(s)* – 1;	(6.4)
POP_FIRST(NUL) = *error;*	(6.5)
POP_LAST (NUL) = *error;*	(6.6)
FIRST(NUL) = *error;*	(6.7)
LAST (NUL) = *error.*	(6.8)

6.1.2   Some functions with two parameters

To construct nontrivial sequences, operations with two parameters are needed.

Clearly, these operations do not suffice for a meaningful data type. The simple reason is, that they do not permit the construction of any but the empty sequence. For the construction of nontrivial sequences, we need a function with two parameters that builds a new sequence by somehow adding an item (one parameter) to a sequence (the second parameter). There are, of course, other types of functions with two parameters, and we will explore some of them later. But first, let us proceed cautiously so that we do not become overwhelmed by their variety and fail to see the forest for the trees. It may do no harm, though, to list the kinds of functions of two parameters that we may wish to consider.

$$t5: Sequence \times Sequence \rightarrow Sequence$$
$$t6: Sequence \times Sequence \rightarrow Item$$
$$t7: Sequence \times Sequence \rightarrow Boolean$$
$$t8: Sequence \times Sequence \rightarrow Integer$$

$$t9: Item \times Sequence \rightarrow Sequence$$
$$t10: Item \times Sequence \rightarrow Item$$
$$t11: Item \times Sequence \rightarrow Boolean$$
$$t12: Item \times Sequence \rightarrow Integer$$

$$t13: Boolean \times Sequence \quad \{it\ is\ difficult\ to\ find\ any\ meaningful$$
$$function\ of\ this\ domain\ type!\}$$

$$t14: Integer \times Sequence \rightarrow Sequence$$
$$t15: Integer \times Sequence \rightarrow Item$$
$$t16: Integer \times Sequence \rightarrow Boolean$$
$$t17: Integer \times Sequence \rightarrow Integer.$$

Operations of the form Item × Sequence → Sequence create arbitrary sequences.

Functions of type *t9* are needed to construct nontrivial sequences. Let us choose the operation *PUSH_FIRST*, familiar to us from stacks, and see how it interacts with the single-argument operations given above in Section 6.1.1. Its form is

function *PUSH_FIRST*(*x:Item*; *s:Sequence*):*Sequence;*

and we assume that it operates upon the front of the sequence, that is, that it adds a new first element. We infer easily, again from our experience with stacks, that,

for all *x* in (*Item* − {*error*}) and
  s in (*Sequence* − {*error*}),

ISMT(PUSH_FIRST(x,s)) = **false,**	(6.9)
POP_FIRST(PUSH_FIRST(x,s)) = *s,*	(6.10)
FIRST(PUSH_FIRST(x,s)) = *x,*	(6.11)

and

$$SIZE(PUSH\_FIRST(x, s)) = SIZE(s) + 1. \qquad (6.12)$$

These axioms describe operations that operate at both ends of a sequence, ...

But what are the values of

$$POP\_LAST(PUSH\_FIRST(x,s))$$

and

$$LAST(PUSH\_FIRST(x,s))?$$

The answer is not difficult if $s = NUL$. Then $PUSH\_FIRST(x,s)$ is a sequence of only one element, x, so that

$$POP\_LAST(PUSH\_FIRST(x,NUL)) = NUL$$

and

$$LAST(PUSH\_FIRST(x,NUL)) = x.$$

Now, if s is a sequence of length > 0, then we can certainly state that we get the same net result from both

$$POP\_LAST(PUSH\_FIRST(x,s))$$

and

$$PUSH\_FIRST(x,POP\_LAST(s)).$$

... but is this description sufficiently complete?

This says that for sequences with at least one element it does not matter whether we first add an element to one end and then delete one from the other, or do it the other way around. But does this observation help us? Does claiming equality for the expressions above precisely describe POP_LAST? It turns out that, indeed, it does! Before we prove this, let us look at the other expression, namely

$$LAST(PUSH\_FIRST(x,s)).$$

Again, we may argue that, if s contains at least one element, the $PUSH\_FIRST$ operation does not influence the result of $LAST$. Hence we may claim

$$LAST(PUSH\_FIRST(x,s)) = \textbf{if not } ISMT(s) \textbf{ then } LAST(s).$$

It seems then that the following assertions are in agreement with our understanding of sequences:

$$POP\_LAST(PUSH\_FIRST(x,s)) \tag{6.13}$$
$$= \textbf{if } ISMT(s)$$
$$\qquad \textbf{then } NUL$$
$$\qquad \textbf{else } PUSH\_FIRST(x,POP\_LAST(s))$$

and

$$LAST(PUSH\_FIRST(x,s)) \tag{6.14}$$
$$= \textbf{if } ISMT(s)$$
$$\qquad \textbf{then } x$$
$$\qquad \textbf{else } LAST(s).$$

Proof of completeness.

We now prove that these assertions are, in fact, sufficient axioms for the definitions of POP_LAST and $LAST$. First we give the

Expressions can be transformed to reduced form, or ...

Definition {*reduced expressions for sequences*}: An expression is said to be reduced if it is either NUL or of the form $PUSH\_FIRST(x, s)$ where s is a reduced expression, and prove

... they have the value *error*.

Lemma: All expressions that denote sequences using NUL, $PUSH\_FIRST$, POP_FIRST, and POP_LAST can be reduced or have the value *error*.

Proof {*by induction over the length of the expression*}: The length of the expression *NUL* equals 1; the length of the expression *F*(...,*s*), where *F* is a function giving a sequence and *s* is an expression denoting a sequence, is 1 + the length of *s*. The only expression of length one is *NUL* and, by definition, *NUL* is reduced. Suppose that all expressions of length *n* are (can be) reduced or have the value *error* and consider an expression of length n + 1. This new expression can have one of the following forms:

> *PUSH_FIRST*(*x*, *s*)
> *POP_FIRST*(*s*)
> *POP_LAST*(*s*),

where *s* is an expression of length *n*. By our (tacit) assumption that our functions are strict, all of these expressions have the value *error* if *s* has the value *error*. Now suppose that *s* is reduced. We obtain

> *PUSH_FIRST*(*x*, *PUSH_FIRST*(*y*, *t*))

and

> *PUSH_FIRST*(*x*, *NUL*)
> {*both are of reduced form*},
>
> *POP_FIRST*(*PUSH_FIRST*(*x*, *t*)) = *t*
> {*where t is of reduced form by the induction hypothesis*},
>
> *POP_FIRST*(*NUL*) = *POP_LAST*(*NUL*) = *error,*
>
> *POP_LAST*(*PUSH_FIRST*(*x*, *t*)) =
> (i) *NUL* {*if t = NUL or*}
> (ii) *PUSH_FIRST*(*x*, *POP_LAST*(*t*))
> {*here POP_LAST*(*t*) *is of length n and can thus by reduced by the induction hypothesis*}

This shows that the axioms for *POP_LAST* are sufficient.

Since we can assume now that in

> *LAST*(*PUSH_FIRST*(*x*,*s*))

the sequence *s* is an expression of reduced form, the proof of completeness is simple and is left as an exercise. □

The addition of *PUSH_LAST* does not change the reduced form.

The obvious next addition to our system is the function *PUSH_LAST*. We obtain the axioms

> *PUSH_LAST*(*x*, *NUL*) = *PUSH_FIRST*(*x*, *NUL*)
>
> *PUSH_LAST*(*x*, *PUSH_FIRST*(*y*, *s*))
>   = *PUSH_FIRST*(*y*, *PUSH_LAST*(*x*, *s*)).

The proof that all expressions for sequences can be reduced is left as an exercise.

Concatenation is an important operation on sequences.

Another interesting kind of functions are those belonging to *t5*. One important member of this family is concatenation:

function *CONCAT(s,t:Sequence):Sequence.*

This function computes the sequence that contains all elements of sequence *s* followed by the elements of sequence *t*. It is defined by the axioms

$$CONCAT(NUL, s) = s,$$

and

$$CONCAT(PUSH\_FIRST(x,s), t) = PUSH\_FIRST(x, CONCAT(s,t)).$$

There are many more interesting functions with two arguments, but by now the reader should be able to continue the systematic analysis of the operations of linear types without further help. Additional functions are discussed in the exercises at the end of this chapter.

If all additions occur at one end and deletions and inspections at the other, ...

We wish to mention, however, that the operations

NUL	{*also called NEW_QUEUE*}
ISMT	{*ISMT_QUEUE*}
PUSH_LAST	{*APPEND or QU*}
FIRST	{*FRONT*}
POP_FIRST	{*POP or DLT_FRONT*}

... a sequence is called a "queue".

are usually considered to be the primitives of the data type *Queue*. If other operations such as *LAST*, *POP_LAST*, or *PUSH_FIRST* are provided, the type is sometimes called a double-ended queue (abbreviated *DEQU*, see [KN68]).

CONCAT is usually considered an operation on a type called *List* or *String* (the latter, if the items are characters).

6.1.3   How to construct specifications

In order to *construct* axioms which are sufficiently complete and consistent (not selfcontradictory), we proceed in two steps:

The reduced forms are designed, not derived.

(i) We define the carrier set of the new type as the set of reduced expressions with the additional member *error*. To this end we first identify the operations that build the reduced expressions. There are no formal rules of how to do this. Reduced expressions reflect our intuitive understanding of the new data type; they are, so to speak, a material version of our idea about the objects of this type. Finding them is a part of designing the type guided by the basic rule of all design: the simplest solution that meets the purpose is the best.

Reduced forms are defined by their operations ...

Although there are no formal rules that tell us which operations to choose as the constituents of reduced expressions, finding these operations is usually not difficult if we have a good understanding of the properties of the new type. Consider the type *natural numbers*. Since all natural numbers can be constructed with the constant *ZERO* and the successor function (and they cannot be constructed with less than that), reduced expressions should consist of exactly these two building blocks. The type *Date* is very similar; all dates can be constructed from some *first* date *FIRST* and a function that returns the next date for a given date.

... and sometimes by their structure.

If we wish to have dates that precede *FIRST* (or numbers that precede *ZERO*) then, in addition to the function that returns the successor of its argument, we need a second function that returns the predecessor.

Since successor and predecessor are inverse functions, that is:

$$SUCC(PRED(n)) = PRED(SUCC(n)) = n, \tag{6.15}$$

there are now many different expressions built with *FIRST*, *SUCC*, and *PRED* that denote any given member of the carrier set. Consequently, we cannot identify the carrier set with the set of all these expressions. That is, we cannot declare that all of them are reduced forms. Instead, we should declare that expressions formed only with either *FIRST* and *SUCC* or with *FIRST* and *PRED* are reduced. We usually arrive at such a result by intuitive reasoning. Here we argue that dates form an infinite sequence, and every date can be reached from a "first" date by some finite number of steps all of which go either forward or backward.

Intuitive results should be validated by proofs.

In order to make sure that our intuition does not lead us astray, we must prove that these forms are good reduced forms by showing that they are unique (i.e. that no two different forms can be transformed into one another) and that expressions that contain both *SUCC* and *PRED* can be reduced uniquely. This poses no problem: each application of transformation rule (6.15) either deletes or creates a *SUCC-PRED* or a *PRED-SUCC* pair. Thus, starting with a reduced expression, we can only construct expressions that are not reduced. Starting with one that is not reduced we can eliminate pairs of different functions so long as there are both *SUCC* and *PRED* functions in the expression. The number of remaining *SUCC* (or *PRED*) functions is independent of the way in which we eliminate the pairs because each application always eliminates one of each kind.

Finally, the kind of *sequences* so far considered can be built from an empty sequence by adding elements to one end. Thus, reduced sequence expressions consist of *NUL* and *PUSH_FIRST*, or, as an equivalent alternative, *NUL* and *PUSH_LAST*. Finding the reduced forms for data types discussed in later sections and chapters will be similarly simple.

Operations are specified one at a time.

(ii) Once the carrier set is defined, the remaining operations are specified one at a time. To specify an operation f, we define its mapping. That is, for each point in f's domain we specify the corresponding value in f's codomain. We refer to values of the participating sets either by variables universally quantified (for all x in *Item*, e.g.) or by reduced expressions. Three examples of increasing complexity will illustrate this method and some of its finer points.

Axioms constructed systematically ...

Consider first the operation *POP* for stacks. The set of all stacks consists of the value *error* and the reduced stack expressions, that is,

NIL STK, and finite expressions of the form *PUSH* (*x,s*) where *x* denotes any item and *s* is another reduced stack expression. Thus we have the specification

function *POP(s:Stack):Stack;*

POP is strict, and
      for all $x \in Item$ and *s* element of *Stack*

POP(NIL_STK) = error,
POP(PUSH(x,s)) = s.

Since this defines *POP* for *error, NIL_STK,* and all expressions of the form *PUSH(x,s)*, it defines *POP* for all elements in *Stack*.

But things are not always this simple. Suppose that instead of *PUSH* we had only the operation *QU* (i.e. *PUSH_LAST*) for building sequences (queues). Now the reduced expressions defining *Queue* – {*error*} are all expressions of the form *NUL* or *QU(x, s)* where *x* denotes any item and *s* is a reduced expression. In this case *POP* must be defined differently:

function *POP(s:Queue):Queue;*

POP is strict and
      for all $x \in Item$ and $s \in Queue$

POP(NUL)   = *error,*
POP(QU(x, s)) =
    if *s = NUL*
        then *NUL*
        else *QU(x, POP(s))*.

... are likely to be complete (which a proof can confirm) ...

Short of a formal proof, do we have some hint that this specification is complete? The axiom does not eliminate *POP* from the expression unless *s* in QU(*x,s*) is *NUL*, so how do we know that *POP* is, indeed, defined for all points in its domain? Well, the axiom expresses what *POP* does with any given queue expression in terms of what *POP* does with a simpler queue expression. Hence, applying the axiom we make *POP*'s problem simpler and, applying it repeatedly we eventually reduce the problem to *POP(QU(x,NUL))*. The formalization of this argument is, of course, the inductive proof. But even without the proof, we can see at a glance that the axiom allows us to make progress toward the final elimination of *POP* from an expression. These quick checks do not make a proof unnecessary, but they are extremely helpful design tools.

We could have stated the previous specification a little differently:

POP(NUL)   = *error,*
POP(QU(x, NUL))   = *NUL,*
POP(QU(x, QU(y, t))) = *QU(x, POP(QU(y, t)))*.

Before, we covered all reduced expressions by considering *NUL* and, for all *x* and *s*, *QU(x,s)*. Here we cover them by considering *NUL, QU(x, NUL)*, and

$QU(x, QU(y, t))$. We have, in effect, subdivided the set of queues s in $QU(x, s)$ into the basic kinds of reduced expressions, namely *NUL* and expressions of the form $QU(y, t)$. Sometimes, this step is not only possible but necessary unless we permit complicated comparisons such as

if, for some $x \in$ *Item* and $t \in$ *Queue, s* $= QU(x,t)$.

Consider, for example, the function *ROTATE* which moves the last item of a queue to the front. *ROTATE* is defined as follows:

function *ROTATE(s:Queue):Queue,*

ROTATE is strict and
  for all $x,y \in$ *Item* and $s \in$ *Queue*

   $ROTATE(NUL)$ $= NUL,$
   $ROTATE(QU(x,NUL))$ $= QU(x,NUL),$
   $ROTATE(QU(x,QU(y,s))) = QU(y, ROTATE(QU(x,s))).$

These axioms pass our quick check since they allow us to make progress with the elimination of *ROTATE* from queue expressions. That they describe the idea of moving an element from the back of a queue to the front cannot formally be shown unless we first define formally what we mean by it. We shall not do this here, and we shall leave the informal argument to the reader as well. It may be helpful to start with a diagram of a queue of the form

  $ROTATE\ (<string\ s > y\ x) = ROTATE\ (<string\ s>x)y.$

Sometimes it may happen that we cannot find axioms for a new operation constructed exclusively from the operations of the reduced form. As an example, consider *ROTATE_LFT* for queues, which moves the first item of the queue to the rear. Here, we are forced to describe the new operation in terms of others already defined. Suppose *POP* and *FIRST* are such operations. Now we obtain

  $ROTATE\_LFT(s) =$
   if $s = NUL$
    then *NUL*
    else $QU(FIRST(s), POP(s))$

These examples are not meant to cover all practical cases but to supply some of the intuitive reasoning that goes into the development of a set of axioms.

... and certain to be consistent.

   We have not yet addressed the problem of consistency. Since an inconsistent specification does not specify anything, we could prove that a set of axioms is consistent by presenting some system that satisfies it. But we do not need to go so far. Since functions are specified one at a time, it suffices to show that each of these function definitions is consistent. We observe that a function is defined inconsistently only if, for at least one point in its domain, the function is defined more than once and differently. Thus, if each axiom is in itself consistent and if different axioms deal with disjoint subsets of the function's domain, then consistency is assured. In our examples above, we have arranged things such that the second condition is guaranteed. The first condition is guaranteed as well. Each axiom is an equality whose right hand side will always yield the same result for the same parameters. Hence, as long as different parameters (including reduced forms) denote different elements, a single axiom cannot specify two different values for the same point in the function's domain.

6.1.4 Sequences with a "point of interest"

A movable access point ...

Earlier we observed that sequences have two naturally distinguished elements, the first one and the last one. By definition, we can introduce other special elements by adding operations such as

function *THIRD(s:Sequence):Item,*

for retrieving the third item in *s*. This distinguishes the third element among all the elements in *s*; but operations of this kind are of doubtful utility. However, it makes good sense to define a *movable* point of interest in a sequence. We can define such a point by adding the following operations:

function *RESTART(s:sequence):sequence*
        {move point of interest to the front of s};

function *NEXT(s:sequence):sequence*
        {advance point of interest toward the end of s};

function *PREV(s:sequence):sequence*
        {move point of interest toward the front of s};

function *CURRENT(s:sequence):Item*
        {retrieve element at point of interest};

function *EOS(s:sequence):Boolean*
        {End Of Sequence: is point of interest at the end of the
        sequence?}.

... allows inspection of entire sequences without destroying them.

These operations are obviously useful since they permit us to inspect all elements of a sequence without changing its contents. Given these, we call two sequences equal only if they contain the same elements in the same order *and* if the points of interest have the same positions within each of the sequences.

We still need operations that do the job of *ISMT, NUL, PUSH,* and *POP* but to avoid later confusion, we should be careful with our choice of names for these operations. In particular, we should not casually reassign, say, the name *PUSH* to an operation that is different from our old *PUSH* even if the difference is rather subtle. Let us view a stack as a sequence where the point of interest is always at the top (or front). Then *TOP* corresponds to *CURRENT*, and *PUSH* and *POP* always keep the point of interest at the front. For a sequence with a movable point of interest, this behavior requires that *PUSH* and *POP* be used only if the point of interest is at the front. A type that does not impose this requirement is simpler and will be considered first. Thus we will not use the operations *PUSH* and *POP* for the modification of a sequence but operations called *SHOVE* and *CLIP* that add and remove items from the front of a sequence without moving the point of interest. We obtain the axioms:

$$ISMT(NUL) \tag{6.16}$$
$$\textbf{not}\quad ISMT(SHOVE(x,s)) \tag{6.17}$$
$$ISMT(RESTART(s)) \qquad = ISMT(s) \tag{6.18}$$

$$EOS(NUL) \tag{6.19}$$
$$EOS(SHOVE(x,s)) \qquad = EOS(s) \tag{6.20}$$
$$EOS(RESTART(s)) \qquad = ISMT(s) \tag{6.21}$$

$$RESTART(NUL) \qquad = NUL \tag{6.22}$$
$$RESTART(RESTART(s)) \ = RESTART(s) \tag{6.23}$$

$$NEXT(NUL) \qquad\qquad = error \tag{6.24}$$
$$NEXT(SHOVE(x,s)) \tag{6.25}$$
$$\qquad = \textbf{if } EOS(s) \textbf{ then } error$$
$$\qquad\qquad\qquad \textbf{else } SHOVE(x,NEXT(s))$$
$$NEXT(RESTART(SHOVE(x,s))) \tag{6.26}$$
$$\qquad = SHOVE(x,RESTART(s))$$

$$PREV(NUL) \qquad\qquad = error \tag{6.27}$$
$$PREV(RESTART(s)) \qquad = error \tag{6.28}$$
$$PREV(SHOVE(x,SHOVE(y,s))) \tag{6.29}$$
$$\qquad = SHOVE(x,PREV(SHOVE(y,s)))$$
$$PREV(SHOVE(x,RESTART(s))) \tag{6.30}$$
$$\qquad = RESTART(SHOVE(x,s))$$

$$CLIP(NUL) \qquad\qquad = error \tag{6.31}$$
$$CLIP(SHOVE(x,s)) \qquad = s \tag{6.32}$$
$$CLIP(RESTART(s)) \qquad = error \tag{6.33}$$

$$CURRENT(NUL) \qquad\quad = error \tag{6.34}$$
$$CURRENT(SHOVE(x,s)) \ = CURRENT(s) \tag{6.35}$$
$$CURRENT(RESTART(SHOVE(x,s))) = x \tag{6.36}$$

With a *point of interest* the reduced form becomes more complex.

These axioms seem to be more complex than those discussed previously. The main reason is simply the number of operations that are involved, but there is another additional complication. The reduced form of a sequence contains, in addition to *NUL* and *PUSH*, the operation *RESTART*. Hence, the proof that the axioms suffice must begin with the demonstration that all expressions that compute a sequence either have the value *error* or can be transformed into the (new) reduced form

NUL,
SHOVE(x,s), or
RESTART(s),

where *s* is a sequence in reduced form. Thereafter, one needs to show that the value of any expression starting with *ISMT*, *EOS*, or *CURRENT* can be determined using these axioms.

INSERT and *SHRINK* allow modifications at the point of interest.

Sometimes we may wish to modify a sequence at the point of interest. Two functions suggest themselves:

function *INSERT(x:Item; s:Sequence):Sequence*;

and

function *SHRINK(s:Sequence):Sequence;*

These functions are defined by the following axioms:

$$INSERT(x,SHOVE(y,s)) \;=\; SHOVE(y,INSERT(x,s)) \qquad (6.37)$$
$$INSERT(x,RESTART(s)) \;=\; RESTART(SHOVE(x,s)) \qquad (6.38)$$

{*INSERT adds x before the "current" item and makes x the new current item*}

$$SHRINK(NUL) \qquad = error \qquad (6.39)$$
$$SHRINK(SHOVE(x,s)) \;\;= SHOVE(x,SHRINK(s)) \qquad (6.40)$$
$$SHRINK(RESTART(SHOVE(x,s))) = RESTART(s) \qquad (6.41)$$
{*SHRINK removes the current item and makes the next item the current one*}.

An axiom for *INSERT(x,NUL)* is not needed. Recall that *RESTART(NUL)* = *NUL*; hence, for *s = NUL*, (6.38) yields

$$INSERT(x,NUL) =$$
$$INSERT(x,RESTART(NUL)) \;=\; RESTART(SHOVE(x,NUL)).$$

Finally, we may wish to move the point of interest to a specific place in the sequence using, for example, the operation *FIND* defined by:

function *FIND(x:Item;s:Sequence):Sequence;*

$$FIND(x,NUL) = NUL; \qquad (6.42)$$
$$FIND(x,SHOVE(y,s)) \qquad (6.43)$$
$$= \textbf{if } (x = y) \textbf{ then } RESTART(SHOVE(y,s))$$
$$\textbf{else } SHOVE(y,FIND(x,s));$$
$$FIND(x,RESTART(SHOVE(y,s))) \qquad (6.44)$$
$$= FIND(x,SHOVE(y,s)).$$

6.1.5 The occasional need for "hidden functions"

Sometimes, the construction of a complete set of axioms ...

Although for many data types we can find a sufficient set of axioms, we may sometimes run into difficulties. While there is no simple recipe for constructing axioms, we gather from our experience with the data types above that we should be able to find all necessary axioms by following the process below:

(i)   we identify the reduced representation of an object of the new type;

(ii)   we make sure that we have enough rules (axioms) for reducing every expression that yields such an object to reduced form;

(iii) we construct rules that permit us to determine the values of expressions that compute objects other than those of the type itself. For example, such an expression could start with *CURRENT, ISMT, EOS,* and so forth.

However, this method does not always succeed. In order to explain why our method of specification sometimes fails, we construct a type even simpler than the sequence with *NEXT, RESTART,* etc. by eliminating the operations *SHOVE* and *CLIP*. Clearly, with *INSERT* and *SHRINK* we can increase and decrease the size of the sequence. Consequently, *SHOVE* and *CLIP* are not actually needed (although they may be convenient).

With a little thought we find that reduced expressions for such a sequence are built from the operations

NUL,
INSERT(*x,s*), and
NEXT(*s*).

In order to construct an arbitrary sequence we start with *NUL* and use *INSERT* repeatedly until all items are added that are required for the sequence. *INSERT*, which makes the new item the current one, keeps the point of interest at the front of the sequences. Finally, we need to apply *NEXT* several times until the point of interest is at the desired position. *RESTART* is no longer needed for the reduced form since reduced expressions that start with *INSERT* always have their point of interest at the front. Further, all applications of *NEXT* precede those of *INSERT*.

Now only a few of the axioms are easily constructed:

$$
\begin{aligned}
NEXT(NUL) \quad\quad &= error \\
RESTART(NUL) \quad\quad &= NUL \\
RESTART(INSERT(s)) &= INSERT(RESTART(s)) \\
RESTART(NEXT(s)) \quad &= RESTART(s)
\end{aligned}
$$

In order to study the problem that arises with most of the other axioms consider the expression

$$CURRENT(NEXT(NEXT(INSERT(x,INSERT(y,$$
$$INSERT(z,NUL)))))).$$

Although we can see intuitively that the result should be *z*, it is not possible to find an axiom that would allow us to transform expressions of this form to *z* without disturbing the other properties of the sequence. We might be tempted to introduce an axiom that permits us to cancel *NEXT* and *INSERT*, namely

$$NEXT(INSERT(x,s)) = s.$$

... unless *hidden* operations are added.

This would certainly achieve our purpose for *CURRENT*, but it would also turn *NEXT* into an operation that modifies the sequence in the same way as *SHRINK* does, which it should not. We might consider modifying our system of specification by allowing the application of certain axioms only to expressions that start with *CURRENT* or *EOS*, but that would destroy its mathematical simplicity. A better solution involves introducing an additional operation. This operation does not need to be implemented; its sole purpose is to facilitate the specification. Because it is not implemented and, hence, is not available to the user, such an operation is termed *hidden*. There are several different operations that, added to the new type, make its specification possible. We shall simply reintroduce *SHOVE*; the reader may enjoy discovering other operations that serve the same purpose.

Recall that *SHOVE* adds an item to the front of a sequence without affecting the point of interest. Now we have regained the previous reduced form — expressions built with *NUL*, *RESTART*, and *SHOVE* — and we can use the previous set of axioms.

The choice of the reduced form is frequently crucial for the successful construction of an axiom set. For the type above we might have chosen the operations *NUL*, *INSERT*, and *SHOVE* for the reduced form. Clearly, we can build all sequences with these functions: starting with *NUL* we first add the items to the right of the point of interest using *INSERT* and then the items to the left using *SHOVE*. Among others, we will need the axiom

$$INSERT(x, SHOVE(y, s)) = SHOVE(y, INSERT(x, s)).$$

Here difficulties arise with the axioms for

$$NEXT(INSERT(x, s)).$$

Turning *INSERT*(x,s) into *SHOVE*(x,s) is correct only if s does not contain any occurrences of *SHOVE*!

But the reduced form does not exclusively determine whether or not an axiom system can be found. Consider a simple sequence where the reduced forms are built with *NUL* and *PUSH*, and try to specify the operation that removes both the top and the bottom element simultaneously:

function *POP_BOTH*(*s*:*Sequence*):*Sequence*.

While

$$POP\_BOTH(NUL) = error,$$

what is the value of

$$POP\_BOTH(PUSH(x,s))?$$

Well, we need to add the function *POP_LAST* unless it is already part of the type and obtain

$$POP\_BOTH(PUSH(x,s)) = POP\_LAST(s).$$

The reader will agree that hiding of operations does not lead to particularly elegant specifications. It should, therefore, be used only as a measure of last resort.

6.1.6   The specification of the Pascal type "file".

Here, Pascal files
are viewed as values
rather than as mutable
objects.
We conclude our discussion of specifications of linear types with the complete specification of Pascal files. While, in reality, files are mutable objects, we again specify them as values since we know from 4.3.1 that this specification can be applied systematically to the object operations of actual files. We represent the "buffer variable" by two special functions that we call *DEPOSIT* and *CONTENT*. *DEPOSIT* performs the assignment of an item to the buffer variable, while *CONTENT* allows the inspection of its contents.

Type: File.

Sets: <u>File</u>, *Item, Boolean;*

Syntax:
> **function** *REWRITE:File*
> **function** *RESET(f:File):File;*
> **function** *EOF(f:File):Boolean;*
> **function** *DEPOSIT(x:Item; f:File):File;*
> **function** *CONTENT(f:File):Item;*
> **function** *GET(f:File):File;*
> **function** *PUT(f:File):File;*

and the hidden function

> **function** *SHOVE(x:Item;f:File):File;*

Axioms: for all f in *File* $-\{error\}$,
> and x,y in *Item* $-\{error\}$

RESET(REWRITE)	= *REWRITE*;
RESET(DEPOSIT(x,f))	= *RESET(f)*;
RESET(PUT(DEPOSIT(x,f)))	= *SHOVE(x,RESET(f))*;
RESET(SHOVE(x,f))	= *SHOVE(x,RESET(f))*;
EOF(REWRITE)	= **true**;
EOF(DEPOSIT(x,f))	= *EOF(f)*;
EOF(PUT(DEPOSIT(x,f)))	= **true**;
EOF(SHOVE(x,f))	= **false**;
CONTENT(REWRITE)	= *error*;
CONTENT(DEPOSIT(x,f))	= *x*;
CONTENT(PUT(f))	= *error*;
CONTENT(SHOVE(x,REWRITE))	= *x*;
CONTENT(SHOVE(x,PUT(f)))	= *x*;
CONTENT(SHOVE(x,SHOVE(y,f)))	= *CONTENT (SHOVE(y,f))*;
GET(REWRITE)	= *error*;
GET(DEPOSIT(x,f))	= *GET(f)*;
GET(PUT(f))	= *error*;

$$GET(SHOVE(x,REWRITE)) = PUT(DEPOSIT(x, REWRITE));$$
$$GET(SHOVE(x,PUT(f))) = PUT(DEPOSIT(x, PUT(f)));$$
$$GET(SHOVE(x,SHOVE(y,f)) \quad SHOVE(x, GET(SHOVE(y,f)));$$

$$DEPOSIT(x,DEPOSIT(y,f))) = DEPOSIT(x,f);$$

$$PUT(REWRITE) = error;$$
$$PUT(PUT(f)) = error;$$

$$PUT(SHOVE(x,s)) = error;$$

$$SHOVE(c,DEPOSIT(y,f)) = DEPOSIT(y,SHOVE(x,f));$$
end {*File*}.

The reader may convince himself that this specification is sufficiently complete. First he needs to show that reduced expressions f are constructed with *REWRITE, DEPOSIT, PUT,* and *SHOVE* using the following recursive procedure:

Replace

f by $DEPOSIT(x, f1)$ or by $f1$,
$f1$ by $SHOVE(x, f1)$ or by $f2$,
$f2$ by $PUT(DEPOSIT(x, f2))$ or by $REWRITE$.

In these forms, x may be replaced by any arbitrary item, and even in the same expression, different items may be chosen for different occurrences of x. For example, the following expression can be derived from $f1$ and thus, from f:

$$SHOVE(x,...$$
$$SHOVE(z, PUT(DEPOSIT(u,...$$
$$PUT(DEPOSIT(w, REWRITE)...).$$

Our file specification follows the least restrictive interpretation of the Pascal report [JW74] by allowing items to be added to a file f whenever $EOF(f)$ is **true**. In contrast, many implementations of Pascal do not permit any alteration of a file after a *RESET* operation has been performed.

6.2   IMPLEMENTATION OF SEQUENCES AS VALUES

Shorter function names improve the readability of programs.

The names for functions that we have used so far were fine for the systematic development of linear types, but they are a little long for practical use. In particular, proofs are sometimes hard to read if they contain an accumulation of long function names. Therefore, in the sequel we will use the following names:

> *NUL*
> *ISMT*
> *PUSH*
> *SHOVE*
> *QU*   = *SHOVE_LAST*
> *POP*   = *POP_FIRST*
> *CLIP*   = *CLIP_FIRST*
> *FIRST*
> *RESTART*
> *NEXT*
> *CURRENT*

While exploring different implementation methods for sequences that permit the user to access both ends, we shall discover that matters are not as simple as they were for stacks.

6.2.1   Implementation based on enumerated types

The implementations of stacks and of sequences by means of enumerated types are quite similar. We need to tabulate all functions and verify the implementation by exhaustively testing each line of every table. Since no particular problems arise, we leave to the reader the construction of the tables for, say, the data type *Queue*.

6.2.2   Implementation based on integer numbers

As for stacks we choose the value 1 for the empty sequence. We assume that the constants *limit* and *base* are suitably declared and *NUL* and *ISMT* are defined in the same fashion as were *NIL_STACK* and *ISMT_STACK* in Section 4.2.3. Thus we need to discuss the functions *QU*, *FIRST* and *POP*. We may decide to implement *QU* in a similar way as we implemented the *PUSH* operation for stacks. In this case, the implementation descriptors *VALID* and *ABSTR* are similar to those for stacks: the specification for *VALID* does not need to be changed at all, the specification of *ABSTR* is adapted to sequences by simply replacing *PUSH* by *QU*. We obtain for *QU*:

> **function** *QU*(*x*:*Item*; *s*:*Sequence*):*Sequence;*
>   **begin**
>   **if** *s* < **limit**
>   **then** *QU*:= *s*∗*base* + *x*
>   **else** *ERROR*('*QU*   ', *overflow*)
>   **end**.

For the implementation of *FIRST* and *POP* we may seek some guidance from the axioms and write:

> **function** *FIRST(s:Sequence):Item;*
> > **begin**
> > > **if** $s = 1$
> > > > **then** *ERROR('FIRST   ', empty)*
> > > > **else**
> > > > > **if** $(s\ DIV\ base) = 1$
> > > > > > **then** *FIRST* $:=\ s\ MOD\ base$
> > > > > > **else** *FIRST* $:=\ FIRST(s\ DIV\ base)$
> > **end;**

> **function** *POP(s:Sequence):Sequence;*
> > **begin**
> > > **if** $s = 1$
> > > > **then** *ERROR('POP   ', underflow)*
> > > > **else**
> > > > > **if** $s\ DIV\ base = 1$
> > > > > > **then** *POP* $:= 1$
> > > > > > **else** *POP* $:=\ PUSH(s\ MOD\ base,$
> > > > > > $POP(s\ DIV\ base))$
> > **end.**

The reader may verify these programs using mathematical induction by the method discussed in section 4.2.3.

Sometimes, elegance
can be expensive!

While the representation of both *FIRST* and *POP* are simple and elegant, they are rather inefficient. Both operate on the front of the sequence, but, instead of accessing the first element directly, they search for it starting at the back. Consequently, their execution time increases with the length of the sequence; that is, their complexity is O(n).

We can compute
the length of a
sequence ...

This waste of time could be avoided if we knew the length of the sequence. Ideally, we would like to know the nth power of the base if the sequence contains $n + 1$ elements. Consider the base of ten with items ranging from zero to nine and suppose that we are given the sequence

15432.

Thus, the sequence contains four elements and the number that we require is 1000. Now,

$FIRST(15432) = 5 = (15432\ DIV\ 1000)\ MOD\ 10,$
and
$POP(15432) = 1432 = 1000 + (15432\ MOD\ 1000).$

... from the value
of the sequence ...

In order to compute this magic number from the value of s, we take advantage of some properties of logarithms. We recall that

$$\log_b(x * b^n) = n + y$$
$$\text{with } 1 \leq x < b \text{ and } 0 \leq y < 1.$$

... by means of
the logarithm.
Thus, we obtain our number by computing the logarithm base *"base"* of *s* and by raising *base* to the power of the integer part of the result minus one. With *base* shortened to *b*, this gives us

$$b^{\,trunc(log_b\,(s)-\,1)}.$$

Since Pascal provides only the natural logarithm and its inverse we recall that

$$log_b\,(x)\;=\;\ln(x)/\ln(b),$$

and

$$b^x\;=\;e^{\ln(b)\cdot x}$$

With this we obtain

$$factor := exp(\ln(base) * trunc(\ln(s)/\ln(base) - 1.0)).$$

Because of the possibility of roundoff errors, we need to add a small correction: instead of 1.0 we subtract 0.9999, and round the result. Hence,

$$factor := round(\,exp(\ln(base) * trunc(\ln(s)/\ln(base) - 0.9999))).$$

NOTE: If the base is greater than 2, then the smallest number representing a sequence of length *n* is much greater than the greatest number representing a sequence of length *n*–1. Therefore, the value of the correction is not very critical; that is, there is no danger that we get an incorrect factor for the greater values of sequences of length *n*–1. Consider, for example, base 3. The smallest value representing a sequence of *n* elements is 3^n while the greatest number that can occur with a sequence of length *n*–1 is $2 * 3^{(n-1)}$.

The programs for *FIRST* and *POP* may be re-expressed as follows:

function *FIRST*(*s*:*Sequence*):*Item;*

　　var *factor*: *Integer;*

　　begin
　　　　if *s* = 1
　　　　　　　then *ERROR*('*FIRST*   ', *empty*)
　　　　　　　else begin
　　　　　　　　　factor := ...;
　　　　　　　　　FIRST := (*s DIV factor*) *MOD base*
　　　　　　　　end
　　　end;

function *POP*(*s*:*Sequence*):*Sequence;*

　　var *factor: Integer;*

　　begin
　　　　if *s* = 1
　　　　　　　then *ERROR*('*POP*   ', *underflow*)

```
                              else begin
                                  factor : = ...;
                                  POP : = factor + (s MOD factor)
                                  end
                 end.
```

The **function** *PUSH* can be programmed recursively as:

```
    function PUSH(x:Item; s:Sequence):Sequence;

        begin
            if s = 1
                then PUSH : = s*base + x
                else
                    if s < limit
                        then PUSH : = PUSH(x,s DIV base)*base
                                                      + s MOD base
                        else ERROR('PUSH        ', overflow)
            end;
```

or with the "magic factor" as:

```
    function PUSH(x:Item; s:Sequence):Sequence;

        var factor: Integer;

        begin
            if s > limit
                then ERROR('PUSH        ', overflow)
                else begin
                    factor : = {base * previous factor}...;
                    PUSH : = (s MOD factor) + factor*(base + x)
                    end
        end.
```

There are several
methods for
implementing "points of
interest".
For the realization of a point of interest, that is, for the implementation of the operations *RESTART, NEXT, CURRENT,* and *EOS* we need to implement a marker of some sort that tells us where the point of interest currently is. There are at least three different approaches to this problem.

(i) Introduce an extra item, the marker, at the appropriate place in the sequence (for example, we could use the number 10 as a marker if our items are the numbers 0 through 9; here, the base would need to have a value of not less than 11).

(ii) for each item, introduce two versions, one with a marker and one without (for example, numbers between 0 and 9 represent items not marked while numbers between 10 and 19 represent those that are marked; here the base would have the value 20).

(iii) At a special place in the sequence store a number that indicates where the point of interest is located.

With the first two solutions, the sequence operations are easy to code, but those that work at the point of interest are slow and inefficient. Therefore, we will not discuss these any further but leave it to the reader to work out the details. For the third solution, we shall go into a little more detail.

Besides the items, we wish to store the index for the point of interest. The maximal size of this index is determined by the number of items that can be stored in the sequence and by the fact that the index itself must also be stored. Its value is computed by the segment below; the second line of code corrects "*max_size*" so that room for the index itself is provided.

$$max\_size := \ln(maxint)\ DIV\ \ln(base);$$
$$max\_size := max\_size - (\ln(max\_size)\ DIV\ \ln(base)).$$

If we decide to store the index at the least significant end of the number, then shoving is accomplished by

$$index\quad := s\ MOD\ max\_size;$$
$$SHOVE := ((s\ DIV\ max\_size)*base + x)*max\_size + index + 1.$$

Figure 6.1 illustrates the method.

s: 5 3 2 7 3 (3) and SHOVE(9,s): 5 3 2 7 3 9 (4)

Figure 6.1 Sequences with a point of interest encoded by integer numbers

NEXT has to test whether the end of the sequence has already been reached, and, if not, to add 1 to *s*. The reader may discover algorithms for the other sequence operations himself.

The predicate *VALID* has the form

$$VALID(n)\ \ iff(n\ MOD\ max\_size \neq 0)$$
$$\text{and } VALID'(n\ DIV\ max\_size);$$

where *VALID'* is the descriptor for the implementation without a point of interest. The **function** *ABSTR* is defined as follows:

$$ABSTR(n)$$
$$= \textbf{if } (n\ DIV\ max\_size = 1)$$
$$\textbf{then } NUL$$
$$\textbf{else}$$
$$\textbf{if } n\ MOD\ max\_size = 1$$
$$\textbf{then } RESTART(ABSTR(n+1))$$
$$\{n+1\text{ only shifts the point of interest one}$$
$$position\ ahead;\ thus\ ABSTR(n+1)\ is\ not$$
$$of\ the\ form\ RESTART(...)\}$$
$$\textbf{else } QU(x,\ ABSTR(m));$$
$$\text{where}$$
$$x\ = (n\ DIV\ max\_size)\ MOD\ base,$$

and
$$m = ((n \; DIV \; max\_size) \; DIV \; base) * max\_size$$
$$+ \; (n \; MOD \; max\_size) - 1.$$

6.2.3   Implementation based on arrays

The required set
of operations
determines the method
of implementation.

The implementation based on arrays follows the same pattern for both stacks and sequences. The main difference occurs with the *POP* operation. While popping a *stack* only requires adding a one to the subscript that represents the stack, removing the front element of a *sequence* (assuming elements are added at the rear) involves copying all array elements that make up the sequence. Thus, if "popping the first element" is one of the required operations, this method is not very attractive, while without *POP* it may be quite advantageous. We conclude that, for the implementation of a data type, the proper choice of the method critically depends on the set of required operations.

We defer the discussion of the use of arrays until the end of this chapter where we shall study the implementation of a practical data type.

6.2.4   Direct implementation of the axioms

Implementing the
axioms of sequences
directly is
straightforward.

In order to keep it simple, we shall restrict our discussion to the implementation of the queue operations

> *NUL,*
> *ISMT,*
> *QU,*
> *FIRST,* and
> *CLIP,*

with the axioms

for all *q* in *Queue,* and *x* in *Item*

ISMT(NUL),	(6.1)
not *ISMT(QU(x,q)),*	(6.45)

FIRST(NUL) = error   (6.7)
FIRST(QU(x,q))   (6.46)
    = **if** *ISMT(q)*
        then *x* **else** *FIRST(q),*

CLIP(NUL) = error   (6.31)
CLIP(QU(x,q))   (6.47)
    = **if** *ISMT(q)*
        then *NUL* **else** *QU(x, CLIP(q)).*

We base our implementation on cells with the operations

NIL_CEL, ISNIL, CELL, HD and *TL*

described in Chapter 5. With these we obtain for the implementation descriptors:

$\quad\cdot\quad$ *ABSTR(NIL_CEL)* = *NUL*,
$\quad\quad$ *ABSTR(CELL(x,s))* = *QU(x, ABSTR(s))*,

and

$\quad\quad$ *VALID(s)* iff *ISNIL (s)*
$\quad\quad\quad$ **or** *VALID(TL(s))*.

The programs for *QU*, *FIRST* and *CLIP* are given next.

type *Queue* = *Cells;*

function *QU(x:Item; q:Queue):Queue;*
$\quad$ **begin** *QU* := *CELL(x,q)* **end;**

function *FIRST(q:Queue):Item;*

$\quad$ **begin**
$\quad\quad$ **if** *ISNIL(q)*
$\quad\quad\quad\quad$ **then** *ERROR('FIRST   ', empty)*
$\quad\quad\quad\quad$ **else**
$\quad\quad\quad\quad\quad\quad$ **if** *ISNIL(TL(q))*
$\quad\quad\quad\quad\quad\quad\quad$ **then** *FIRST* := *HD(q)*
$\quad\quad\quad\quad\quad\quad\quad$ **else** *FIRST* := *FIRST(TL(q))*
$\quad\quad$ **end;**

function *CLIP(q:Queue):Queue;*

$\quad$ **begin**
$\quad\quad$ **if** *ISNIL(q)*
$\quad\quad\quad\quad$ **then** *ERROR('CLIP   ', underflow)*
$\quad\quad\quad\quad$ **else**
$\quad\quad\quad\quad\quad\quad$ **if** *ISNIL(TL(q))*
$\quad\quad\quad\quad\quad\quad\quad$ **then** *CLIP* := *NIL_CEL*
$\quad\quad\quad\quad\quad\quad\quad$ **else** *CLIP* := *CELL(HD(q), CLIP(TL(q)))*
$\quad\quad\quad\quad\quad\quad\quad\quad\quad\quad$ {= *QU(HD(q), CLIP(TL(q)))*}
$\quad\quad$ **end.**

6.2.5   Linked implementation

With the direct implementation, *CLIP* and *FIRST* are 0(*n*) ...

There are two fundamental problems with the direct implementation of queues: both *FIRST* and *CLIP* execute with a time complexity O(n), where n is the number of items in the queue, and *CLIP* always creates a new copy of the queue whenever it is invoked.

... because the front
of a sequence must be
found by searching
from the back.

These problems are caused in part by the fact that we cannot access the front of the queue directly and must search for it starting at the rear. We can improve the situation by keeping track of where the front is.

If we do this, we arrive at a method that, although related to the previous one, no longer directly implements the axioms. Therefore, we choose a different name, *linked implementation,* for it, suggesting that the cells containing the items are linked together by their *TL*-fields.

Access to the
front and rear is
accomplished by an
extra cell.

Earlier in this chapter queues were represented by their rear cells. Now, in order to maintain access also to the front of the queue, we represent a queue by an extra cell of a different kind: one that has two cell fields, rather than an item field and a cell field. Then we link these two cell fields to the front and the rear cell of the queue proper (Figure 6.2). We define this new cell type as a variant of *Cells* by adding the operations

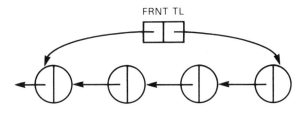

FRNT TL

Figure 6.2   A queue implementation that allows access to both front and rear

function *PAIR(c,d:Cells):Cells*
     {creates an instance of the new variant},

function *KIND(c:Cells):Ilk*

function *FRNT(c:Cells):Cells,*

where
     type *Ilk* = *(empty, c_cel, p_cel)*

with the additional axioms

$$
\begin{aligned}
KIND\,(NIL\_CEL) &= empty, \\
KIND\,(CELL\,(x,d)) &= c\_cel, \\
KIND\,(PAIR\,(c,d)) &= p\_cel, \\
FRNT(PAIR\,(c,d)) &= c, \\
TL\quad(PAIR\,(c,d)) &= d, \\
HD\quad(PAIR\,(c,d)) &= error, \\
FRNT(CELL\,(x,d)) &= error.
\end{aligned}
$$

With these operations, linked implementation of queues is described as follows:

$$
\begin{aligned}
&ABSTR\,(NIL\_CEL) = NUL, \\
&ABSTR\,(PAIR\,(c,d)) \\
&\quad\quad = \textbf{if } (c = d)
\end{aligned}
$$

$$\textbf{then } QU(HD(d), NUL)$$
$$\textbf{else } QU(HD(d), ABSTR(PAIR(c, TL(d)))),$$

and

$$VALID(NIL\_CEL), \qquad\qquad\qquad\qquad \{v1\}$$
$$VALID(PAIR(c,d))$$
$$\textbf{iff } KIND(d) = c\_cel \textbf{ and } (c = d \qquad\qquad \{v2\}$$
$$\textbf{or } VALID(PAIR(c, TL)(d)))). \qquad\qquad \{v3\}$$

Facts about queues can be proved ...

For valid pairs we can define the function *LNGTH* which associates an integer number with a nonempty queue. This number is useful for inductive proofs of program correctness. We define

$$LNGTH(PAIR(c,d))$$
$$= \textbf{if } (c = d)$$
$$\textbf{then } 1 \textbf{ else } 1 + LNGTH(PAIR(c, TL(d))).$$

If $VALID(PAIR(c, d))$, then $LNGTH(PAIR(c, d))$ is some finite number. To see this, interpret *VALID* as meaning *LNGTH-is-finite*. This interpretation is consistent since, if $c = d$, $LNGTH = 1$, so it is finite. Otherwise,

$$LNGTH(PAIR(c,d)) = 1 + LNGTH(PAIR(c, TL(d))),$$

which is finite if $LNGTH(PAIR(c, TL(d)))$ is finite. $\square$

... by induction over LNGTH.

Consequently, for valid *queues q* we may induce over $LNGTH(q)$. We obtain for the code of *QU* and *FIRST* with

```
type Queue = Cells,

function QU(x:Item; q:Queue):Queue;

    var qq: Cells;

    begin
        if KIND(q) = empty
            then begin
                qq := CELL(x, NIL_CEL);
                QU := PAIR(qq, qq)
            end
            else QU := PAIR(FRNT(q), CELL(x,TL(q)))
    end.
```

Since the front is now directly accessible, the **function** *FIRST* is very simple

```
function FIRST(q:Queue):Item;
    begin
        if KIND(q) = empty
            then ERROR('FIRST        ', empty)
            else FIRST := HD(FRNT(q))
    end.
```

Verification
of *QU* and *FIRST*
Next we verify that *QU* and *FIRST* are programmed correctly. We start
with *QU* by showing that $ABSTR(QUc(x,q)) = QU(x,ABSTR(q))$ and that
$VALID(q)$ implies $VALID(QUc(x,q))$. (The suffix "c" again distinguishes
the programmed, "concrete" function from the abstract function specified
by the axioms.) We distinguish three cases:

$$q = NIL\_CEL; \tag{i}$$
$$q = PAIR(c,c) \text{ with } c = CELL(x,NIL\_CEL); \text{ and} \tag{ii}$$
$$q = PAIR(c,d) \text{ with } KIND(d) = c\_cel$$
$$\text{and } VALID(PAIR(c,TL(d))). \tag{iii}$$

We first show that $ABSTR(QUc(x,q)) = QU(x,ABSTR(q))$ and obtain for
(i)

$$ABSTR(QUc(x,NIL\_CEL))$$
$$= ABSTR(PAIR(qq,qq)) \text{ where } qq = CELL(x, NIL\_CEL)$$
$$\hspace{8cm} \{by\ code\}$$
$$= QU(HD(CELL(x,NIL\_CEL)),NUL) \hspace{1.5cm} \{by\ ABSTR\}$$
$$= QU(x,NUL) = QU(x,ABSTR(NIL\_CEL)) \hspace{1cm} \{by\ axiom\},$$

and for (ii) and (iii)

$$ABSTR(QUc(x,PAIR(c,d)))$$
$$= ABSTR(PAIR(c,CELL(x,d))) \hspace{3cm} \{by\ code\}$$
$$= QU(HD(CELL(x,d)), ABSTR(PAIR(c,TL(CELL(x,d)))))$$
$$\hspace{8cm} \{by\ ABSTR\}$$
$$= QU(x, ABSTR(PAIR(c,d))). \ \square$$

Now we demonstrate that $VALID(q) \Rightarrow VALID(QUc(x,q))$ and obtain for (i)

$$QUc(x,q) = PAIR(qq,qq) \text{ with } qq = CELL(x,NIL\_CEL),$$

thus $VALID(QUc(x,q))$ by line $\{v2\}$,

for (ii)

$$QUc(x,q) = PAIR(FRNT(q), CELL(x,TL(q)))$$
$$= PAIR(c,CELL(x,c)),$$

thus $VALID(QUc(x,q))$ by line $\{v3\}$, and
for (iii) with $VALID(q)$

$$QUc(x,q) = PAIR(FRNT(q), CELL(x,TL(q)))$$
$$= PAIR(c,CELL(x,d))$$
$$\text{with } VALID(PAIR(c,d)),$$

and $VALID(QUc(x,q))$ again by line $\{v3\}$.
   Showing the correctness of *FIRST* using the relationship

$$VALID(q) \Rightarrow (FIRST(ABSTR(q)) = FIRSTc(q))$$

requires an inductive proof except for the special case

$$q = NIL\_CEL.$$

We leave the verification of this special case, that is, of

$$FIRST(ABSTR(NIL\_CEL)) = FIRSTc(NIL\_CEL)$$

as an exercise to the reader. If q is not NIL_CEL, then it is of the form $PAIR(c, d)$; thus we must show that

$VALID(PAIR(c,d))$ implies
$\qquad FIRST(ABSTR(PAIR(c,d))) = FIRSTc(PAIR(c,d)).$

We do this by induction over $LNGTH(PAIR(c, d))$. That $LNGTH$ is some finite natural number is assured because of the premise $VALID(PAIR(c,d))$. We obtain for the

Base case: $LNGTH(PAIR(c,d)) = 1$, that is, $c = d$.

Left hand side

$\quad FIRST(ABSTR(PAIR(c,\ c)))$
$= FIRST(QU(HD(c),\ NUL))$ *{by def. of ABSTR}*
$= HD(c)$ *{by axiom (6.46)}*

Right hand side

$\quad FIRSTc(PAIR(c,c))$
$= HD(FRNT(PAIR(c,c)))$ *{by code of FIRST}*
$= HD(c).$

Induction hypothesis:

$\quad$ If $LNGTH(PAIR(c,d)) = n$,
$\qquad$ then $FIRST(ABSTR(PAIR(c,d))) = FIRSTc(PAIR(c,d))$

Inductive step: consider (*valid*) $PAIR(c,CELL(x,d))$

Left hand side

$\quad FIRST(ABSTR(PAIR(c,\ CELL(x,d))))$
$= FIRST(QU(HD(CELL(x,d)),ABSTR(PAIR(c,d))))$
$\qquad\qquad\qquad\qquad\qquad\qquad\qquad\qquad$ *{by def. of ABSTR}*
$= FIRST(ABSTR(PAIR(c,d)))$ *{by axiom (6.46)}*
$= FIRSTc(PAIR(c,d))$ *{by ind hyp}*

Right hand side

$\quad FIRSTc(PAIR(c,\ CELL(x,d)))$
$= HD(FRNT(PAIR(c,\ CELL(x,d))))$ *{by code}*
$= HD(c)$
$= HD(FRNT(PAIR(c,\ d)))$
$= FIRSTc(PAIR(c,d))$ *{by code}.*

Despite access to the front, CLIP is still O(n).

Knowing where the front is does not help us with the implementation of *CLIP* since we need to update the element next to the front. The location of this element cannot be found other than by searching through the entire queue starting at the rear. Figure 6.3(a) gives an arrow diagram of a number of queues as they typically occur after some queuing and popping, and Figure 6.3(b) illustrates the result of the transitions

$$q1 := QU(a,q1); q4 := CLIP(q3).$$

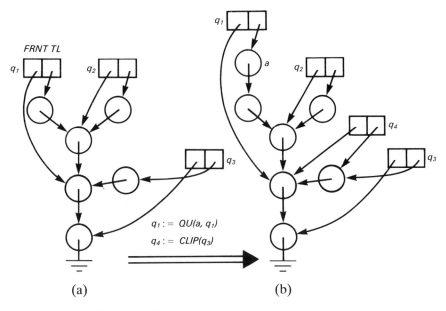

(a)   (b)

Figure 6.3   Queues sharing common elements

function *CLIP(q:Queue):Queue;*

var *next,front*: *Cells;*

    begin
        if *KIND(q)* = *empty*   {p1}
           then *ERROR('CLIP   ', underflow)*   {p2}
        else
           if *FRNT(q)* = *TL(q)*   {p3}
             then *CLIP* := *NIL_CEL*
           else begin
             next := *TL(q); front* := *FRNT(q);*   {p5}
             while *front* < > *TL* (*next*) **do**   {p6}
               next := *TL(next);*   {p7}
             CLIP := *PAIR(next, TL(q))*   {p8}
           end
      end.

Figure 6.4   Function *CLIP* for linked implementation

We will see that clipping can only be done by searching from the rear for the new front cell, that is, for the cell which contains the same index in its *"TL"* field as the head cell in its *"FRNT"* field. Figure 6.4 gives the code of *CLIP*. While it is easy to see that

$$CLIPc(NULc) = CLIPc(NIL\_CEL) = error$$

and

$$CLIPc(QUc(x, NUL))$$
$$= CLIPc(PAIR(qq,qq)) = NUL,$$

Proof of correctness
of a program with a
while-loop.

it is not quite as simple to verify that the implementation of *CLIP* satisfies

$$VALID(qq) \Rightarrow ABSTR(CLIPc(qq)) = CLIP(ABSTR(qq))$$

where *qq* is not empty, because of the use of a **while**-loop in the code.

In order to prove a property of the computation evoked by a **while**-loop, we need a formal statement that specifies its semantics. The following axiom suffices:

> **while** *p* **do** *S*
> = **if** *p* **then begin** *S*; **while** *p* **do** *S* **end**

where *p* is some logical expression and *S* is some statement. Thus, if *p* is false, **while** has no effect, otherwise the statement *S* is executed and **while** is performed again. In our particular case, we can modify this axiom a little by interpreting **while** as a function. This is possible since, except for changing *next*, **while** has no side effects, and *next* is used when the **while**-loop terminates only to communicate the result. Because of this particular property of our code we are allowed to interpret **while** as the function *fwhile* with the parameters *next* and *front*.

With this (pseudo) function *fwhile*, *CLIP* is expressed as

```
function CLIP(q:Queue):Queue;
  begin
    if KIND(q) = empty
      then ERROR(...)
      else
        if FRNT(q) = TL(q)
          then CLIP := NIL_CEL
          else CLIP :=
            PAIR(fwhile(TL(q),FRNT(q)), TL(q))
            {fwhile(...) computes the index of the record next to
              the front}
  end.
```

where *fwhile* satisfies the axiom

$$fwhile(next,front)$$ {a1}
$$= \textbf{if } (TL(next) = front)$$ {a2}

$$\textbf{then } next \qquad \{a3\}$$
$$\textbf{else } fwhile(TL(next), front). \qquad \{a4\}$$

We shall now prove the following assertion:

$$VALID(PAIR(c,CELL(x,d)))$$
$$\Rightarrow ABSTR(CLIPc(PAIR(c,CELL(x,d))))$$
$$= CLIP(ABSTR(PAIR(c,CELL(x,d)))).$$

Proof by induction over $LNGTH(PAIR(c,CELL(x,d)))$:
$\{VALID(PAIR(...))$ *assures that* $LNGTH(...)$ *is some natural number*$\}$.

Base case: $LNGTH(PAIR(c,CELL(x,d))) = 2$, thus $c = d$.

Left hand side
$$ABSTR(CLIPc(PAIR(c,CELL(x,c))))$$
$$= ABSTR(PAIR(fwhile(CELL(x,c), c),CELL(x,c))) \qquad \{by\ code\}$$
$$= ABSTR(PAIR(CELL(x,c), CELL(x,c))) \qquad \{by\ a2,\ a3\}$$
$$= QU(x,NUL) \qquad \{by\ ABSTR\}$$

Right hand side

$$CLIP(ABSTR(PAIR(c,CELL(x,c))))$$
$$= CLIP(QU(x, ABSTR(PAIR(c,c)))) \qquad \{by\ ABSTR\}$$
$$= QU(x, CLIP(ABSTR(PAIR(c,c)))) \qquad \{by\ axiom\ (6.47)\}$$
$$= QU(x, CLIP(QU(HD(c), NUL))) \qquad \{by\ ABSTR\}$$
$$= QU(x, NUL) \qquad \{by\ axiom\ (6.47)\}$$

Induction hypothesis:

$$VALID(PAIR(c,\ CELL(x,d)))$$
$$\text{and } LNGTH(PAIR(c,\ CELL(x,d))) = n$$

implies that

$$ABSTR(CLIPc(PAIR(c,CELL(x,d))))$$
$$= CLIP(ABSTR(PAIR(c,CELL(x,d)))).$$

Inductive step:

Consider $CLIPc(PAIR(c,CELL(y,CELL(x,d))))$
$$\{now\ LENGTH(PAIR(...)) = n + 1\}$$
Left hand side
$$ABSTR(CLIPc(PAIR(c,CELL(y,CELL(x,d)))))$$
$$= ABSTR(PAIR(fwhile(CELL(y,CELL(x,d)),c),$$
$$CELL(y,CELL(x,d)))) \qquad \{by\ code\}$$
$$= ABSTR(PAIR(fwhile(CELL(x,d),\ c),$$
$$CELL(y,CELL(x,d)))) \qquad \{by\ a2,\ a4\}$$
$$= QU(y, ABSTR(PAIR(fwhile(CELL(x,d), c), CELL(x,d)))) \{by\ ABSTR\}$$
$$= QU(y, ABSTR(CLIPc(PAIR(c, CELL(x,d))))) \qquad \{by\ code\}$$
$$= QU(y, CLIP(ABSTR(PAIR(c,CELL(x,d))))) \qquad \{by\ ind\ hyp.\}$$
$$= CLIP(QU(y, ABSTR(PAIR(c,CELL(x,d))))) \qquad \{by\ axiom\ (6.47)\}$$

Right hand side

$$CLIP(ABSTR(PAIR(c,CELL(y,CELL(x,d)))))$$
$$= CLIP(QU(y, ABSTR(PAIR(c,CELL(x,d)))))$$ *{by ABSTR}.* □

The complexity of *CLIP* is made O(1) by rearranging the elements of the sequence periodically.

Whereas the maintenance of access to both ends of the sequence improves the efficiency of *FIRST*, the complexity of *CLIP* is still O(n). It turns out that we can achieve a complexity O(1) for *CLIP* if we use a structure of the kind depicted as an arrow diagram in Figure 6.5. Such a structure can be accessed at both ends for adding, inspecting, and deleting elements. A problem occurs only if several deletions have moved a point of access down to the cell common to both sides and *CLIP* is applied again. If it happens, we restack the sequence (Fig. 6.5(c)) in such a way that the old bottom becomes the top. If

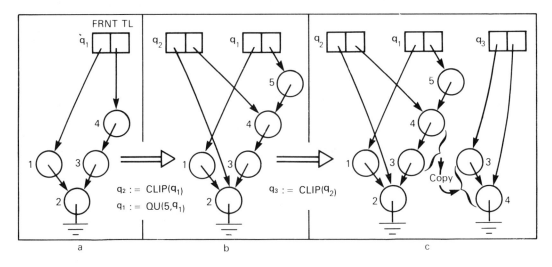

Figure 6.5 Value implementation of queues with a time complexity of O(1) for CLIP

the sequence is used as a proper queue, that is to say, if all additions are made at one end and all deletions at the other, then every record of the queue is restacked exactly once. The total time needed for the occasional restacking process can therefore be subdivided into constant portions (those needed for restacking a single record) and charged to the operation that adds this record to the queue. By this accounting method all queuing operations take the same constant amount of time (that is, their execution time does not depend on the number of items in the queue).

The implementation of this method is no more complex than the previous one. In fact, both *QU* and *FIRST* are not changed at all. Figure 6.6 shows the code for the **function** *CLIP*.

function *CLIP(q:Queue):Queue;*

  var *old_q*, *new_q*, *new_rear*: *Cells;*

begin
  if *KIND(q)* = *empty*
  then *ERROR(..., underflow)*
  else
    if not *KIND(TL(FRNT(q)))* = *empty*
    then *CLIP* := *PAIR(TL(FRNT(q)), TL(q))*
    else
      if *KIND(TL(TL(q)))* = *empty*
      then *CLIP* := *NUL*
      else begin
        old_q := *TL(q)*;
        new_rear := *CELL(HD(old_q),NIL_CEL)*;
        new_q := *new_rear*;
        old_q := *TL(old_q)*;
        while not *(KIND(TL(old_q))* = *empty)* **do**
          begin
            new_q := *CELL(HD(old_q), new_q)*;
            old_q := *TL(old_q)*
          end;
      CLIP := *PAIR(new_q, new_rear)*
      end
  end.

Figure 6.6   Implementation of *CLIP* with an O(1) time complexity

In spite of the similarities between this implementation and the simpler linked implementation discussed earlier, the implementation descriptors *VALID* and *ABSTR* are considerably different:

VALID(NIL_CEL),
VALID(PAIR(q1,q2))
  iff *q1* = *q2* and *q1* = *CELL(x, NIL_CEL)*
  or *KIND(TL(q2))* = *empty*
    and *VALID(PAIR(TL(q1), q2))*
  or *VALID(PAIR(q1, TL(q2)))*;

ABSTR(NIL_CEL) = *NUL*,
ABSTR(PAIR(q1,q2))
  = **if** *q1* = *q2*
    then *PUSH(HD(q1), NUL)*
    else
      if *KIND(TL(q2))* = *empty*
        then *PUSH(HD(q1),ABSTR (PAIR(TL(q1),q2)))*
        else *QU (HD(q2),ABSTR(PAIR(q1,TL(q2))))*.

For sequences
interpreted as values,
either *RESTART* or
INSERT and *SHRINK*
are O(*n*).

As an exercise, the reader may explore linked (and direct) implementations of operations that involve a point of interest. Some of them, such as *INSERT* and *SHRINK*, may suggest programs of complexity O(n), which require that portions of the sequence be copied for each such change. It turns out that either *RESTART* or *INSERT* and *SHRINK* are O(n). The obvious implementation leads to an efficient program (O(1)) for *RESTART* and less efficient programs for *INSERT* and *SHRINK*. However, if we represent our sequence by two smaller pieces, one containing the leading elements up to the point of interest and the other containing the tail end that starts at the point of interest, then *INSERT* and *SHRINK* are O(1) while *RESTART* is O(n). This follows because *INSERT* and *SHRINK* are now implemented as *PUSH* and *POP* functions for the second sequence, but *RESTART* must be implemented as the concatenation of the two pieces. The operation *NEXT* queues the front of the second piece at the rear of the first (and pops it off the front of the second piece).

6.3 IMPLEMENTATION OF SEQUENCES AS OBJECTS

Most programmers will implement sequences (and other data types) as mutable objects. The advantages seem to be obvious: all operations can be performed in constant time (O(1)) and cells that are no longer needed are recycled rather than lost. The disadvantages are more subtle. We discussed this problem in some detail in Chapter 4 and we also gave a general method for deriving the specifications of the object type from the properties of functions of the corresponding value type. Hence we concern ourselves here only with the *implementation* of sequence objects.

We shall build the programs for operations such as *QU*, *INSERT*, and so forth by using again the cell operations

PAIR, *CELL*, *FRNT*, *HD*, and *TL*,

together with the new operations

> **procedure** *SET_FRNT*(*p*:Queue; *x*:Cells)
>   {*changes the front of p to x*};

> **procedure** *SET_HD*(*c*:Cells; *x*:Item)
>   {*changes the HD field of cell c to x*};

> **procedure** *SET_TL*(*c,d*:Cells)
>   {*changes the TL field of cell c to d*};

> **procedure** *DELETE*(*c*:Cells)
>   {*returns cell c to pool of available cells; details are described in Chapter 5*}.

We shall describe each implementation by *ABSTR*. When discussing actual code we will not give complete programs but code skeletons to show how the cells and indices are manipulated. We shall deal with four basic representations of sequences: two for sequences that do not have a point of interest and two for those that do.

6.3.1   A simple implementation of queue objects

Consider Figure 6.7.

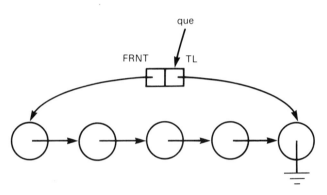

Figure 6.7   Simple implementation structure of queue objects

This representation seems similar to the "linked implementation" discussed above, but there is an important difference: the arrows point from the front to the rear rather than the other way. Consequently, *ABSTR* is easier to express in terms of *PUSH* than in terms of *QU* and has the form:

$ABSTR(PAIR(NIL\_CEL,\ q)) = NUL\ \{for\ any\ q\},$

$ABSTR(PAIR(q1,\ q2))\ \{with\ KIND(q1) = c\_cell\}$
    $= $ **if** $q1 = q2$
        then $PUSH(HD(q1),\ NUL)$
        else $PUSH(HD(q1),\ ABSTR(PAIR(TL(q1),q2)))$.

This implementation makes clipping (removing the first element) very simple:

CLIP:
    $temp := FRNT(que)$;
    if $KIND(temp) = empty$
        then $ERROR(...)$;
        else begin
            $SET\_FRNT(que,\ TL(temp))$; $DELETE(temp)$
        end.

Queuing a new item at the rear is also straightforward:

QU:
  temp := *CELL*(*x*,*NIL_CEL*);
  if *KIND*(*FRNT*(*que*)) = *empty*
    then *SET_FRNT*(*que, temp*)
    else *SET_TL*(*TL*(*que*), *temp*);
  SET_TL(*que, temp*).

6.3.2   A queue as a circularly linked list

If we replace the *NIL_CEL* link in the last element of the previous queue by a link back to the first element (Figure 6.8), then we can save a field in the head

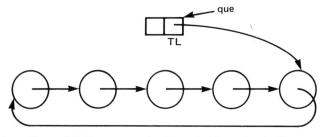

Figure 6.8   A sequence implemented by a circular list

cell. We interpret the cell to which the head cell points as the last element of the queue. Now we obtain for *ABSTR*:

ABSTR(*PAIR*(*p,q*))
  =**if** *KIND*(*q*) = *empty*
      then *NUL* **else** *ABSTRa*(*TL*(*q*),*q*)

ABSTRa(*p,q*)
  = **if** *p* = *q*
      then *PUSH*(*HD*(*p*), *NUL*)
      else *PUSH*(*HD*(*p*), *ABSTRa*(*TL*(*p*),*q*))

and for *CLIP*

CLIP:
  if *KIND*(*TL*(*que*)) = *empty*
      then *ERROR*(...)
      else begin
          temp := *TL*(*TL*(*que*));
          if *temp* = *TL*(*que*)
              then *SET_TL*(*que, NIL_CEL*)
              else *SET_TL*(*TL*(*que*), *TL*(*temp*));
          DELETE(*temp*)
      end.

Queuing an element to the rear is performed as follows:

QU:

         $temp := CELL(x, NIL\_CEL)$;
         if $KIND(TL(que)) = empty$
             then $SET\_TL(temp, temp)$
             else begin
                 $SET\_TL(temp, TL(TL(que)))$;
                 $SET\_TL(TL(que), temp)$
             end;
       $SET\_TL(que, temp)$.

If we interpret the element $TL(TL(que))$ not as the first element of a queue but as the "point of interest" in some other kind of sequence, then the operations $CLIP$ and QU become the operations $INSERT$ and $SHRINK$, respectively. Now the operation $NEXT$ is quite simple:

$NEXT$:

         if $KIND(TL(que)) = empty$
             then $ERROR(...)$
             else $SET\_TL(que, TL(TL(que)))$.

Note that this implementation of $NEXT$ behaves slightly differently from the "$NEXT$" described by the axioms 6.24–6.26 (page 130). This version of $NEXT$ does not recognize the end of a sequence but "wraps around". The axiomatic specification for this variant is not as simple as the original one; it requires an extra hidden function that moves the point of interest back to the front when $NEXT$ shifts it beyond the end of the sequence.

     If we wish to keep track of a distinguished point *front*, we simply need a second field in the head cell of the sequence that points to the cell that, in turn, points to the front.

6.3.3   Sequences with PREV as singly linked lists

Being able to move the point of interest efficiently back and forth seems to call for arrows pointing in both directions. It turns out that this is not true. Consider Figure 6.9.

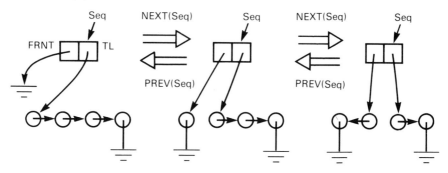

Figure 6.9   **Singly linked implementation sufficient for both NEXT and PREV**

Here we take full advantage of the fact that we may modify a sequence object as we process it. Looking toward the end of the sequence from the point of interest, *HD* points to the subsequence ahead while *TL* points to the part already traversed (using *NEXT*). This implementation is formally described by

$$ABSTR(PAIR(NIL\_CEL, NIL\_CEL)) = NUL,$$

$$
\begin{aligned}
ABSTR(PAIR(q1, q2)) &\ \{q1\ or\ q2\ are\ nonempty\} \\
&= \textbf{if}\ KIND(q1) = empty \\
&\quad \textbf{then}\ PUSH(HD(q2), \\
&\qquad\qquad ABSTR(PAIR(NIL\_CEL, TL(q2)))) \\
&\quad \textbf{else}\ NEXT(INSERT(HD(q1), \\
&\qquad\qquad ABSTR(PAIR(TL(q1), q2)))).
\end{aligned}
$$

The reader is urged to apply *ABSTR* to sample sequences in order to understand completely how it works. Note that *PUSH* keeps the point of interest in front. The implementations of *INSERT* and *SHRINK* are left as exercises. For *NEXT* and *PREV* we obtain:

NEXT:
      temp := *TL*(*seq*);
      if *KIND*(*temp*) = *empty*
            then *ERROR*(...)
            else begin
                  SET_TL(*seq*, *TL*(*temp*));
                  SET_TL(*temp*, *FRNT*(*seq*));
                  SET_FRNT(*seq*, *temp*)
            end;

PREV:
      temp := *FRNT*(*seq*);
      if *KIND*(*temp*) = *empty*
            then *ERROR*(...)
            else begin
                  SET_FRNT(*seq*, *TL*(*temp*));
                  SET_TL(*temp*, *TL*(*seq*));
                  SET_TL(*seq*, *temp*)
            end.

Again, if we wish to have immediate access to the front (or the rear) of the sequence, then we may add one or two fields to the head cell to hold the indices of the front and/or rear cell.

6.3.4   Sequence objects as doubly linked lists

While implementation based on single links allows efficient execution of *NEXT* and *PREV* as well as *INSERT* and *SHRINK*, the operation

RESTART takes O(n) steps. If the rapid execution of all these operations is equally important to the extent that the expense of extra storage space is justified then we may use doubly linked lists. Figure 6.10 shows the linking

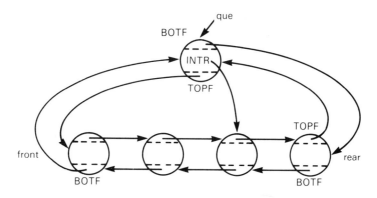

Figure 6.10   A sequence implemented by a doubly linked list

structure of such an implementation. We give the code for *NEXT, PREV, INSERT* and *SHRINK*. For the following code segments, we need cells with additional fields. For reasons of simplicity, we assume that the head cell and the actual sequence cells have the same type. Each cell is assumed to have (at least) three fields, accessed by *"INTR"* (point of interest link), *"TOPF"* and *"BOTF"*. The head cell uses the *"INTR"* field to keep track of the point of interest; the other cells may use it for storing other data. In analogy to our previous cell operations, we assume that we may use the following functions and procedures:

    CELL, INTR, TOPF, BOTF, SET_INTR, SET_TOPF, SET_BOTF.

The axioms

    INTR (*CELL*(a,b,s)) = a,
    TOPF(*CELL*(a,b,c)) = b, and
    BOTF(*CELL*(a,b,c)) = c

explain how the parameters of *CELL* are to be interpreted. As before, a *SET_xxx* operation changes the specified field of the cell denoted by its first parameter to the value of its second parameter. With these conventions we obtain for *NEXT, PREV, INSERT,* and *SHRINK*:

    NEXT:
        SET_INTR(*que, TOPF*(*INTR*(*que*)));

    PREV:
        SET_INTR(*que, BOTF*(*INTR*(*que*)));

    INSERT:

        temp := *CELL*(*x*, *INTR*(*que*), *BOTF*(*INTR*(*que*)));
        SET_TOPF(*BOTF*(*INTR*(*que*)), *temp*);
        SET_BOTF(*INTR*(*que*), *temp*);
        SET_INTR(*que*, *temp*);

    SHRINK:

        temp := *INTR*(*que*);
        if *temp* = *que*
            then *ERROR*(...)
            else begin
                SET_INTR(*que*, *TOPF*(*temp*));
                SET_TOPF(*BOTF*(*temp*), *TOPF*(*temp*));
                SET_BOTF(*TOPF*(*temp*), *BOTF*(*temp*));
                DELETE(*temp*)
            end.

Note that neither the empty sequence nor the end-of-sequence condition gives rise to special cases. Note also that this implementation does not satisfy all of the error conditions of the pertinent axioms. As an exercise modify (i) the implementation, so that the axioms are satisfied, and (ii) the axioms, so that the above implementation is correct.

6.4   THE FILE OF TOKENS: A CASE STUDY

We conclude this chapter with an example of a data type that is useful for a great number of programs that deal with manual input. This example is to show how a data type can be constructed from several layers of programs. We state our problem as follows.

    A program (for example, a text editor or command processor) reads pieces of information from a keyboard and, depending on the information it finds, invokes specific actions. As it proceeds, it subdivides the information read into character strings and classifies these strings into commands and data (parameters). Such character strings are commonly called "tokens". Typical tokens are identifiers, numerals and, perhaps, other types of strings, as well as special symbols that serve as separators, operators or brackets. In short, looked at from a sufficiently high level, the data items read from the keyboard are tokens rather than characters. Consequently, we wish to look at the input file associated with the keyboard not as a file of characters but as a file of tokens.

    Since Pascal does not give us the data type "file of tokens", we have to create it ourselves using what Pascal provides: the text file. The goal is a set of operations that resemble the usual file operations and that can be used, for example, as follows:

> **var** *infile*: *text; nxt_tkn*: *Token;*
> **begin**
>   ...
>   *RESET_TOKEN*(*infile*);
>   **repeat**
>   *READ_TOKEN*(*infile*, *nxt_tkn*);
>   ...
>   **until** *EOF_TOKEN*(*infile*);
>   ...

Using existing notations is better than introducing new ones.

By choosing names for our operations similar to those used for Pascal files (*RESET_TOKEN, READ_TOKEN, EOF_TOKEN*), we wish to indicate that our operations should behave in exactly the same manner as those provided by Pascal. The only difference is that our items are "tokens". Borrowing the specifications from Pascal itself has at least two advantages: we do not need to work out the details of the specification ourselves, and we do not impose a new notation on the user. Thus, we assume that both the token file and the underlying text file are defined by the specification given in 6.1.6. The type of *Item* is *Token* and *Char*, respectively.

Remark: Programming is a rather difficult business; we can ease the problems somewhat by not introducing new concepts or new notations unnecessarily. Put positively, we should consider good established concepts and notations and adapt them to our purpose provided that they are appropriate.

Like notations must have like meanings.

   A word of caution is in order: if we borrow an existing notation for a new purpose, then we ought to use it in exactly the same way as it is used elsewhere; otherwise we are doing something much worse than inventing our own new notation (which makes the user memorize new rules): we are misleading the user and, thus creating conditions that may cause unnecessary problems and even errors.

   For this reason we have not chosen an operation similar to *get* (instead of *read*). Because of the restrictions that most Pascal implementations impose on external files — they cannot be part of a record — identifying the buffer variable (needed with *get*) using the file identifier is not possible. Hence, the correspondence between the Pascal operation *get* and a *GET_TOKEN* procedure cannot be complete.

We know from our previous discussion, that the set of operations consisting of *RESET*, *READ*, and *EOF* cannot be defined by our style of axiomatic specification. Hence, we may decide to enlarge this set by including the operations *REWRITE*, *WRITE*, etc. or we may simply look upon these additional operations as being "hidden".

The type *file of tokens ...*

   Our next step is to decide on a method of implementation for our new file operations. A study of the theory of "lexical analysis" (that is the technique of recognizing tokens described by quite general rules) would go beyond the scope of this book. We therefore simplify the task by defining a token to be any character string delimited by blank spaces. A sequence of spaces is not considered to be a token and is ignored whenever it occurs.

... is based on the type *Token*, ...

Earlier we said that tokens are classified into identifiers, numerals, and so on. Therefore, we need a function

$$CLASS(t: Token): Class\_of\_token$$

to decide to which class a particular token belongs.

Usually, the class of a token is determined by the lexical analyzer at the time when the token is isolated from the input file. Since saving this result seems to be more reasonable than recomputing it each time that we need it, we store the class of a token together with its string using a packing function. Thus we define *Token* to be the following data type:

Sets: <u>*Token*</u>, *String, Class_of_token;*

Syntax:

$$NEW\_TOKEN(s: String; \ c: Class\_of\_token): Token;$$
$$T\_STRING(t: Token): String;$$
$$T\_CLASS(t: Token): Class\_of\_token;$$

Axioms: for all *s* in *String* and *c* in *Class_of_token*
$$T\_STRING(NEW\_TOKEN(s, \ c)) \ = \ s;$$
$$T\_CLASS(NEW\_TOKEN(s, \ c)) \ = \ c.$$

... which is based on the type *String*.

For the time being, we assume that the type *String* provides at least the operations

function *NUL*: *String*
    {*create a new empty string*}

function *APPEND*(*x:Char*; *s:String*):*String*;
    {*append x to the end of s*}.

Ensuring like meanings for like notations requires close attention to details.

We now go back to the implementation of our new file operations. It seems that the implementation of *RESET_TOKEN* and *EOF_TOKEN* is simply the invocation of *reset* and *eof*. But wait! Suppose that the input file contains nothing but a few blank characters, that is, the file contains no tokens. Viewed as a file of tokens, this file must be considered empty, and, by the rules of *reset* and *eof*, "*read(f,tkn)*" should cause an error condition while *eof(f)* should be true.

While our axiomatic definition of a (Pascal) file in Section 6.1.6 did not involve *READ* (because we did not wish to discuss the complications caused by functions with side effects), it does describe the behavior of *RESET* and *EOF* properly. The empty file, represented by *REWRITE*, gives rise to the axioms

$$RESET(REWRITE) \ = \ REWRITE, \text{ and}$$
$$EOF(REWRITE) \qquad = \ \textbf{true},$$

which address the problem described above. Unfortunately, the Pascal *eof* will not be true after *reset* if the file contains blank spaces; as a text file, it is not empty!

We can solve the problem in one of two ways, namely, by having either *RESET_TOKEN* or *EOF_TOKEN* read all leading blanks. In the first case, *READ_TOKEN* must read all blanks that follow a token, in the second case, *READ_TOKEN* must read the blanks that precede a token. In any case, if it does not find a token, *READ_TOKEN* should report an error.

For our example, we choose to have *RESET_TOKEN* read all leading blanks. With this we obtain the following code for the three operations:

```
procedure RESET_TOKEN(var f: Text);

    var blank: Boolean;

    begin
        reset(f);
        if not eof(f)
            then repeat
                    blank := (f↑= ' ');
                    if blank then get(f)
                until eof(f) or not blank
    end;

procedure READ_TOKEN(var f:Text; var tkn: Token);

    var blank: Boolean; strng: String;

    begin
        strng := NUL;
        if not eof(f) then
            repeat
                    strng := APPEND(f↑, strng);
                    get(f); blank := (f↑ = ' ')
            until blank or eof(f);
        if not eof(f) then
            repeat
                    blank := (f↑ = ' ');
                    if blank then get(f)
            until not blank or eof(f);
        if ISNUL(strng)
            then ERROR('READ_TOKN', end_of_file)
            else tkn := NEW_TOKEN(strng, KIND(strng))
            {KIND computes the class of strng.
             A regular lexical analyzer would do this in the course
             of isolating the token}
    end;

procedure EOF_TOKEN(f:Text):Boolean;

    begin EOF_TOKEN := eof(f) end.
```

The implementation descriptors *VALID* and *ABSTR* are rather complex. This is not surprising since they have to describe the nature of a token. In the following specification we have separated the part that defines the concept of a token from the rest by means of the functions

$$LAST\_TOKEN(f:Text):Token;$$

and

$$TAIL\_FILE(f:Text):Text;$$

where *LAST_TOKEN(f)* is the token added last to the file *f* using either *SHOVE*(...) or *PUT*(*DEPOSIT*(...)) one or more times, and *TAIL_FILE(f)* is the file that remains after removing *LAST_TOKEN(f)* from *f*. With these operations we obtain

$$ABSTR(REWRITE) = REWRITE\_TOKEN;$$
$$ABSTR(SHOVE(x, f))$$
$$= \textbf{if } (x = \text{ ' '})$$
$$\qquad \textbf{then } ABSTR(f)$$
$$\qquad \textbf{else } SHOVE\_TOKEN(APPEND$$
$$\qquad\qquad\qquad\qquad (x, LAST\_TOKEN(f)), TAIL\_FILE(f));$$

$$ABSTR(PUT(DEPOSIT(x, f)))$$
$$= \textbf{if } (x = \text{ ' '})$$
$$\qquad \textbf{then } ABSTR(f)$$
$$\qquad \textbf{else } PUT\_TOKEN($$
$$\qquad\qquad DEPOSIT\_TOKEN(APPEND$$
$$\qquad\qquad\qquad\qquad (x, LAST\_TOKEN(f)), TAIL\_FILE(f))).$$

For *LAST_TOKEN* and *TAIL_FILE* we obtain

$$LAST\_TOKEN(REWRITE) = NUL;$$

$$LAST\_TOKEN(SHOVE(x, f))$$
$$= \textbf{if } (x = \text{ ' '})$$
$$\qquad \textbf{then } NUL$$
$$\qquad \textbf{else } APPEND(x, LAST\_TOKEN(f))$$

$$LAST\_TOKEN(PUT(DEPOSIT(x, f)))$$
$$= \textbf{if } (x = \text{ ' '})$$
$$\qquad \textbf{then } NUL$$
$$\qquad \textbf{else } APPEND(x, LAST\_TOKEN(f))$$

$$TAIL\_FILE(REWRITE) = REWRITE;$$

$$TAIL\_FILE(SHOVE(x, f))$$
$$= \textbf{if } (x = \text{ ' '})$$
$$\qquad \textbf{then } f$$
$$\qquad \textbf{else } TAIL\_FILE(f);$$

$$TAIL\_FILE(PUT(DEPOSIT(x, f)))$$
$$= \textbf{if } (x = \text{‘ ’})$$
$$\textbf{then } f$$
$$\textbf{else } TAIL\_FILE(f);$$

A text file is a valid representation of a token file, if the point of interest is at the beginning of a token or if the file is exhausted. We express this fact using the **function** $REST(f:Text):Text$ which removes trailing blanks from f.

$$REST(REWRITE) = REWRITE;$$

$$REST(SHOVE(x, f))$$
$$= \textbf{if } (x = \text{‘ ’})$$
$$\textbf{then } REST(f)$$
$$\textbf{else } SHOVE(x, f);$$

$$REST(PUT(DEPOSIT(x, f)))$$
$$= \textbf{if } (x = \text{‘ ’})$$
$$\textbf{then } REST(f)$$
$$\textbf{else } PUT(DEPOSIT(x, f)).$$

Now we obtain for *VALID*:

$$VALID(REWRITE);$$

$$VALID(SHOVE(x, SHOVE(y, f)))$$
$$\text{iff } (x <> \text{‘ ’}) \textbf{ and } VALID(REST(SHOVE(y, f)));$$

$$VALID(SHOVE(x, PUT(DEPOSIT(y, f))))$$
$$\text{iff } (x <> \text{‘ ’}) \textbf{ and } (y = \text{‘ ’});$$
$$VALID(PUT(DEPOSIT(x, PUT(DEPOSIT(y, f)))))$$
$$\text{iff } (x <> \text{‘ ’}) \textbf{ and }$$
$$VALID(REST(PUT(DEPOSIT(y, f)))).$$

Notice that $PUT(DEPOSIT(x, SHOVE(y, f)))$ is not a properly reduced expression; hence *VALID* is not defined for it. Also notice that $REST(f) = f$ if f ends with a (part of a) token.

Token strings: their specification ...   We now turn our attention to the type *String*. Besides *NUL* and *APPEND*, we need an operation that permits us to compare two strings for equality (*EQ*). Since tokens are atomic items, we do not need operations that take characters of a string or that concatenate strings. In fact, the only reason for having *APPEND* is for use in the function *READ*, which assembles a string from single characters.

We may wish to convert tokens of type *numeral* to numbers (*Integer* or *Real*, as the case may be) which requires that we be able to inspect all characters in the token string. This may be done by providing operations that maintain a "point of interest" or by means of an operation that gives us access to the *i*th character of the string (*CHAR_AT(i, s)*). To facilitate character by character processing of a string using a **for**-loop, a function that computes the length (*LENGTH*) of the string is also needed. We now define the type String:

Sets: <u>String,</u> *Char, Integer, Boolean*

Syntax:
> **function** *NUL* :*String;*
> **function** *ISNUL* (*s*:*String*):*Boolean;*
> **function** *APPEND*(*c*:*Char; s*:*String*):*String;*
> **function** *EQ*(*s, t*:*String*):*Boolean;*
> **function** *CHAR_AT*(*i*:*Integer; s*:*String*):*Char;*
> **function** *LENGTH*(*s*:*String*):*Integer;*

Axioms: For all *s, t* in *String* − {*error*} and
> > > > *c, d* in *Char* − {*error*}

> *ISNUL* (*NUL*)
> ¬*ISNUL* (*APPEND*(*c,s*))

> *EQ*(*s,NUL*) = *ISNUL* (*s*)
> *EQ*(*NUL,t*) = *ISNUL* (*t*)
> *EQ*(*APPEND*(*c,s*),*APPEND*(*d,t*))
> > = (*c* = *d*) **and** *EQ*(*s, t*)

> *LENGTH*(*NUL*) = 0
> *LENGTH*(*APPEND*(*c,s*)) = 1 + *LENGTH*(*s*)

> *CHAR_AT*(*i,NUL*) = *error*
> *CHAR_AT*(*i,APPEND*(*c,s*))
> > **if** *LENGTH*(*s*) = *i*−1
> > > **then** *c*
> > > **else** *CHAR_AT*(*i,s*)

... and implementation. The implementation of this type becomes particularly simple and efficient if we exploit the peculiar way token strings are created: A token string is built by a series of successive *APPEND* operations and is never altered thereafter. Moreover, while space is being allocated to a particular string, no space is being allocated to any other string. Therefore, we can afford to use an implementation based on arrays that tightly packs the characters into contiguous array locations. *APPEND*, by adding characters to the most recent string, simply extends the used part of the array (recall that a similar array implementation of stacks required that the entire stack be copied each time *PUSH* was invoked; in contrast, *APPEND* does not need to produce copies due to the way token strings are created). In a way, we treat the latest string as a mutable object but all other (older) strings as values. Figure 6.11 shows the configuration of the array space.

As with earlier implementations, we represent a string as a pair of numbers where the first component is the index of the first character and the

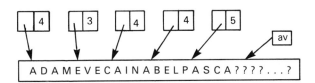

Figure 6.11 The implementation of token strings

second component is the (current) length of the string. The empty string is represented by zero.

We shall write *APPEND* in such a way that only the string *PASCA* (Figure 6.11) can be modified. Note that this is a restriction imposed by our implementation; it is not required by our formal specification. With these conventions and the following definitions

const *max* = 1000; *factor* = 1001 {*max* + 1};

type *Supply* = 0..*max*; *Range* = 1..*max*;
　　　String = 0..1002000 {*max∗factor* + *max*};

var *space:* **array** [*Range*] **of** *Char*; *av: Supply;*
　　　　　　　　　　　　　　　{*av is to be initialized to* 1}

we obtain for *APPEND*:

function *APPEND*(*c:Char*; *s:String*):*String;*

var *new_strng*: 0..*max*;

begin
　　　if *av* > *max*
　　　　then *ERROR*('*APPEND*　　', *overflow*)
　　　　else begin
　　　　　if *s* = 0
　　　　　　then *new_strng* := *av∗factor*
　　　　　　else
　　　　　　if *av* = (*s DIV factor*) + (*s MOD factor*)
　　　　　　　　　　　　　　{*successive use of APPEND?*}
　　　　　　　　then *new_strng* := *s*;
　　　　　　　　else *ERROR*('*APPEND*　　', *bad_use*);
　　　　　　space[*av*] := *c*; *av* := *av* + 1;
　　　　　　APPEND := *new_strng* + 1
　　　　end
　　end.

The other operations are very simple:

function *NUL*:*String*;
　　begin *NUL* := 0 **end**;

```
function ISNUL(s : String) : Boolean;
    begin ISNUL : = (s = 0) end

function LENGTH(s:String):Integer;
    begin LENGTH : = s MOD factor end;

function CHAR_AT(i:Integer; s:String):Char;
    begin
        if i <1 or (s MOD factor)< i
            then ERROR('CHAR_AT    ',position)
            else CHAR_AT : = space[s DIV factor + i−1]
    end;

function EQ(s,t:String):Boolean;

    var i, j, n:Integer;

    begin
        if (s MOD factor)< >(t MOD factor)
            then EQ : = false
            else begin
                i : = s DIV factor;
                j : = t DIV factor;
                n : = i + s MOD factor;
                while (space[i] = space[j])and (i + 1 < n)
                    do begin i : = i+1; j : = j+1 end;
                EQ : = (space[i] = space[j])
            end
    end.
```

We leave the specification of *VALID* and *ABSTR* for strings as an exercise for the reader.

This concludes our discussion of linear types. The reader should now be able (i) to create the particular types appropriate for his applications and (ii) to specify them formally. In designing new types, a programmer should always strive for conceptual simplicity; simplicity is the mother of correctness.

EXERCISES

Theoretical exercises

T6.1 For the following functions on linear types, develop algebraic axioms and prove that they are sufficiently complete:

function *ROTATE*(s:Sequence):Sequence
    {remove the first element from s and append it to the rear};

> **function** *SUFFIX*(*s*:*Sequence*; *n*:*Integer*):*Sequence*
> {*return subsequence of s starting with nth item; if length(s) < n, return NUL*};
>
> **function** *PREFIX*(*s*:*Sequence*; *n*:*Integer*):*Sequence*
> {*return leading subsequence of s of length n*};
>
> **function** *FREQ*(*x*:*Item*;*s*:*Sequence*):*Integer*
> {*count number of occurrences of x in s*};
>
> **function** *SPLIT*(*s*,*t*:*Sequence*):*Sequence*
> {*find the first occurrence of t in s and return the part of s that precedes this occurrence*}

T6.2   Invent five other functions for sequences, give algebraic specifications for them, and prove that these specifications are sufficiently complete.

T6.3   Prove that the axioms (6.16)–(6.36) on page 130 are sufficiently complete.

Hint: Show first that all valid expressions that compute sequences can be reduced to *NUL*, *SHOVE*(*x*,*s*), or *RESTART*(*s*) where *s* is a reduced sequence.

T6.4   Prove that axioms (6.37)–(6.44) on page 131 for *INSERT*, *SHRINK*, and *FIND* are sufficiently complete.

T6.5   Prove that the specification of the *PASCAL* file (Section 6.1.6) is sufficiently complete.

T6.6   Change the axioms for *NEXT*, *PREV*, *INSERT*, and *SHRINK* so that the implementation of sequences by doubly linked lists, as described in Section 6.3.4, satisfies them.

T6.7   Give the implementation descriptors *VALID* and *ABSTR* for the implementation of token strings depicted in Figure 6.10.

Programming exercises

P6.1   Implement the operations *SHOVE*, *QU*, *CLIP*, *FIRST*, *NEXT*, *PREV* and *RESTART* according to the implementation descriptors given at the end of Section 6.2.2 (page 140).

P6.2   Implement queue values with a point of interest using linked implementation (Section 6.2.5, page 143). Begin by designing the implementation descriptors *ABSTR* and *VALID*.

P6.3   Implement the operation *SPLIT* as described in problem T6.1 using (i) integers, (ii) direct implementation of the axiom, (iii) the method depicted in Figure 6.7, and (iv) linked implementation (P6.2).

P6.4   Implement *QU, SHOVE, RESTART, NEXT, PREV* and *PREFIX* for sequence objects using the method depicted in Figure 6.9 (page 155). Modify this method by maintaining pointers to the front and to the rear of the sequence. Begin with the specification of *ABSTR* and *VALID*!

P6.5   Design, specify and implement the following data type useful for the implementation of a screen editor.

     Basically, the type required is a sequence of lines. A line is a sequence (string) of characters or alternatively, a sequence of words, where a word is a string of characters delimited by suitable symbols (blanks, punctuation symbols).

     The sequence of lines has a point of interest. One of the operations at the point of interest is retrieving a "frame", that is, a subsequence of a fixed length for display on the screen.

     From your experience with screen editors you may wish to invent other operations that might be useful for writing the editor. However, the most important problem is to identify the fundamental operations of the type (and its supporting types), and the development of the implementation descriptor.

     Guided by the descriptor, you may then write the code for some of the type primitives.

NOTE: Develop the implementation descriptors before writing any code for the primitive operations. This is best accomplished by drawing a diagram describing the intended representation of a typical instance of the type. This diagram will probably not describe all special cases; so be careful. Remember that the implementation descriptors are thinking tools that help you to find a simple and good implementation. Hence they are not as beneficial as they could be if they are produced when the implementation is finished. At that point, you, the programmer, may be less inclined to modify your work and you may consider the new insights gained while producing the implementation descriptors to be inconveniently late.

7 Binary Trees

The concept of a
sequence, ...

In Chapters 4 and 6 we have seen that all instances of linear types can be
produced by expressions of the form

$$NUL \text{ and } PUSH(i, s), \text{ (or } NUL \text{ and } QU(i,s)),$$

unless there is a "point of interest". Furthermore, every sequence that can be
produced with *PUSH* can also be produced with *QU* (or even *INSERT* if we
ignore the position of the point of interest). Thus, a nonempty sequence
consists of an item and another (shorter) sequence. A sequence can be
constructed from two or more sequences (by *CONCAT*) but the same result
can be achieved with *PUSH* or *QU*. Similarly, the operations used to
decompose a sequence give us either an item (*TOP, REAR, CURRENT*) or a
sequence shorter by one element (*POP, POP_LAST, SHRINK*).

... suitably
generalized, ...

In this chapter, we shall explore a new family of types which are slightly
more complex than sequences. A new instance of such a type is constructed
by combining not just one but *two or more* smaller instances of the same
type, and an item.

... leads to the
concept of a tree.

These new types are called *trees*. If each nonempty tree is built from an
item and exactly two smaller trees, then the type is called *binary tree*.

Examples of
applications of trees are
deferred.

At this point we may be tempted to present and illustrate a number of
practical uses of trees, in part, to stress their importance as a data type, and
also in order to help the reader develop an intuition for this important
structure. Unfortunately, an illustration of the use of a structure often has the
devilish property of suggesting an implementation of this structure. As a
result, the reader's freshly acquired intuition may be too firmly associated
with such an implementation scheme and consequently limit his imagination
rather than widen it. Therefore, we begin by showing that the formal
structure (that is to say, the collection of operations) of binary trees is
strikingly similar to that of stacks. Later we shall have and exploit many
opportunities to discuss and illustrate practical applications of trees.

7.1 BINARY TREES AND LINEAR TYPES

Now, since linear types, such as stacks, and binary trees seem to differ only by the number of objects (stacks and trees, respectively) used to construct the next larger object, let us try to derive the primitive operations for a simple version of binary trees by generalizing the primitives of stacks. We begin with the syntax of the operations.

Stack primitives	**Tree primitives**
NIL_STACK: Stack;	*NIL_TREE: Bitree;*
ISMT_STACK(s:Stack):Boolean;	*ISMT_TREE(t:Bitree):Boolean;*
TOP(s:Stack):Item;	*ROOT(t:Bitree):Item;*
POP(s:Stack):Stack;	*LEFT (t:Bitree):Bitree;*
	RGHT(t:Bitree):Bitree;
PUSH(x:Item; s:Stack):Stack;	*TREE(x:Item; lt,rt:Bitree):Bitree.*

The axioms for these tree operations can be similarly derived from the stack axioms by analogy.

Stack axioms

ISMT_STACK(*NIL_STACK*)

not *ISMT_STACK(PUSH(x,s))*

$TOP(PUSH(x,s)) = x$

$POP(PUSH(x,s)) = s$

$TOP(NIL\_STACK) = error$

$POP(\text{NIL\_STACK}) = error$

Tree axioms

ISMT_TREE (*NIL_TREE*),   (7.1)

not *ISMT_TREE (TREE(x,lt,rt))*,   (7.2)

$ROOT(TREE(x,lt,rt)) = x,$ (7.3)

$LEFT(TREE(x,lt,rt)) = lt,$ and   (7.4)

$RGHT(TREE(x,lt,rt)) = rt,$ (7.5)

$ROOT(NIL\_TREE) = error,$ (7.6)

$LEFT(NIL\_TREE) = error,$ and   (7.7)

$RGHT(NIL\_TREE) = error.$ (7.8)

In order to see that these axioms are sufficiently complete, observe that reduced tree expressions are of the forms

$$NIL\_TREE \text{ or } TREE(x,lt,rt)$$

where *lt* and *rt* are reduced tree expressions.

Binary trees, though similar to stacks, have a much richer structure.

At this point we may conclude that binary trees are not much different from stacks and, hence, we may be tempted not to bother studying them further. This, however, would be a great mistake. As we will see, although they are similar to stacks, trees have a much richer structure and, consequently, properties that stacks do not have. This, in turn, makes trees incomparable with stacks for many practical applications.

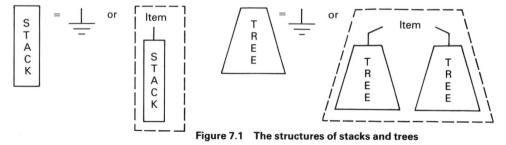

Figure 7.1   The structures of stacks and trees

The similarities and differences between stacks and binary trees that are apparent with our present knowledge are illustrated in Figure 7.1.

A binary tree has a root (a label), and a left and a right subtree.

In *TREE*(*x,lt,rt*), *x* is called the root item or the *label* of the tree, *lt* and *rt* are called the *left and right subtree*, respectively. Thus *LEFT*(*t*) and *RGHT*(*t*) are *t*'s left and right subtrees; *ROOT*(*t*) is *t*'s label. While Figure 7.1. compares the general structures of stacks and trees, Figure 7.2 depicts specific stacks and trees. Note that trees are drawn "upside down".

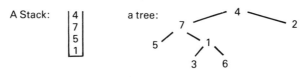

Figure 7.2   A specific stack and tree

To argue about programs on trees *NEVER* use specific trees.

When arguing about programs that process trees, we should always use the general model of trees as depicted in Figure 7.1 rather than specific trees such as those in Figure 7.2. The general model usually leads to a shorter argument, and, more importantly, it leads to an argument that does not depend on the accidental properties of the (specific) tree chosen. We shall see examples of this rule throughout this chapter.

Number of labels in a binary tree

We now continue our comparison of properties of stacks and trees. A simple property of a specific stack is the number of items on the stack. This number can be computed by the recursive rule

$N\_O\_ITEMS(NIL\_STACK) = 0$, and
$N\_O\_ITEMS(PUSH(x,s)) = 1 + N\_O\_ITEMS(s)$.

For trees let us try the analogous pair of specifications

$N\_O\_LABELS(NIL\_TREE) = 0$,
$N\_O\_LABELS(TREE(x,lt,rt))$
$\quad = 1 + N\_O\_LABELS(lt) + N\_O\_LABELS(rt)$.

In words, this says that

(1) there are no labels in an empty tree, and
(2) the number of labels in a nonempty tree is
    1 + the number of labels in the left subtree
    + the number of labels in the right subtree.

As an exercise, we shall now turn the specification for *N_O_ITEMS* into a program and prove its correctness. The reader may do the same with *N_O_LABELS*.

```
function N_O_ITEMS(s:Stack):Integer;
    begin
        if ISMT_STACK(s)
            then N_O_ITEMS := 0
            else N_O_ITEMS := 1 + N_O_ITEMS(POP(s));
    end.
```

In order to show that our program satisfies the specification, we compute (1)

$N\_O\_ITEMS(NIL\_STACK)$ {*which should equal* 0}
    = **if** $ISMT\_STACK(NIL\_STACK)$ {*which is true*}
        then 0   {*so it* does *equal*}   0

and (2)

$N\_O\_ITEMS(PUSH(x,s))$ {*should equal* 1 + ...}
    = **if** $ISMT\_STACK(PUSH(x,s))$ {*false by ax.2*}
        else 1 + $N\_O\_ITEMS(POP(PUSH(x,s)))$
            = 1 + $N\_O\_ITEMS(s)$ {*by ax.4*}.

Thus, our program is correct.

In Chapter 6 we observed that linear types have two distinguished elements: the first and the last one. A tree, on the other hand, has a clearly defined first element, usually called the *root*, but generally many last elements. Because of this, stacks and binary trees differ fundamentally with regard to another property: the number of steps that it takes to find the bottom of the stack and an empty subtree. Obviously, for the stack this is the same number as the number of items on the stack. Not so for the tree! Since there is no unique last element, there is no unique number of steps that takes us to the bottom of the tree (or should we say to its top?); this number depends on the path that we choose.

We seem to have exhausted the obvious similarities of stacks and binary trees, so that any further comparison will probably not give us any more understanding of either sequences or trees. Hence we shall give up comparing the two types and concentrate on trees.

7.2   MORE PROPERTIES OF BINARY TREES

Definitions:

Before we continue with the computation of the number of steps from the root of a tree to a last element, we wish to introduce two additional terms by formal definitions: *path* and *leaf*.

path, ...

Definition: A *path* (of tree t_1 to its subtree t_k is the sequence

$t_1, t_2, \ldots, t_k$

of trees where, with i $\geq$ *1*,

t_{i+1} equals either *LEFT* t_i or *RIGHT* t_i

leaf, ...

Definition: A tree *t* is called a *leaf* if

$ISMT\_TREE(LEFT(t))$ **and** $ISMT\_TREE(RGHT(t))$.

NOTE: There is a difference between a leaf and what we call a *last* element. For the latter it suffices that

$$ISMT\_TREE(LEFT(t)) \text{ or } (!) ISMT\_TREE(RGHT(t)).$$

Since there is no unique number of steps for the walk from the root of a tree to one of its last elements, let us compute the two extremes:

(1) the greatest number of steps (longest path)

{this number is usually called the *depth* or the *height* of the tree}, and

(2) the smallest number of steps.

We specify

depth (height), and ...

$$DEPTH(NIL\_TREE) = 0;$$
$$DEPTH(TREE(x,lt,rt))$$
$$= 1 + max(DEPTH(lt), DEPTH(rt)), \text{ and}$$

$$MIN\_PATH(NIL\_TREE) = 0;$$
$$MIN\_PATH(TREE(x,lt,rt))$$
$$= 1 + min(MIN\_PATH(lt), MIN\_PATH(rt)).$$

NOTE: Most implementations of Pascal provide the functions *max* and *min* as standard library functions, where *max* returns the greatest and *min* the smallest of its arguments.

Do these specifications express what we want them to express?

Clearly, the depth of an empty tree is zero. If the tree is not empty, then the depth is at least one since we have to apply *LEFT* or *RGHT* at least once. Now the longest path has to go down into one of the two subtrees and the deeper of the two subtrees will supply this longest path as 1 plus its own longest path. Hence, the specification correctly defines the depth of the tree as the depth of the deeper of the subtrees plus one.

The argument that the specification of *MIN_PATH* is correct, is quite similar and is left as an exercise.

The program that computes the depth is straightforward:

```
function DEPTH(t:Bitree):Integer;
    begin
        if ISMT_TREE(t)
            then DEPTH := 0
            else  DEPTH  :=  1  +  max(DEPTH(LEFT(t)),
                                        DEPTH(RGHT(t)))
    end.
```

The proof that this program is correct is also left as an exercise.

perfect balance.

If both *DEPTH* and *MIN_PATH* have the same value, then all paths down the tree must have the same length. Such a tree is called *perfectly balanced*.

Lemma: A tree t of depth k is perfectly balanced if and only if it is empty (*if* $k = 0$) or if it has two perfectly balanced subtrees both of depth $k - 1$.

(7.9)

Proof: That the *if* part of the lemma is correct follows directly from the definition of "perfectly balanced". For the *only-if* part, we prove $p \Rightarrow q$ by showing $\neg q \Rightarrow \neg p$. Suppose that one of the subtrees is not perfectly balanced (without loss of generality assume that this is the left subtree), now:

$$MIN\_PATH(LEFT(t)) \ < \ DEPTH(LEFT(t));$$

Consequently,

$$min(MIN\_PATH(LEFT(t)), \ MIN\_PATH(RGHT(t)))$$
$$< max(DEPTH(LEFT(t)), \ DEPTH(RGHT(t))),$$

thus

$$MIN\_PATH(t) \text{ is not equal to } DEPTH(t).$$

The proof that both subtrees have a depth of $k - 1$ is left as an exercise. $\square$ Suppose we find that some given tree t is perfectly balanced and that its depth is k. Can we predict the value computed by $N\_0\_LABELS(t)$? Of course!

Number of labels in a perfectly balanced binary tree

Lemma: The number of labels in a perfectly balanced tree of depth k is

$$n = 2^k - 1. \tag{7.10}$$

Proof {*by induction over k*}:

Base case: $k = 0$.
An empty tree is balanced ($DEPTH = MIN\_PATH$). The above formula gives $n = 1 - 1 = 0$; since the empty tree has no labels, the base case is established.

Induction hypothesis:

if $DEPTH(t) = m$, then $n = 2^m - 1$.

Induction step: Suppose $DEPTH(t) = m+1$. Then $DEPTH(LEFT(t)) = DEPTH(RIGHT(t)) = m$, because the tree is perfectly balanced. Hence the total number of labels is

$$1 + N\_O\_LABELS(LEFT(t)) + N\_O\_LABELS(RGHT(t))$$
$$= 1 + (2^m - 1) + (2^m - 1) \ \{by \ ind. \ hypothesis\}$$
$$= 1 + 2*(2^m - 1) = 2^{m+1} - 1. \ \square$$

Depth of a perfectly balanced binary tree

Corollary: A perfectly balanced tree with n labels has a depth of

$$k = \log_2(n + 1). \ \square \tag{7.11}$$

This result is of practical interest because many algorithms that work with trees involve following a path from the root to some leaf. Clearly, a bound for the number of steps needed is the depth of the tree.

Perfect balance gives us the smallest depth for a given number of labels (since $DEPTH = MIN\_PATH$), that is, the most favorable case. Hence, it is unfortunate that trees are rarely perfectly balanced.

The other extreme (the worst case) is a tree that has a depth of n where n is the number of its labels. Such a tree has one empty subtree, and the other subtree is a worst-case tree or it is empty. But this result is not very useful either!

What we would like to know is the depth that we have to expect for a tree chosen at random. In order to make the notion of "expected depth" precise, we will first define the term *random tree*.

Random trees

Definition: A random tree t with a set L of $n > 0$ labels (all distinct) is constructed as follows. The probability that a label $a \in L$ which is not at the root is inserted into the left (or right) subtree of t is 0.5, and the left and the right subtree of t are empty or are constructed as random trees.

Depth of a random tree

Lemma: The expected depth of a random tree with n labels is

$$k \leq 2.41 * \log_2(n + 1). \tag{7.12}$$

The derivation of this result is discussed as an exercise at the end of this chapter (T7.19). The factor 2.41 is rather conservative. The main substance of the result is not this factor but the logarithmic law: even if a tree is not balanced, its depth can be expected to grow no faster than the logarithm of the number of labels in the tree.

Sometimes the following lemma is quite useful:

Number of leaves in a perfectly balanced binary tree

Lemma: A perfectly balanced tree of depth $k > 0$ has 2^{k-1} leaves. (7.13)

Proof: If the tree has a depth of 1, then the tree *is one* leaf. This is the base case of our inductive argument.

Suppose (induction hypothesis) that perfectly balanced trees of depth k have 2^{k-1} leaves.

For the inductive step, remember that, by (7.9), a perfectly balanced tree of depth $k + 1$ has two perfectly balanced subtrees, both of depth k. Since $k > 0$, the subtrees are not empty and, hence, the leaves of the whole tree are the leaves of its subtrees.

Since each subtree contributes 2^{k-1} leaves, the tree has $2*2^{k-1} = 2^k$ leaves. □

For an arbitrary tree, there is a simple relationship between the number of items stored in the tree and the number of empty (sub)trees:

Number of empty subtrees in a binary tree

Lemma: A tree with n labels has $n + 1$ empty (sub)trees. {*we put "sub" in parentheses because we wish to include the special case where the tree itself is empty*} (7.14)

Proof {*by induction over the number of items in the tree*};

Base case: if $n = 0$, that is, if there are no items in the tree, then there is one empty tree, namely the tree itself.

Induction hypothesis: trees with m items, where $n \geq m \geq 0$, have $m + 1$ empty trees.

Induction step: Consider the tree $TREE(x, lt, rt)$ with $n + 1$ items where the subtrees lt and rt have $m(lt) \leq n$ and $m(rt) \leq n$ items, respectively; hence $m(lt) + m(rt) = n$. The total number of items is

$$N\_O\_LABELS = 1 + m(lt) + m(rt) = n + 1,$$

and the number of empty trees is, using the induction hypothesis,

$$N\_O\_EMPTIES = (m(lt) + 1) + (m(rt) + 1)$$
$$= (1 + m(lt) + m(rt)) + 1$$
$$= (n + 1) + 1. \ \Box$$

Definition:
the *n*th level of a binary
tree

Finally we define the term *level of a tree*. Be especially careful not to confuse "depth" and "level". While these concepts are rather different, experience teaches that they are easily confused. *DEPTH*(t) is a number, *LEVEL*(t,n) is a sequence of items. The *n*th level, $n > 0$, of a tree t is defined as follows:

Syntax:

  $LEVEL(t:Bitree;\ n:Integer):Sequence;$

Axioms:
  $LEVEL(NIL\_TREE, k) = NUL;$
  $LEVEL(TREE(x,lt,rt),\ 1) = PUSH(x,NUL);$
  $LEVEL(TREE(x,lt,rt),\ n+1)$
      $= CONCAT(LEVEL(lt,n),\ LEVEL(rt,n)).$

For example, if t is the tree of Figure 7.2 (page 171), then

  $LEVEL(t,\ 3) = PUSH(5,\ PUSH(1,\ NUL)).$

7.3   A SIMPLE METHOD OF IMPLEMENTING TREES

For experiments
with trees ...,

While we are going to discuss several methods for implementing trees in a later section, we outline one rather simple (and rather common) method here before we start talking in depth about applications of binary trees. This gives the reader the tools to program the tree operations, and, thus, may encourage him to experiment with trees as he reads on.

... the direct
implementation of the
tree axioms is well
suited.

An obvious method of implementing trees is what we used to call the direct implementation of the axioms. Each nonempty tree is represented by a cell with three fields, one for the root item and one for each of the two subtrees. Thus we have

  type *Bitree* = *T_cells* where *T_cells* provides the usual operations:

  function *NIL_CEL*: *T_cells*
  function *IS_NIL*(t:*T_cells*):*Boolean*
  function *T_CELL*(x:*Item*; s,t:*T_cells*):*T_cells*
  function *INF*(t:*T_cells*):*Item*
  function *LFT*(t:*T_cells*):*T_cells*
  function *RGT*(t:*T_cells*):*T_cells*

with the obvious axioms. Trees implemented by *T_cells* are described by

  $ABSTR(NIL\_CEL) \quad = NIL\_TREE$
  $ABSTR(T\_CELL(x,s,t)) = TREE(x,ABSTR(s),\ ABSTR(t))$

and

> *VALID(NIL_CEL)* and
> *VALID(T_CELL(x,s,t))*.

We see that the only difference between trees and cells is one of interpretation. Turning cells into trees amounts to calling *T_cells Bitrees* and renaming the cell operations. Data types that can be converted into each other simply by renaming their constituents are called *isomorphic*.

We hasten to point out that only the value types of cells and trees are isomorphic; we will see later that mutable cell and tree objects are *not isomorphic*.

Frequently, one refers to a cell (other than *NIL_CEL*) that occurs in a tree as a *node* of the tree. Thus, the meaning of the term "node" is similar to that of the phrase "nonempty (sub)tree". The term "root node" or simply *root* refers to the cell that represents the entire tree.

7.4 APPLICATIONS OF BINARY TREES

Tree structures occur naturally in many practical problems.

Binary trees occur quite naturally in all kinds of practical instances. Consider the following examples:

(1) *A pedigree* that is not empty consists of a reference to an individual (the root label), as well as the pedigree of the father, and the pedigree of the mother of the individual.

(2) Any *finite set* can be represented as a tree: the empty set is represented by the empty tree; if a set is not empty, one of its elements is chosen as the root label, the remaining elements of the set are arranged in two (disjoint) subsets which, represented as trees, become the left and right subtree.

(3) *A tournament schedule* is the name of a contestant (a leaf of the tree) or the date of a game and two tournament schedules. Here, the special case of an empty schedule is not meaningful. The next example shares this property:

(4) An *expression* built with binary operators is either a single object (for example, a number or a variable) or it consists of a binary operator and two (operand) expressions.

7.4.1 Trees and arithmetic expressions: a case study

With a simple convention about associativity, ...

Let us analyze this last example more closely. Expressions are commonly given as a sequence of symbols that denote operands and operators. Sometimes parentheses are used to indicate groupings that do not conform to the usual conventions. The decomposition of a given expression into subexpressions is not always unique unless we adopt some rule that resolves the ambiguity. For example, we could agree to evaluate operators from left to right unless some other rule tells us otherwise. By this rule, we evaluate

$a + b + c$

as if it were given as

$(a + b) + c.$

... expressions can be uniquely converted to trees.

This convention is used by most programming languages. Figure 7.3 gives an expression in both its usual representation and in a representation that emphasizes its tree character.

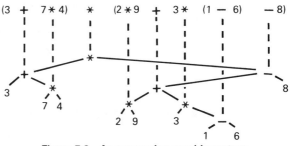

Figure 7.3   An expression as a binary tree

As a tree, an expression needs neither precedence rules nor parentheses, and ...

We make two observations:

(i) the tree representation does not contain (nor needs to contain) parentheses;
(ii) in order to interpret the tree representation properly, precedence rules for operators (such as multiply before adding) are not needed.

... it is easy to evaluate.

In fact, the evaluation of an expression given as a binary tree is a rather simple affair. It proceeds by two rules:

(i) If the tree is a leaf, then the value of the tree (the value of the expression) is the value of the item labelling the leaf;
(ii) otherwise, none of the subtrees is empty (unless the tree is ill-formed). Now, the value of the tree is the value of the left subtree and the value of the right subtree combined by the operator that labels the root.

This recursive specification leads directly to the following program:

```
type Expression = Bitree;

function VALUE(E:Expression):Real_or_something;
    begin
        if ISMT_TREE(LEFT(E))
            then VALUE := ROOT(E)
            else VALUE := COMBINE(ROOT(E),
                          VALUE(LEFT(E)), VALUE(RGHT(E)))
    end.
```

The function *COMBINE* simply applies the operator found at the root of the tree to the values of the left and right subtree. Since *ROOT* returns a value of type *Real_or_something*, the operators must be encoded by such values (we shall discuss a different method further below). Suppose values are, indeed, of type *real*; then *COMBINE* could be coded as follows.

function *COMBINE(OP,LO,RO: Real):Real*;
    begin {*suppose* 1.0 *denotes* +,
                       2.0   ''   −,
                       3.0   ''   ∗,
                       4.0   ''   / }
        case round(OP) of

1{ + }:   *COMBINE* := *LO* + *RO*;
2{ − }:   *COMBINE* := *LO* − *RO*;
3{ ∗ }:   *COMBINE* := *LO* ∗ *RO*;
4{ / }:   *COMBINE* := *LO* / *RO*
           end {*case*}
           end.

A proof of
correctness

With the assumption that *COMBINE* works correctly, the correctness of the function *VALUE* is verified by induction over the depth d of the tree as follows:

Base case: $d = 1$,

    $E = TREE(\{some\ number\}\ x,\ NIL\_TREE,\ NIL\_TREE)$.

Then, since

    $ISMT\_TREE(LEFT(E)) = ISMT\_TREE(NIL\_TREE) =$ **true**
    $= ISMT\_TREE(RGHT(E)) = ...,$

we obtain

    $VALUE(E) = ROOT(E) = x.$

Induction hypothesis: *VALUE* properly computes the values of expressions of a depth d where $1 \leq d \leq k$.

Inductive step: Consider the expression

    $E = TREE(\{some\ operator\}\ q,\ E1,\ E2)$

of the depth $k + 1$. By the definition of depth, the depths of $E1$ and $E2$ are at most k.

Now, *VALUE(E)* exercises the else-part of the **if**-statement since (**not** *ISMT_TREE(E1)*). Thus, we obtain

    $COMBINE(ROOT(TREE(q,\ E1,\ E2)),$
              $VALUE(LEFT(TREE(q,\ E1,\ E2))),$
              $VALUE(RGHT(TREE(q,\ E1,\ E2))))$
    $=\ COMBINE(q,\ VALUE(E1),\ VALUE(E2)).$

Since the expressions $E1$ and $E2$ are of depth $d \leq k$, *VALUE* computes the proper results (by the induction hypothesis) and *COMBINE* applies the operator denoted by q to these two values.

The automatic
conversion of an
expression into a
tree ...

Unfortunately, expressions are usually not given as trees but as textual lines (of characters). Hence, the next important problem is to transform an expression given as a textual line into its tree representation. In order to accomplish this transformation, we will use not only the type *tree* but also the type *stack*. The algorithm, that we are about to develop uses a stack as an intermediate storage device in which it retains partial trees, operators and parentheses. When the algorithm is finished, then the final stack contains only one item: the complete tree.

... suitably
simplified ...

In order to keep some of the technicalities of translating expressions out of our discussion, we assume that all operators have the same precedence, that is to say, we assume that expressions are evaluated from left to right unless they contain parentheses that override this rule.

... is best
described by
"snapshots"

The algorithm is best described by a number of "snapshots" of intermediate stages of the process, shown in Figure 7.4. First, the input contains the expression

$$((3 + 4) * (1 + 9) + 7)$$

and the stack is empty (a).

The tree version
of the expression can
be constructed bottom-
up.

As the process reads characters from the input, it assembles subexpressions to trees. In (b), for example, the symbols up to the digit "1" of the second sum have been read. The complete subexpression found so far is

$$(3 + 4).$$

Note that the parentheses around "3 + 4" have been removed from the stack; the parentheses left on the stack are those of which the matching counterparts have not yet been found. As scanning progresses, the expression "1 + 9" is transformed into a tree (c). The next step, that is, reading the next right parenthesis consists of two parts:

(i) the right parenthesis removes the matching left one from the stack (d1). As a result, the stack contains the complete subexpression

$$E1 * E2 \text{ where } E1 = 3 + 4 \text{ and } E2 = 1 + 9;$$

(ii) E1 * E2 is converted to a tree (d2).

Next "+" moves to the stack (e); then "7" completes an expression (f); finally the outer parentheses drop off (g). The fact that the input is empty and that the stack contains a single tree signals that the process has finished without error.

The actual
conversion program
needs the type *Mixed_
bag*, which can store
different types of data.

We are now ready to design the program that performs the transformation of an expression given as a line of characters into a tree. There are a great number of details that we would like to keep out of our program since they are not relevant to the highest level of concern. First, by contemplating

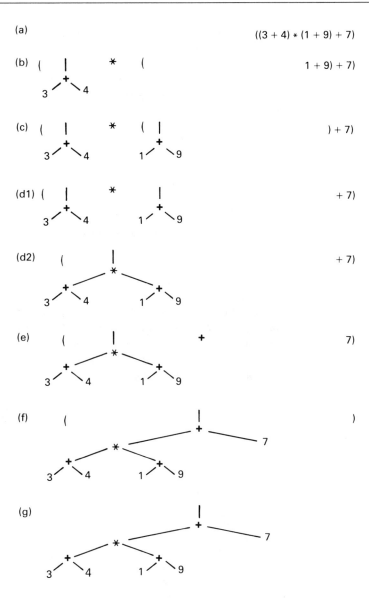

Figure 7.4   **The transformation of a textual line
into a tree**

Figure 7.4 again, we observe that the stack is used for quite different types of data simultaneously. It is used to store trees, operators, and parentheses. If we want to use the stack operations described in Chapter 4, then items have to be things that could be any of the above data objects. Such a *mixed bag* could be defined as a variant cell type (see Chapter 5) with a different variant for each of the types to be stacked.

The items of a
stack can behave like
mixed bags ...
Here, we consider instead yet another alternative for stacking items of
different types onto the same stack: we create a "variant stack" type, that is a
stack that combines the properties of a regular stack with that of a mixed bag.
This type of stack has several different *PUSH* and *TOP* functions, and a
function *TOP_KIND* that retrieves the sort of the item currently on top. This
operation can even be combined with the *ISMT_STACK* function by having
TOP_KIND return the value *EMPTY* if the stack is empty. Figure 7.5 gives
the definition of this type.

type   *Sort*   = (*empty, a_parn, an_op, a_tree*);
     Operator = (*plus, minus, times, div_by*);

Type: M_stack

Sets: M_stack, Bitree, Operator, Sort

Syntax:

function *NIL_STACK: M_stack;*
function *TOP_KIND(s:M_stack): Sort;*
function *PUSH_PARN(s:M_stack): M_stack;*
function *PUSH_OPER(op:Operator; s:M_stack):M_stack;*
function *PUSH_TREE(t:tree; s:M_stack):M_stack;*
function *TOP_OPER(s:M_stack):Operator;*
function *TOP_TREE(s:M_stack):Bitree;*
function *POP(s:Bitree):Bitree;*

Axioms:

TOP_KIND(NIL_STACK)	= *empty;*	(7.15)
TOP_KIND(PUSH_PARN(s))	= *a_parn;*	(7.16)
TOP_KIND(PUSH_OPER(q,s))	= *an_op;*	(7.17)
TOP_KIND(PUSH_TREE(t,s))	= *a_tree;*	(7.18)
TOP_OPER(PUSH_PARN(s))	= *error*	(7.19)
TOP_OPER(PUSH_OPER(q,s))	= *q;*	(7.20)
TOP_OPER(PUSH_TREE(t,s))	= *error;*	(7.21)
TOP_TREE(PUSH_PARN(s))	= *error;*	(7.22)
TOP_TREE(PUSH_OPER(q,s))	= *error;*	(7.23)
TOP_TREE(PUSH_TREE(t,s))	= *t;*	(7.24)
POP(PUSH_...(...,s))	= *s;*	(7.25)

end {*M_stack*}.

Figure 7.5 The data type M_stack

For our program, we shall use this third solution to the stacking problem.
From Chapter 6 we borrow the type *token file* assuming that

type *Class_of_token* =   (*LPR*   {*left parenthesis*},
                  RPR   {*right parenthesis*},
                  NUM   {*numeral*},
                  OPR   {*operator*}).

function *EXPRESSION_TREE*(*var f*:*Token_file*):*Bitree;*
  var *tokn: Token; s: M_stack*; *LT,RT*: *Bitree;*
    OP : *Operator;*
  begin *s* : = *NIL_STACK*;
    while not *EOF_TOKEN*(*f*) **do begin**
      READ_TOKEN(*f, tokn*);
      case *T_CLASS*(*tokn*) **of**

LPR: **if** *TOP_KIND*(*s*) <> *a_tree*
      then *s* : = *PUSH_PARN*(*s*)
      else *ERROR*({*syntax error in input*});

RPR,NUM: **begin case** *T_CLASS*(*tokn*) **of**

    RPR: **if** *TOP_KIND*(*s*) = *a_tree* **then**
          begin
             RT : = *TOP_TREE*(*s*); *s*   POP(*s*);
             if *TOP_KIND*(*s*) = *a_parn*
               then *s*: = *POP*(*s*)
               else *ERROR*({*mismatch*})
          end
          else *ERROR*({*syntax error*});

    NUM: **if** *TOP_KIND*(*s*) <> *a_tree*
          then *RT* : = *NEW_LEAF*(*CONVERT*(*tokn*))
          else *ERROR*({*syntax error*})
        end {*inner* **case** *T_CLASS*};

    if *TOP_KIND*(*s*) = *an_op* **then**
      begin
        OP: = *TOP_OPER*(*s*); *s* : = *POP*(*s*);
        LT: = *TOP_TREE*(*s*); *s* : = *POP*(*s*);
        s : = *PUSH_TREE*(*NEW_EXPR*(*OP,LT,RT*), *s*)
      end
      else *s* : = *PUSH_TREE*(*RT, s*)
    end {*RPR, NUM:* **begin**};

OPR: **if** *TOP_KIND*(*s*) = *a_tree*
      then *s* : = *PUSH_OPER*(*ENCODE*(*tokn*), *s*)
      else *ERROR* ({*syntax error*})

    end {**case** *T_CLASS*}
  end {**while**};

EXPRESSION_TREE : = *TOP_TREE*(*s*);
if not *ISMT*(*POP*(*s*)) **then** *ERROR* ({*syntax error* })
end.

Figure 7.6 Translation of expressions from text form to tree form

We further assume that for tokens the following two operations are defined with their obvious meaning:

> **function** *CONVERT*(*t*:*Token*):*Integer;*
> {*defined for numerals*}

and

> **function** *ENCODE*(*t*:*Token*):*Operator*
> {*defined for operators*}.

*... and so can
the labels of a tree.*

Finally, we still have to solve the problem of storing both operators and operands (numbers) in the same tree. The method of encoding operators as numbers, which we had used before, is a rather poor solution to the problem. It not only lacks flexibility (adding additional operators requires changes of programs not concerned with the types and numbers of operators), but it also burdens the user of the tree operations (that is, the programmer of the translation program) with the details of encoding and decoding operators. In order to eliminate this problem, we use the same method that we developed above for stacks: We introduce two operations *NEW_TREE*:

> **function** *NEW_LEAF*(*x*:*Integer*):*Bitree*;

and

> **function** *NEW_EXPR*(*q*:*Operator*; *lt*,*rt*:*Bitree*):*Bitree*.

We also need, of course, two *ROOT* functions and operations that can test what kind of tree we are given. But since these operations do not occur in the translation program that we are about to write (Figure 7.6), we leave the formulation of these operations as an exercise for the reader.

While this program is not overly complex, it is certainly not as easily understood as many of the earlier programs. In particular, an (even informal) proof of correctness would certainly be rather lengthy and complex.

*A simpler
solution to the parsing
problem which divides
the task ...*

Clearly, if we did not have parentheses, then the translation from the text to the tree would be much easier to program. In order to translate an expression of the form

> <*term*><*op*><*term*><*op*>...<*op*><*term*>,

We only need a procedure of the following form:

> **function** *TERM*(*var input*:*Token_file*):*Bitree*; **forward**;
>
> **procedure** *EXPRESSION*(*var input*: *Token_file*; *var t*: *Bitree*; *var
> tokn*: *Token*);
>   **var** *done*: *Boolean;*

```
begin
  t := TERM(input) {creates leaf for next term};
  done := false;
  while not done and not EOF_TOKEN(input) do begin
    READ_TOKEN(input, tokn);
    if T_CLASS(tokn) = OPR
      then t := NEW_EXPR(ENCODE(tokn), t, TERM(input))
      else done := true
  end
end.
```

… into the conversion of expressions …

This program does not even need a stack for keeping track of intermediate results; it creates the tree "on the fly". As an extra service to the calling program, this procedure also returns the token that follows the expression translated. For example, if the input file contains the text "$3 + 5 - 7 * 19$;" then, upon completion of *EXPRESSION*, *t* contains the tree corresponding to $(((3 + 5) - 7) * 19)$ and *tokn* contains the token with the value ";". Only if the file *input* is exhausted after the expression has been read, is *tokn* undefined or meaningless.

Unfortunately, if *TERM* delivers only leaves, then the expressions that we can translate are simply too trivial to be of much use.

… and the conversion of terms …

Perhaps we could program the function *TERM* to translate not only single numbers but also arbitrary expressions that are enclosed in parentheses. But this seems to be a rather ambitious plan! Can translating expressions in parentheses be any simpler than translating unrestricted expressions? Hardly — unless we use the program *EXPRESSION* above to translate what is between the parentheses. This leads to a process of two programs that call each other in a recursive fashion with the following code for *TERM*:

```
function TERM {(input: Token_file): Bitree see "forward" definition
above};

  var tokn: Token; t:Bitree;

  begin
    READ_TOKEN(input, tokn);
    if T_CLASS(tokn) = NUM
      then TERM := LEAF(CONVERT(tokn))
      else
        if T_CLASS(tokn) = LPR
          then begin  {left parenthesis}       *
                EXPRESSION(input, t, tokn);
                TERM := t;
                if T_CLASS(tokn) <>RPR
                  then ERROR({mismatch})
              end
          else ERROR({syntax error})
  end.
```

Here, *TERM* produces the required leaf if it finds a numeral, but, if it finds a left parenthesis, then it calls *EXPRESSION* in order to read what follows. Now, if *EXPRESSION* returns with a right parenthesis as its terminating token, then *TERM* returns the tree computed by *EXPRESSION*; otherwise it reports an error.

... is called "parsing by recursive descent".

This method of translating expressions can be extended and used for the transformation of program text of quite general programming languages (Pascal for one) into tree representation. This method is called parsing by recursive descent.

A proof of correctness

In order to convince ourselves that these two programs do indeed compute the proper tree we construct an informal inductive proof over the number of nested parentheses in the original input text.

Base case: There are no parentheses in the text. *EXPRESSION* will continue to execute the body of the **while**-loop as long as it finds operators $(+,-,*,/)$ between terms, and, since there are no parentheses in the input, *TERM* will always execute the **then** part of its first **if** and return a leaf with the converted numeral found in the input.

Induction hypothesis: *EXPRESSION* properly translates expressions with not more than k levels of nested parentheses returning the terminating token.

Inductive step: Given the text of an expression that contains nestings of parentheses of up to $k+1$ levels, *EXPRESSION* will rely on *TERM* to find the terms enclosed in parentheses. Such a term, handed to *TERM*, contains not more than $k+1$ levels of parentheses. *TERM* removes the outermost left parenthesis and gives the remaining input to *EXPRESSION*. The latter, by the induction hypothesis, can handle the text preceding the matching right parenthesis since this text will have no more than k levels of parentheses. *EXPRESSION* will return the tree version of this text and the right parenthesis as its terminating symbol. This symbol indicates to *TERM* that the syntax is correct (parentheses match), so that *TERM* returns the tree computed by *EXPRESSION*.

Thus, if *EXPRESSION* can handle expressions with k *nested parentheses*, *TERM* can handle terms with k + 1 levels of parentheses, which, in turn, allows *EXPRESSION* to handle expressions with $k + 1$ levels. □

As an alternative, consider ...

A comparison of this method with the previous one (which used a stack as intermediate storage) seems to be heavily biased toward parsing by recursive descent. It turns out, however, that the other method can be refined and made attractive enough to become a successful competitor. While we are not interested here in parsing methods as an end in itself, we will nevertheless look at this refined version because it teaches us a lot about programming and identifying levels of concern. The basic idea of this program is as follows.

Depending upon the item on top of the stack and the token next in the input three different cases can be distinguished:

(i)   The next input symbol is moved to the stack (this operation is called a *shift*);

(ii)   some items on top of the stack are combined to form a new tree (this operation is called a *reduction*);

(iii)   the configuration is illegal, that is, an error is to be reported.

"shift-reduce"
parsing.
Because of the two alternative actions "shift" and "reduce" the method is called *shift-reduce parsing*. The program *EXPRESSION_TREE*, thus, has the following form:

function *EXPRESSION_TREE* (*var f*:*Token_file*):*Bitree*;

    var *s*: *M_stack; tokn*: *Token;*

    function *SHIFT*(*tokn*:*Token*; *s*:*M_stack*):*M_stack;*
    begin
        if *T_CLASS*(*tokn*) = *OPR*
        then *SHIFT* := *PUSH_OPER*(*ENCODE*(*tokn*), *s*)
        else *SHIFT* := *PUSH_PARN*(*s*)
            {SHIFT is invoked only for
            operators and parentheses}
    end   *{SHIFT}*;

    function *REDUCE*(*tokn*:*Token*; *s*:*M_stack*):*M_stack;*

    var *LT,RT*: *Bitree; OP*:*Operator;*

    begin
        if *T_CLASS*(*tokn*) = *RPR*
        then begin
            RT := *TOP_TREE*(*s*); *s* := *POP*(*s*);
            if *TOP_KIND*(*s*) = *a_parn*
                then *s* := *POP*(*s*)
                else *ERROR* (*{mismatch}*)
            end
        else
            RT := *NEW_LEAF*(*CONVERT*(*tokn*));
        if *TOP_KIND*(*s*) = *an_op*
        then begin
            OP := *TOP_OPER*(*s*); *s* := *POP*(*s*);
            LT := *TOP_TREE*(*s*); *s* := *POP*(*s*);
            RT := *NEW_EXPR*(*OP, LT, RT*)
            end;
        REDUCE := *PUSH_TREE*(*RT, s*)
        end *{REDUCE}*;

    begin *{EXPRESSION_TREE}*
        s := *NIL_STACK*;
        while not *EOF_TOKEN*(*f*) **do**
            begin
                READ_TOKEN(*f, tokn*);

case *ACTION(T_CLASS(tokn), TOP_KIND(s))* **of**
{*ACTION is a tabulated function that determines which of the three actions (shft,redce, err) ought to be chosen*}

shft: *s* := *SHIFT(tokn, s)*;
redce: *s* := *REDUCE(tokn, s)*;
err: *PARSE_ERROR(tokn, s)* {*suitably defined*};
              end {**case**}
          end {**while**};
    EXPRESSION_TREE := *TOP_TREE(s)*;
    if not *ISMT(POP(s))* **then** *error...*
    end.

This team of three programs, while not together shorter than the first program, is much easier to understand, since levels of concern are properly separated. We can look at the different activities and agree that they are correct one at a time. We may take this program as an example to illustrate that the discovery of the proper levels is by no means always a trivial matter; it has taken the community of computer science researchers quite a number of years before they discovered this — form (for a moment, I was considering saying "this final form", but who is to say that there is not an even more elegant method yet to be discovered?!).

7.4.2   Printing a tournament schedule

Suppose that we have managed to set up a binary tree that represents the schedule of a Roman chariot tournament and would like to print it out. We decide to print schedules in the manner illustrated in Figure 7.7.

```
        Crassus
                            Date 1
        Cato
                                        date 2
        Ben Hur
```

FIGURE 7.7.   The printout of a tournament schedule

How can we do this?

How to construct a recursive program

We notice that the different versions of the problem can be classified by their respective sizes, where the size of a version is the depth of the tree to be printed. The solution to problems of this sort is best constructed as a recursive algorithm. We find such an algorithm by constructing the solution of a problem of size *k* (in this case printing a schedule tree of depth *k*) from the solution of the problem of size $k-1$. If we can do this and can solve the smallest meaningful version of the problem, then we are finished; we have an algorithm!

In approaching the specifics of our problem, let us first keep the somewhat messy details of printing a name or a date out of our consideration. We do this assuming that we have a program which, given an item (i.e. a name or a date), prints it out using a unit of space, where a "unit" is some number of columns sufficient for such an item. We further assume that this program can be given an integer number k to indicate that the item is to be printed k units to the right of the left margin. Suppose that the header line of the definition of this print program has the form

>   **procedure** *PRINT_ITEM*(*x*:*Item*; *gap*:*Integer*);

Now we can write the program that prints a schedule with the final match *place* units off the left margin of the paper:

>   **procedure** *PRINT_S_TREE*(*t*:*Bitree*; *place*:*Integer*);
>   **begin**
>   **if not** *ISMT*(*t*)
>   **then begin**
>   *PRINT_S_TREE*(*LEFT*(*t*), *place*–1);
>   *PRINT_ITEM*(*ROOT*(*t*), *place*);
>   *PRINT_S_TREE*(*RGHT*(*t*), *place*–1)
>   **end**
>   **end.**

The program that not only prints the schedule but also decides where to print it on the paper has the following form.

>   **procedure** *PRINT_SCHEDULE*(*t*:*Bitree*);
>
>   **var** *DPTH*: *Integer*;
>
>   **procedure** *PRINT_S_TREE*(...);
>   **begin** ... {*same as PRINT_S_TREE above*}
>   **end**;
>   **begin**
>   *DPTH* := *DEPTH*(*t*);
>   **if** *DPTH* > *max_depth*
>   **then** *ERROR*({*does not fit on paper*})
>   **else** *PRINT_S_TREE*(*t*, *DPTH*)
>   **end.**

7.4.3   Printing a tree root-first

Before we can print a tree root-first ...

In the previous section we have printed a tree lying on its side. An even more challenging problem is to draw it as we draw an expression tree with the root item on top and the items on the second level in the line below and so on.

we need to know how
to print a single level.

We approach this problem in two steps. First we develop a program that prints the kth level of a tree with some given width around a center. Since we want to use this procedure in a program that can print an entire tree, we must make sure that we space the items properly, that is, we must make sure that we leave the proper number of blank spaces if a subtree is missing. An example may help to clarify the problem. Consider Figure 7.8. In order to print level 4 correctly, we have to leave an extra space between the 9 and the 5 and another one between the 2 and the 8. Furthermore, we must leave some room at the right end because an item is missing there also.

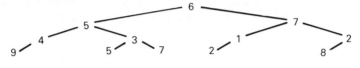

Figure 7.8   A tree to be printed

All this looks rather difficult but, as it turns out, there is a surprisingly simple solution for it. Suspecting that this solution is a recursive one, we again ask ourselves the question: "can we construct the solution for the nth level using the solution for the $n-1$st level?"

Suppose the program, called *PRINT_LEVEL*, has the header

procedure *PRINT_LEVEL* (*t*:*Bitree*; *level,ctr,wdth*:*Integer*);

It is obvious that we have to print *ROOT(t)* at the position *"ctr"* if *"level"* has the value 1. In order to do this, we need some operation that can print an item at a given position. Since we know that such an operation can be programmed, we shall not worry about its details but assume that there is a procedure that can be called by

PRINT_THING (*x*{: *Item*},*k* {:*Integer*}).

For the recursive part of the program we observe that: printing the $n-1$st level of the left subtree into the left half of the specified width, and printing the $n-1$st level of the right subtree into the right half of the specified width should give us the entire level printed into the field provided.

Thus we obtain the program

```
procedure PRINT_LEVEL (t:Bitree; level,ctr,wdth:Integer)
      begin if not ISMT_TREE then
            if level = 1
                  then PRINT_THING(ROOT(t), ctr)
                  else begin
                        PRINT_LEVEL(LEFT(t),   level–1,
                                               ctr – wdth/4,
                                               wdth/2);
```

$$PRINT\_LEVEL(RGHT(t), \quad level{-}1,$$
$$ctr + wdth/4,$$
$$wdth/2)$$

end

end.

The reader may enjoy designing the program that prints the entire tree and working out the details of the routine *PRINT_THING*. Questions to be asked include "do we need a print buffer in which to prepare a printed line?" and "how deep a tree can we print?".

7.4.4   Binary search trees

The data type *Set*

Rather frequently, programmers have to implement the data type *Set*. Three fundamental operations are needed:

(i)   adding an element to a set;

(ii)   deleting an element from the set; and

(iii) testing if a given element is a member of (has been added to) a given set.

This problem is so important that we shall devote much of Chapter 9 to it. Here we look at only one of its solutions; one that involves binary trees.

The three set operations are called *INSERT*, *DELETE*, and *MEMBER*. In order to get things started we also need an operation that creates a new empty set and one that lets us test whether a set is empty. These operations are called *NIL_SET* and *ISMT_SET*. The specification of the type *Set* is given in Figure 7.9.

A set expression is in reduced form if it is either

NIL_SET or *INSERT*(x,s) where s is reduced.

But notice that this form is not unique, because there is more than one reduced expression for any particular set except the empty set. In order to see this, prove (Exercise T7.8) that

INSERT$(x,INSERT(y,s))$ and *INSERT*$(y,INSERT(x,s))$

are equivalent with respect to the behaviour of *MEMBER* and *ISMT_SET*.

As with the other types, *Set* can be implemented in many different ways (think about an implementation based on sequences!).

The implementation of sets by trees leads to ...

Here we want to implement it using binary trees. Of course, the empty set is modelled by the empty tree. In order to make the *MEMBER* operation efficient, we shall use the tree to keep some order among the items inserted so that we do not need to look through the whole tree in order to decide if *MEMBER*(x,s) is **true** or **false**. We go about this in the following way:

Suppose that the items can be put into some sequential order, that is to say, suppose we can define an operation *GREATER*(x,y) that, given a pair (x,y) of items, returns **true** or **false**. This is not a very serious requirement

Type: Set

Sets: Set, Item, Boolean

Syntax:

> *NIL_SET: SET;*
> *ISMT_SET(s:Set):Boolean;*
> *INSERT   (x:Item; s:Set):Set;*
> *DELETE   (x:Item; s:Set):Set;*
> *MEMBER(x:Item; s:Set):Boolean;*

Axioms:

> *ISMT_SET(NIL_SET);*   (7.26)
> $\neg$*ISMT_SET(INSERT(x,s));*   (7.27)
> *DELETE(x,NIL_SET) = NIL_SET;*   (7.28)
> *DELETE(x,INSERT(y,s))*   (7.29)
> = **if** $(x=y)$
>   **then** *DELETE(x,s)*
>   **else** *INSERT(y, DELETE(x,s));*
> $\neg$*MEMBER(x,NIL_SET);*   (7.30)
> *MEMBER(x,INSERT(y,s))*   (7.31)
> = **if** $x = y$
>   **then true**
>   **else** *MEMBER(x,s).*

Figure 7.9   The data type *"Set"*

since numbers, character strings and enumerated types all have a natural ordering. For other objects, such as stacks, sequences, vectors, or even other trees we can certainly develop some method of putting them into a sequential order. In fact, mathematics tells us that this is always possible as long as the set of all items has certain very general properties, which we can take for granted for all sets of items used in computations.

Having decided on some ordering we compute *INSERT* as follows: the first item added to an empty set is put at the root of the tree that models the set. If the tree is not empty, then we compare the item at the root with the item to be added. Three cases can occur:

if *ROOT(s)* and x {*the new item*} are equal, then x is already a member of the set, and no action is needed.

if $x <$ *ROOT(s)*, then we *INSERT* x into the left subtree.

if $x >$ *ROOT(s)*, then we *INSERT* x into the right subtree.

Here is our program:

> **type** *Set = Bitree;*

function *INSERT*(*x*:*Item*; *s*:*Set*):*Set*;
begin
  if *ISMT_TREE*(*s*)
    then *INSERT* := *TREE*(*x*, *NIL_TREE*, *NIL_TREE*)
    else
      if *x* = *ROOT*(*s*)
        then *INSERT* := *s*
        else
          if *x* < *ROOT*(*s*)
            then *INSERT* := *TREE*(*ROOT*(*s*),
                              INSERT(*x*,*LEFT*(*s*)),
                              RGHT(*s*))
          else *INSERT* := *TREE*(*ROOT*(*s*),
                              LEFT(*s*),
                              INSERT(*x*,*RGHT*(*s*)))

  end.

Figure 7.10 may help to illustrate the effect of the function *INSERT*. We see that the new tree shares much of its parts with the original tree, and that new cells need to be created only along the search path from the root down to the place where the new node is attached.

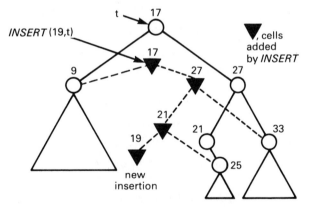

Figure 7.10   Trees *t* and *INSERT* (19, *t*)

Readers who have studied graph theory may object to calling the structure resulting from the application of *INSERT* a tree because some nodes are reached from more than one place. But this objection is unfounded. We should remember that we are severely constrained in analyzing the structure because of our particular set of primitive tree operations. In fact, since we are not allowed to modify a node once it has been created, we have no means of proving (using just our primitives) that the two trees *t* and *INSERT*(19, *t*) have any nodes in common.

... the concept of binary search trees.
    The tree constructed by *INSERT*(*x*,*s*) is called a *binary search tree* provided that *s* is empty or is already a search tree. We could use this

statement as a definition of the concept "search tree"; however, restating the definition in a different way can only help to make the concept clearer.

Definition: *Binary search tree*

A binary search tree is either the empty tree or all labels in the left subtree are less than the label at the root, all labels in the right subtree are greater than the label at the root, and both the left subtree and the right subtree are binary search trees. □

Formally we specify our implementation method by providing the functions *ABSTR* and *VALID*:

$$ABSTR(NIL\_TREE) = NIL\_SET; \tag{7.32}$$
$$ABSTR(TREE(x, lt, rt)) \tag{7.33}$$
$$= INSERT(x, UNION(ABSTR(lt), ABSTR(rt)));$$

where *UNION* is a hidden function defined as follows:

function *UNION*(*s*, *t*:*Set*):*Set;*

$$UNION(NIL\_SET, s) = s;$$
$$UNION(INSERT(x, t), s) = INSERT(x, UNION(t,s)).$$

For the function *VALID*, we obtain

$$VALID(NIL\_TREE) \quad \{is\ true\}; \tag{7.34}$$
$$VALID(TREE(x, lt, rt)) \tag{7.35}$$
$$\text{iff } MAXL(lt) < x < MINL(rt)$$
$$\textbf{and } VALID(lt) \textbf{ and } VALID(rt);$$

where *MAXL* and *MINL* (which retrieve the greatest and the smallest label of a search tree) are defined as follows:

$$\text{for all } x.\ MAXL(NIL\_TREE) < x;$$
$$\text{for all } x.\ MINL(NIL\_TREE) > x;$$
$$MAXL(TREE(y,lt,rt))$$
$$= \textbf{if } ISMT\_TREE(rt) \textbf{ then } y \textbf{ else } MAXL(rt);$$
$$MINL(TREE(y,lt,rt))$$
$$= \textbf{if } ISMT\_TREE(lt) \textbf{ then } y \textbf{ else } MINL(lt).$$

In order to show that all valid trees are, in fact, search trees, we would have to demonstrate that

$$VALID(t) \text{ implies:}$$
$$\text{for all } labels\ x\ of\ the\ tree\ t,$$
$$MAXL(t) \geq x \geq MINL(t).$$

The verification of this as well as a number of other propositions about search trees is left as an exercise (see Exercises T7.9–T7.12).

This type of tree is called a search tree because searching it for a particular label is very efficient. We go about this search by comparing the item in question, x, with $ROOT(s)$. If we are particularly lucky, then we find the item right there; but even without luck our task is reduced to searching either the left or the right subtree (never both) depending on whether x is less or, respectively, greater than $ROOT(s)$. Thus $MEMBER$ is programmed as follows:

```
function MEMBER(x:Item; s:Set):Boolean;
  begin
    if ISMT_TREE(s)
      then MEMBER := false
      else
        if x = ROOT(s)
          then MEMBER := true
          else
            if x < ROOT(s)
                then MEMBER := MEMBER(x, LEFT(s))
                else MEMBER := MEMBER(x,RGHT(s))
  end.
```

The functions NIL_SET and $ISMT\_SET$ have the simple forms:

```
function NIL_SET:Set;
    begin NIL_SET := NIL_TREE end;
```

```
function ISMT_SET(s:Set):Boolean;
    begin ISMT_SET := ISMT_TREE(s) end.
```

Finally, we give the code for $DELETE$. Here, the recursive part of the algorithm is straightforward: if the item to be deleted is in the left or in the right subtree (that is, if it is smaller or greater than the item at the root), then $DELETE$ must be applied to the left or the right subtree, respectively. Further, if the tree is empty, then nothing needs to be done. However, if the item to be deleted is found at the root of the search tree, then the item at the root cannot simply be eliminated. It must be replaced by some appropriate item taken from the left or the right subtree. The nontrivial case occurs if both subtrees are nonempty. In this case, a suitable new root item is the greatest item in the left subtree or the smallest item in the right subtree. With these observations we obtain for $DELETE$:

```
function DELETE(x:Item; s:Set):Set;

    var R_SMALL :Item;

    begin
      if ISMT(s)
        then DELETE := NIL_TREE;
        else
          if x = ROOT(s)
```

```
            then
              if ISMT(LEFT(s))
                then DELETE : = RGHT(s) else
              if ISMT(RGHT(s))
                then DELETE : = LEFT(s) else
              begin
                R_SMALL : = MINL(RGHT(s));
                DELETE : = TREE(R_SMALL,
                                  LEFT(s),
                                  DELETE(R_SMALL,RGHT(s)))
              end
            else
              if x < ROOT(s)
                then
                    DELETE : = TREE(ROOT(s),
                                  DELETE(x,LEFT(s)),
                                  RGHT(s))
                else
                    DELETE : = TREE(ROOT(s),
                                  LEFT(s),
                                  DELETE(x,RGHT(s)))
        end.
```

We leave the proof that *NIL_SET, ISMT_SET, INSERT, DELETE,* and *MEMBER* satisfy the axioms (7.26)–(7.31) as an exercise for the reader.

Since the labels of a search tree are easy to print alphabetically, ...   It is very easy to print the labels of a search tree in ascending (or descending) order. We find the algorithm by the following observation.

(i)   Printing the labels of the empty tree in ascending order is trivially doing nothing.

(ii)   Printing the labels of a search tree which is not empty in ascending order is accomplished by: printing the labels of the left subtree in ascending order, printing the label at the root (notice that the sequence printed this far is still in ascending order because, by the definition of a search tree, the label at the root is greater than all labels in the left subtree), and printing the right subtree in ascending order.

Assuming that *PRINT_LABEL*(x : *Item*) is a given routine that prints a single label in some appropriate fashion, we obtain the print program as

```
procedure PRINT_TREE(s : Bitree);
    begin
        if ¬ ISMT(s)
            then begin
                    PRINT_TREE(LEFT(s));
                    PRINT_LABEL(ROOT(s));
```

$$PRINT\_TREE(RGHT(s))$$
    end
  end.

... search trees
can be used for sorting.

This method
of sorting is called a *tree
sort.*

We observe that we can put a set of items in ascending order, (that is, we can sort it) by first inserting all items into a search tree and then extracting them in ascending order. This method of sorting is called a *tree sort*. It is fairly efficient. *INSERT* follows a path from the root to a leaf. By Lemma 7.12 the expected length of such a path is $O(\log(n))$ where n is the current number of labels in the tree. Thus, on the average, inserting an item into a tree costs of the order of $\log(n)$ steps. Hence inserting N items into a tree which is originally empty costs, on the average, $O(N*\log(N))$ steps. Further, we can easily show by induction that extracting all N items from a search tree in ascending order costs $O(N)$ steps. Thus, the complete sorting process costs

$$O(N*\log(N)) + O(N) = O(N*\log(N))$$

steps.

7.4.5 Traversing binary trees

A tree can be
traversed in ...

Many algorithms that operate on trees apply the same given operation to all labels of a given tree. The evaluation of expressions and the printing of trees are two examples. Since these algorithms process the labels one at a time, they have to visit them in some systematic fashion. Basically, there are three ways of doing this recursively:

... preorder, ...

Preorder traversal. First visit (operate on) the root, then traverse the left and the right subtree in preorder.

... inorder, or ...

Inorder traversal. First traverse the left subtree in inorder, then visit the root, and finally traverse the right subtree in inorder.

... postorder.

Postorder traversal. First traverse the left and the right subtree in postorder and visit the root afterwards.

Of course, traversing the empty tree using any of the three methods amounts to doing nothing. Notice that evaluating an expression tree is a postorder traversal, while alphabetically printing a search tree is an inorder traversal. As an example of a preorder traversal consider the task of printing a tree as an indented list (Figure 7.11).

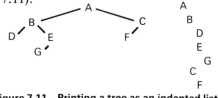

Figure 7.11   Printing a tree as an indented list

7.5 OTHER PRIMITIVE OPERATIONS ON TREES

Up to this point, we have written all of our tree programs with the six primitive operations *NIL_TREE, ISMT_TREE, TREE, LEFT, RGHT* and *ROOT.*

In Chapter 6 we were able to generalize the concept of a stack to that of a sequence by the systematic construction of additional primitives. Can we do anything similar with binary trees? Since a tree has only one distinguished element, the root, many operations on sequences do not have natural counterparts for trees. It is difficult, if not impossible, to generalize and adapt to trees such operations as queueing, rotating, or concatenating.

However, we can easily define and realize a "point of interest". For this we need the functions *RESET, MOVE_LEFT, MOVE_RGHT* and *MOVE_BACK* that move the point of interest; and we need some suitable operations that inspect and modify the tree at the point of interest.

We can extend the type *binary tree* in a second way by generalizing those sequence operations that modify (inspect) the *n*th element of a sequence. Since it does not make much sense to talk about the *n*th label of a tree, we need to replace the integer parameter *n* by some other parameter that identifies a place within a tree. We call such an entity either a *trace* or a *site*. Trace and site are two distinct concepts. A trace describes the path from the root of a tree to the place in question; a site describes the place in question directly. Therefore, a trace, which is a sequence of instructions such as *GO_LEFT* and *GO_RIGHT*, can be used with all trees that are deep enough so that the trace does not lead beyond a leaf. A site, on the other hand, points directly to a label in a particular tree; thus, a site can be used only with "its own" tree.

Are these modifications of and additions to the data type *tree* useful or are they unnecessary complications of a previously simple and elegant concept? If we work with trees as values, then we may as well restrict our set of primitives to the original six functions. However, as we will see in the next section, if we want to use trees as mutable objects, then extensions seem indispensable.

Many operations on sequences do not have counterparts for trees.

Trees can have points of interest, ...

... traces, and sites.

7.6   TREES AS MUTABLE OBJECTS

The simple conversion of the six operations for tree values to operations for tree objects ...

In Section 4.3.1 we described a method of deriving procedures for a type of mutable objects from the functions of the corresponding type of values. If we use this method for trees starting with the six functions defined in 7.1, then we obtain a type of doubtful utility. The new type would consist of the following operations:

> **procedure** *NEW_TREE*(*var t*: *Bitree_obj*);
> **procedure** *NIL_TREE*(*t*: *Bitree_obj*);
> **function**   *ISMT_TREE*(*t*: *Bitree_obj*): *Boolean*;
> **function**   *ROOT*(*t*: *Bitree_obj*): *Item*
> **procedure** *LEFT*(*var t*: *Bitree_obj*);
> **procedure** *RGHT*(*var t*: *Bitree_obj*);
> **procedure** *TREE*(*x*: *Item*; *var lt*: *Bitree_obj*; *rt*: *Bitree_obj*);

Objections must be raised against the way the procedures *LEFT* and *RGHT* treat tree objects, and against the inherent inefficiency of the procedure *TREE*. *LEFT* and *RGHT* replace the given tree *t* by its left or, respectively, right subtree, that is, they work analogously to the stack procedure *POP*. However, while *POP*(*s*) removes only the top element of the stack *s*, *LEFT*(*t*) and *RGHT*(*t*) eliminate both the root label and the other subtree of the original tree *t*. Hence, *LEFT* and *RGHT* cannot be used to traverse a tree without destroying it. The function *MEMBER*, for example, can be programmed only by first producing a copy of the original tree; otherwise this tree will be lost.

Further, the implementation of *TREE* (which replaces *lt* by the newly constructed tree) has to ensure that the parameter *rt* is maintained; that is, *TREE* must produce a complete copy of *rt* when it constructs the new tree.

... even with modifications ...

One might consider giving *LEFT* and *RGHT* two parameters so that these functions do not alter the original tree but return (a copy of) the desired subtree by the second parameter. However, this solution is out of the question. It combines the worst features of objects and values: conceptual complexity of objects and poor space efficiency. In fact, the space efficiency of this solution is even worse than that of values because the sharing of substructures, natural with value implementations, is impossible for objects.

... does not yield a useful type.

We have to conclude that the transformation of the six tree value primitives to tree object primitives does not yield a useful type. At this point we have two philosphically different options to pursue: (i) we tailor tree objects in a way similar to cell objects and accept that the resulting type, which would need to allow for both the arbitrary creation and deletion of objects, is similarly unsafe, or (ii) we redesign the type by adding a point of interest, traces, or sites.

(i) The first option is acceptable if we view trees as auxiliary types that are used only as a stepping stone to some higher type with a safe set of primitive operations. In this case we would use the tree operations only in a small well isolated part of a program and, thus, have a good chance of avoiding errors by using trees strictly as objects of the first kind. Sets implemented as search trees are a typical case where this approach is possible. (Recall from 4.3 that objects of the first kind cannot be shared among different parts of a program.)

These "unsafe" tree objects have the same operations as the corresponding cell objects, but still, the two types are not isomorphic. The reason is that not all cell objects make valid tree objects. This is expressed by the following definition of *VALID*:

$$VALID(t)$$
$$\text{iff } IS\_NIL(t)$$
$$\text{or } VALID(LFT(t)) \text{ and } VALID(RGT(t)) \text{ and}$$
$$\text{for all } r,s \in Bitree$$
$$\text{and } f,g \in \{LFT,RGT\}:$$
$$f(r) = g(s) = t \text{ implies } r=s \text{ and } f=g.$$

This not only excludes structures with nodes accessed by more than one other node, but also circular structures such as the one in Figure 7.12. For such a structure *VALID* is undefined: if we assume that *VALID(LFT(t))*, then

$$VALID(t) = VALID(LFT(t)) \textbf{ and } VALID(NIL\_TREE)$$
$$\textbf{and (for all ...)}$$

is **true** if (for all ...) is **true**. But it is **false** if we assume that *VALID(LFT(t))* is **false**.

Figure 7.12   VALID (t) is undefined
for circular structures.

Tree objects must
be extended in one of
three ways.

(ii) In order to construct a "safe" object type, we have to extend the set of primitive operations substantially and contend with a rather complex construction. We have at least three choices:

install a point of interest:
add the concept of a trace; or
add the concept of a site.

This facilitates
nondestructive tree
traversing.

All three choices solve our basic problem: they permit the nondestructive traversal of trees. None the less, the last choice seems to be superior to the first two for the following reasons.

With a point of interest, we can record only one place in the tree at a time. This makes the implementation of certain recursive algorithms clumsy. Instead of code segments of the form

$$DO\_IT\_TO(LEFT(t));$$
$$DO\_IT\_TO(RGHT(t));$$

we have to use segments of the form

$$MOVE\_LEFT(t);$$
$$DO\_IT\_TO(t);$$
$$MOVE\_BACK(t);$$
$$MOVE\_RGHT(t);$$
$$DO\_IT\_TO(t).$$

The reader may discover for himself that usually either the operation *MOVE_BACK* or the operation *RESET* (which moves the point of interest to the root of the tree) is expensive to implement.

The second choice, the use of traces, solves this problem. But with most implementations a trace is an inefficient device because accessing a label requires a walk starting at the root of the tree.

The concept of a "site" avoids both of these problems (for an informal description of sites see subsection 7.5). It seems that intuitively many programmers treat tree objects as trees with sites. Yet it is the explicit distinction between (i) trees (subtrees) and (ii) sites of trees that promotes clear concepts and avoids errors.

Specification of
trees with sites

Below we give a specification of trees with sites. In choosing the set of operations we have to be rather modest; in particular, we cannot allow deleting a node from a tree because this leads to the severe complication discussed next.

We wish to think of a site as a direct reference to a cell that represents a node in a tree. Thus, if the node is deleted, the site that refers to it becomes invalid. This by itself does not pose a problem. But consider the following sequence of operations:

delete a leaf with some label x that is referenced by the site s;
add a leaf at the same place with the same label x.

Clearly, the value of the tree is first changed but then restored, yet the site s is no longer valid. As a result, we can write procedures with a rather disturbing behavior: they do not change the value of a given tree object but they cause sites to become invalid. If we wanted to describe this effect correctly, we would need a store that is more than a mapping from tree objects to tree values; it would have to record the history of modifications as well.

Since addressing this complication goes beyond the scope of this book we will not permit deletions. In practice, sites are (or should be) used only locally, that is, in relatively small program segments. Consequently, the validity of a site can be checked by careful tracing and, hence, deletion may (cautiously) be used.

In the specification below, we again write the axioms not for the procedures of the type *tree object* but for the functions of the type *tree value* recalling that these axioms can be used to analyze programs for tree objects by the method described in 4.3.1. If we apply the specification for values to mutable objects, we must observe that a site derived for a tree object $t1$ is invalid for a different tree object $t2$. Further, because of the discussion above, the object operation *NEW_TREE* ($t:Tree\_obj$) can only be used to initialize t; it cannot assign the empty tree to an already initialized tree object. In short, we must ensure that the value of any given tree object can only be made larger not smaller.

Since it consists of two carrier sets (trees and sites) this data type is somewhat more complex than the simple tree type defined in 7.1. However, we shall see that programs that use sites are quite natural and easy to understand.

Type *Tree* {*with sites*}

Sets: *Tree, Site* {*note that two types are being defined*}, *Item, Boolean*

Syntax:
> **function** *NEW_TREE:Bitree;*
> **function** *TREE(x:Item; lt,rt:Bitree):Bitree;*
> **function** *SET_LEAF(t:Bitree;x:Item):Bitree;*
> > *{turns empty tree into leaf labeled "x"}*
>
> **function** *SET_ROOT(t:Bitree;s:Site;x:Item):Bitree;*
> > *{changes label at site to x}*
>
> **function** *SET_LFT(t:Bitree;s:Site;x:Item):Bitree;*
> > *{adds new leaf at left of site}*
>
> **function** *SET_RGT(t:Bitree;s:Site;x:Item):Bitree;*
> **function** *ORG(t:Bitree):Site;*
> > *{computes site of root of t}*
>
> **function** *LFT(t:Bitree;s:Site):Site;*
> > *{computes site at left of current site in t}*
>
> **function** *RGT(t:Bitree;s:Site):Site;*
> > *{computes site at right of current site in t}*
>
> *{hidden}* **function** *LT(t:Bitree;s:Site):Site;*
> > *{computes site in TREE(x,t,t') from site in t;*
> > *needed since expressions with LFT and RGT are*
> > *useless for certain axioms; also ensures that*
> > *sites are used only with "their own" trees}*
>
> *{hidden}* **function** *RT(t:Bitree;s:Site):Site;*
> > *{computes site in TREE(x,t',t) from site in t }*
>
> **function** *ISMT_TREE(t:Bitree):Boolean;*
> **function** *IS_NIL(s:Site):Boolean;*
> > *{tests for a nil site}*
>
> **function** *ROOT(t:Bitree;s:Site):Item;*

Axioms:

> *ISMT_TREE(NEW_TREE)*   (7.36)
>
> **not**   *ISMT_TREE(TREE(x,a,b))*   (7.37)

> *IS_NIL(ORG(NEW_TREE))*   (7.38)
>
> **not**   *IS_NIL(ORG(TREE(x,a,b)))*   (7.39)
>
> *IS_NIL(LT(t,s)) = IS_NIL(RT(t,s))*   (7.40)
> > *= IS_NIL(s)*

> *ROOT(TREE(x,a,b), ORG(t))*   (7.41)
> > *= **if** (t = TREE(x,a,b))*
> > > **then** *x* **else** *error;*
>
> *ROOT(TREE(x,a,b), LT(c,d))*   (7.42)
> > *= **if** (a = c)*
> > > **then** *ROOT(a,d)* **else** *error;*
>
> *ROOT(TREE(x,a,b), RT(c,d))*   (7.43)
> > *= **if** (b = c)*
> > > **then** *ROOT(b,d)* **else** *error;*

$$LFT(TREE(x,a,b),\ ORG(t)) \qquad (7.44)$$
$$= \textbf{if } (t\ =\ TREE(x,a,b))$$
$$\textbf{then } LT(a,\ ORG(a))\ \textbf{else } error;$$
$$LFT(TREE(x,a,b),\ LT(c,d)) \qquad (7.45)$$
$$= \textbf{if } (a\ =\ c)$$
$$\textbf{then } LT(a,\ LFT(a,d))\ \textbf{else } error;$$
$$LFT(TREE(x,a,b),\ RT(c,d)) \qquad (7.46)$$
$$= \textbf{if } (b\ =\ c)$$
$$\textbf{then } RT(b,\ LFT(b,d))\ \textbf{else } error;$$

$$RGT(TREE(x,a,b),\ ORG(t)) \qquad (7.47)$$
$$= \textbf{if } (t\ =\ TREE(x,a,b))$$
$$\textbf{then } RT(b,\ ORG(b))\ \textbf{else } error;$$
$$RGT(TREE(x,a,b),\ LT(c,d)) \qquad (7.48)$$
$$= \textbf{if } (a\ =\ c)$$
$$\textbf{then } LT(a,\ RGT(a,d))\ \textbf{else } error;$$
$$RGT(TREE(x,a,b),\ RT(c,d)) \qquad (7.49)$$
$$= \textbf{if } (b\ =\ c)$$
$$\textbf{then } RT(b,\ RGT(b,d))\ \textbf{else } error;$$

$$SET\_ROOT(TREE(x,a,b),\ ORG(t),y) \qquad (7.50)$$
$$= \textbf{if } (t\ =\ TREE(x,a,b))$$
$$\textbf{then } TREE(y,\ a,\ b)\ \textbf{else } error;$$
$$SET\_(TREE(x,a,b),\ LT(c,d),\ y) \qquad (7.51)$$
$$= \textbf{if } (a\ =\ c)$$
$$\textbf{then } TREE(x,\ SET\_ROOT(a,d,y),\ b)$$
$$\textbf{else } error;$$
$$SET\_ROOT(TREE(x,a,b),\ RT(c,d),\ y) \qquad (7.52)$$
$$= \textbf{if } (b\ =\ c)$$
$$\textbf{then } TREE(x,\ a,\ SET\_ROOT(b,d,y))$$
$$\textbf{else } error;$$

$$SET\_LEAF(NEW\_TREE,\ x) \qquad (7.53)$$
$$\cdot= TREE(x,NEW\_TREE,NEW\_TREE);$$
$$SET\_LEAF(TREE(x,a,b),\ y)\ =\ error; \qquad (7.54)$$

$$SET\_LFT(TREE(x,a,b),\ ORG(t),\ y) \qquad (7.55)$$
$$= \textbf{if } (t\ =\ TREE(x,a,b)\ and\ ISMT\_TREE(a))$$
$$\textbf{then } TREE(x,\ TREE(y,NEW\_TREE,NEW\_TREE,\ b)$$
$$\textbf{else } error;$$
$$SET\_LFT(TREE(x,a,b),\ LT(c,d),\ y) \qquad (7.56)$$
$$= \textbf{if } (a\ =\ c)$$
$$\textbf{then } TREE(x,\ SET\_LFT(a,d,y),\ b)$$
$$\textbf{else } error;$$
$$SET\_LFT(TREE(x,a,b),\ RT(c,d),\ y) \qquad (7.57)$$
$$= \textbf{if } (b\ =\ c)$$
$$\textbf{then } TREE(x,\ a,\ SET\_LFT(b,d,y))$$
$$\textbf{else } error;$$

$$SET\_RGT(TREE(x,a,b), ORG(t), y) \qquad (7.58)$$
$$= \textbf{if } (t = TREE(x,a,b) \text{ and } ISMT\_TREE(a))$$
$$\quad \textbf{then } TREE(x,a, TREE(y,NEW\_TREE,NEW\_TREE))$$
$$\quad \textbf{else } error;$$
$$SET\_RGT(TREE(x,a,b), LT(c,d),y) \qquad (7.59)$$
$$= \textbf{if } (a = c)$$
$$\quad \textbf{then } TREE(x, SET\_RGT(a,d,y), b)$$
$$\quad \textbf{else } error;$$
$$SET\_RGT(TREE(x,a,b), RT(c,d), y) \qquad (7.60)$$
$$= \textbf{if } (b = c)$$
$$\quad \textbf{then } TREE(x, a, SET\_RGT(b,d,y))$$
$$\quad \textbf{else } error;$$

$$SET\_ROOT, SET\_LFT, SET\_RGT, ROOT, LFT, RGT \qquad (7.61)$$
$$applied\ to\ (NEW\_TREE, ...)\ yield\ error.$$

It turns out that

(i) reduced expressions for trees are of the form *NEW_TREE* or *TREE(x,a,b)* where *a* and *b* are reduced tree expressions, and that

(ii) reduced expressions for sites are of the form *ORG(t)* where *t* is a reduced tree expression, or they are of the form *LT(t,s)* or *RT(t,s)* where *t* is a reduced tree expression and *s* is a reduced site expression.

With this as a hypothesis, sufficient completeness of the specification can be verified in the usual way (see Exercise T7.7).

Quite understandably, the reader may feel rather confused at this point. Although most of the functions may seem to be straightforward, and most of the axioms may seem to make some sense, the sheer size of the specification is certainly overwhelming. Let us, therefore, try to bring some order into this plethora of formulas.

The axioms (7.36) to (7.39) are simple enough. We will comprehend axiom (7.40), after we understand the purpose of the somewhat mysterious functions *LT* and *RT*. The remaining axioms come in groups of three, one for each of the forms of a reduced site expression. The simplest example is the set (7.41) − (7.43). These axioms specify the value of *ROOT(TREE(x,a,b),s)* depending on the value of the site *s*.

If the site is at the root of *TREE(x,a,b)*, then, (7.41), the root label is *x* itself {so far so good!};

If the site expression is of the form *LT(a, d)*, then, by (7.42), the site is in the left subtree and it has the value *d* with respect to the top of the left subtree. Thus, we may replace

ROOT(TREE(x,a,b), LT(a,d)) by *ROOT(a,d)*.

The case (7.43), symmetric to (7.42), deals with a site in the right subtree.

We see that the outermost function of a site expression built with *LT* and *RT* conveniently tells us if the site is at the root or in the left or the right subtree of a tree. If we wanted to extract this information from an expression built with *LFT* and *RGT,* we would have to examine the function next to the innermost function of the expression. This is not a mere inconvenience, but it makes expressions built with *LFT* and *RGT* useless for the construction of axioms and, consequently, expressions built with *LT* and *RT* indispensable. We might view the expressions with *LT* and *RT* as the "inside-out" version of expressions with *LFT* and *RGT.* Exercises T7.13 – T7.17 deal with these questions in some more detail.

As a last remark about these axioms we should point out that the specifications for functions that take both a tree and a site as parameters enforce that the given site is in the given tree. If we had to implement our operations so that these tests are always actually performed, then sites would be even less efficient than traces. This is so because, for a tree with n labels, following a trace takes $O(\log(n))$, while verifying a site takes $O(n)$. We will see, however, that, with a little discipline on the part of the programmer, the proper use of sites can be verified before the program is executed. In this case, the actual testing of validity at runtime is unnecessary.

Examples of trees with sites

How these operations are used in practice is demonstrated by the following code for the previously defined operations *INSERT* and *MEMBER* of the type *search tree (Set).* The functions *ABSTR* and *VALID* are defined by the axioms (7.32) – (7.35) given in section 7.4.4.

```
type Set = Bitree;
function INSERT(x:Item;t:Set):Set;

  function INSRT(x:Item;t:Set;s:Site):Set;
  begin
    if x = ROOT(t,s)
      then INSRT := t
      else
        if x < ROOT(t,s)
          then
            if IS_NIL(LFT(t,s))
              then INSRT := SET_LFT(t, s, x)
              else  INSRT := INSRT(x,t,LFT(t,s))
          else
            if IS_NIL(RGT(t,s))
              then INSRT := SET_RGT(t,s,x)
              else  INSRT := INSRT(x,t,RGT(t,s))
  end;
  begin
    if ISMT(t)
      then INSERT := SET_LEAF(t, x)
      else  INSERT := INSRT(x, t, ORG(t))
  end.
```

The transformation of this program to one for tree objects (set objects) is now straightforward. Instead of the functions *SET_LEAF, SET_LFT,* and *SET_RGT,* tree objects have the primitive procedures

> **procedure** *SET_LEAFo(t:Bitree_obj; x:Item);*
> **procedure** *SET_LFTo (t:Bitree_obj; s:Site; x:Item);*
> **procedure** *SET_RGTo (t:Bitree_obj; s:Site; x:Item);*

and, with this, we obtain

> **type** *Set_obj = Bitree_obj;*

> **procedure** *INSERTo(x:Item; var t:Set_obj);*

> **procedure** *INSRTo(x:Item;var t:Set_obj; s:Site);*
> **begin**
>   **if** *x = ROOT(t,s)*
>   **then** *{t : = t}*;
>   **else**
>   **if** *x < ROOT(t,s)*
>   **then**
>   **if** *IS_NIL(LFT(t,s))*
>   **then** *SET_LFTo(t, s, x))*
>   **else** *INSRTo(x,t,LFT(t,s))*
>   **else**
>   **if** *IS_NIL(RGT(t,s))*
>   **then** *SET_RGTo(t, s, x)*
>   **else** *INSRTo(x,t,RGT(t,s))*
>   **end;**
> **begin**
>   **if** *ISMT_TREE(t)*
>   **then** *SET_LEAFo(t,x)*
>   **else** *INSRTo(x,t,ORG(t))*
>   **end.**

The code for the **function** *MEMBER* is given next. It may be used with both tree values and tree objects.

> **function** *MEMBER(x: Item; t:Set):Boolean;*

> **function** *MEMBR(x:Item; t:Set; s:Site):Boolean;*
> **begin**
>   **if** *IS_NIL(s)*
>   **then** *MEMBR : =* **false**
>   **else**
>   **if** *x = ROOT(t,s)*
>   **then** *MEMBR : =* **true**
>   **else**
>   **if** *x < ROOT(t,s)*
>   **then** *MEMBR : = MEMBR(x,t,LFT(t,s))*
>   **else** *MEMBR : = MEMBR(x,t,RGT(t,s))*
>   **end;**

> **begin** *MEMBER : = MEMBR(x,t,ORG(t))* **end.**

If programs are carefully written ...

We make the following observation. Each of the three programs consists mainly of the invocation of a subprogram which performs the actual work. Let us take *MEMBER* as an example. Compared with the calling program *MEMBER*, the subprogram *MEMBR* has the additional parameter s of type *Site*, which is initialized by *MEMBER* to the site of the root of the given tree (by $ORG(t)$). From the way the parameters of type *Bitree* and *Site* are used by *MEMBR*, we see that the given site must belong to the given tree. This is clearly satisfied for the outer reference $MEMBR(x,t,ORG(t))$. That it is also fulfilled for all subsequent calls can easily be seen: $MEMBR(x,t,LFT(s))$ and $MEMBR(x,t,RGT(s))$ are only invoked if $LFT(t,s)$ or, respectively, $RGT(t,s)$ are not nil-sites. Thus, with s a site in t, $LFT(s,t)$ or $RGT(s,t)$ are also sites in t.

... run-time tests for the validity of sites are not needed.

Therefore, we know that *MEMBER* (and for similar reasons *INSERT*) will never use a site improperly. Hence we may implement sites simply as pointers to the cells of the "sites"; an actual runtime check for validity is not needed.

7.7   MORE ON IMPLEMENTING TREES

Implementation based on enumerated types or on integers is not interesting.

If we would follow the pattern of the previous chapters, then we would first discuss the implementation of trees based on enumerated types and based on integers. While these implementations are possible, they are not very interesting, because, in practice, they severely limit the size of the trees that can be built. Hence we begin with the discussion of implementation methods that are based on arrays.

7.7.1   Implementation based on arrays

The first method is excellent if the tree is nearly balanced.

There are at least two ways in which we can implement trees by arrays. One way is particularly efficient if the tree is nearly perfectly balanced. This method assigns an array subscript to the root of every subtree (see Figure 7.13).

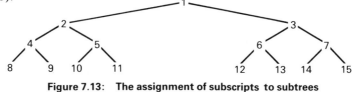

Figure 7.13:   The assignment of subscripts to subtrees

Figure 7.14 gives an example for the array representation of a specific tree. The symbol "?" in the array denotes "subtree does not exist". Since the only types of elements stored in the array are labels, this symbol must be a distinguished element in the set of possible labels.

This particular assignment of subscripts has a very useful property: let n be the subscript of the subtree t in some tree; then the subscript of $LET(t)$ is $2\,n$ and the subscript of $RGHT(t)$ is $2\,n + 1$.

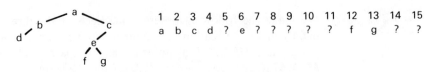

Figure 7.14: Array representation of a particular tree

Because of this relationship, we obtain for the abstraction function

$ABSTR(k)$
= **if** $T\_ARRAY[k]$ = '?'
then NEW_TREE
else $TREE\ (T\_ARRAY[k],\ ABSTR(2*k),\ ABSTR(2*k + 1))$.

It allows the efficient implementation of traces, sites, and points of interest.

With this implementation each subscript is in fact, a trace! This implementation of a trace allows immediate access to a denoted label; it does not require walking there from the root. Also, a point of interest can be efficiently implemented. Let n be the current point of interest; then $2*n$ and $2*n + 1$ are the points of interest after *MOVE_LEFT* and *MOVE_RGHT*, respectively $n\ DIV\ 2$ after *MOVE_BACK*, and "1" after *RESET*.

Coding the various tree operations is straightforward and is left as an exercise. The advantages of this method are: fast access to all labels; and no need for explicit links to subtrees: The main disadvantage is the poor space efficiency if the tree is not (nearly) balanced.

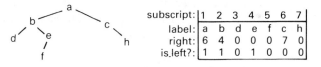

Figure 7.15: Array representation of trees with right links only

The second method does not require balanced trees, but ...

The second method, which represents trees by means of arrays, eliminates the disadvantage of the previous method by, unfortunately, sacrificing most of its advantages. Still, some space for links is saved. However, most kinds of modifications become costly. The basic idea is simple: always store the left subtree adjacent to the root label and provide a link for the right subtree.

... it does not save as much space ...

This saves about half of the space that the direct method requires for links. Besides the link to the right subtree, this method needs a single bit which indicates if there is a left subtree associated with the given label. Figure 7.15 gives an example of this representation.

The bit *is_left* can easily be stored with the link to the right subtree by defining a negative link denoting that there is no left subtree. Of course, zero can no longer be used as a link (since $0 = -0$). Instead, we may use the value "1" to indicate that there is no right subtree (why?).

... and is useful only for trees which are rarely modified.

This method is advantageous if the tree is frequently traversed but rarely altered. While changing a label is not difficult, adding a subtree (even if it is only a single leaf) frequently requires a major reorganization of the storage.

7.7.2 Implementation based on sequences

Trees may be represented by sequences ...

We can also represent trees as sequences of labels interspersed with punctuation symbols that record the structure of the tree. For example, we could represent the empty tree by the null sequence and nonempty trees by a sequence consisting of a left parenthesis, the root label, the two subtrees, and a right parenthesis. This can be done in three different ways, one way for each of the three methods of tree traversal:

{*preorder*}	(*root, left_subtree, right_subtree*)
{*inorder*}	(*left_subtree, root, right_subtree*),
{*postorder*}	(*left_subtree, right_subtree, root*).

Figure 7.16 gives an example for an inorder representation.

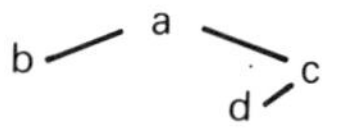

Figure 7.16: Inorder representation of a tree.

... for economical preservation in archives.

With an economical encoding of the parentheses, this method of representation can save some storage space. Further, if most of the tree processing consists of traversing the tree in, for example, inorder, then the inorder representation can also save some time, since traversing the tree is realized by simply scanning the list sequentially. In general, however, we represent a tree as a sequence if we wish to store it economically (for example, in an archive) and if we do not expect to process it frequently.

Besides parentheses, there are other means for punctuating trees. While we cannot deal here with all of them, we will discuss one other method because of its economy. The abstraction function of this method is defined as

$$ABSTR(PUSH(`.`,NUL)) = NEW\_TREE;$$
$$ABSTR(PUSH(x, s))$$
$$= \textbf{if } (\textit{for some } s1,s2) \ VALID(s1) \textbf{ and } VALID(s2)$$
$$\textbf{and } s = CONCAT(s1,s2)$$
$$\textbf{then } TREE(x, ABSTR(s1), ABSTR(s2))$$
$$\textbf{else } \textit{undefined};$$

and the invariant *VALID* has the form

$$VALID(PUSH(`.`,NUL));$$
$$VALID(PUSH(x, s))$$
$$\text{iff } (\textit{for some } s1,s2) \ VALID(s1) \textbf{ and } VALID(s2)$$
$$\textbf{and } s = CONCAT(s1,s2).$$

With this representation we obtain for the tree of Figure 7.16 the sequence depicted in Figure 7.17.

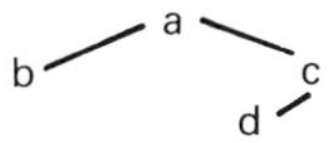

Figure 7.17: A tree recorded by the dot representation

7.7.3   Cell implementation of tree objects with sites

Tree objects
built with cells need a
head cell, and ...

... they have to
satisfy another stringent
limitation.

In section 7.3 we discussed a method of implementing tree *values* by cells. We are now going to adapt this method for tree *objects with sites*. First, we have to introduce a head cell which represents the tree object (see Figure 7.18).

Furthermore, we have to impose the requirement that for each cell there is no more than one variable that refers to this cell as a tree value. To be sure, there may be many variables that refer to a cell as a *site value* but there may be only one that refers to it as a *tree value*. You may recall that we had to impose similar requirements for stack objects and sequence objects in previous chapters. As we did not formalize the rules then, we will not formalize them now.

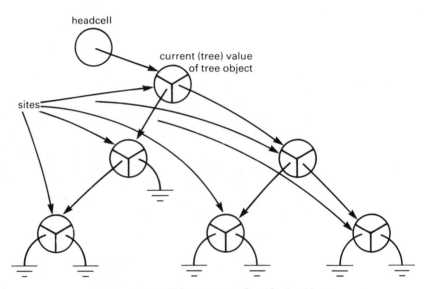

headcell

current (tree) value
of tree object

sites

Figure 7.18:   Cell representation of tree objects

The representation
is specified by *ABSTR*
and *VALID* and is
illustrated by ...

We will now describe the details of our implementation by specifying the implementation descriptors for both tree and site values. Since we deal with two carrier sets within the same type, we distinguish between

$ABSTR_t(c:Cells):Bitree$

and

$ABSTR_s(c:Cells):Site.$

Since cells that are valid trees are also valid sites, we need only one version of *VALID*. We obtain

$ABSTR_t(NIL\_CELL) = NEW\_TREE;$
$ABSTR_t(CELL(x,a,b)) = TREE(c,ABSTR_t(a),ABSTR_t(b));$

$$ABSTR_s(NIL\_CELL) = NIL\_SITE;$$
$$ABSTR_s(c) = ORG(ABSTR_t(c));$$

$$VALID(NIL\_CELL) = true$$
$$VALID(CELL(x,a,b))$$

         iff *the stated informal requirements are met.*

... two examples.

As examples of tree primitives implemented with cells, it may suffice to consider the actual code of the two operations *SET_LFT* and the utility function *CHK* that tests if a given site *s* is in a given tree *t*.

We assume that we are given the following cell operations for three-field cells and one-field head cells with the obvious meanings:

```
function   NIL_CEL:Cells;
function   IS_NILC(c:CELLS):Boolean;
function   CELL(x:Item; a,b:Cells):Cells;
function   INFO(c:Cells):Item;
function   LCEL(d:Cells):Cells;
function   RCEL(d:Cells):Cells;
procedure SET_INFO(c:Cells;x:Item);
procedure SET_LCEL(c{modified}, d: Cells);
procedure SET_RCEL(c{modified}, d: Cells);
procedure DELETE(var c:Cell);
procedure NEW_HEAD(var h: Headcell; c:Cell);
         {creates the new headcell h pointing to c}
function   HEAD_LNK(h:Headcell):Cells;
         {retrieves cell pointed to from headcell}
procedure SET_HEAD_LNK(h:Headcell; c:Cells)
         {makes headcell point to c}
```

The code for *CHK* and *SET_LFT* follows:

type *Bitree = Headcell; Site = Cells;*

function *CHK(t:Bitree; s:Site):Boolean;*

```
   function  CK(t:Cells; s:Site):Boolean;
     begin
       if t = s
         then CK := true
         else
           if IS_NILC(t)
             then CK := false
             else  CK := CK(LCEL(t),s) or CK(RCEL(t),s)

     end {CK};
   begin CHK := CK(HEAD_LNK (t), s) end {CHK};
```

> **procedure** *SET_LFT*(*t:Bitree; s:Site; x:Item*);
>   **begin**
>   **if** *CHK*(*t,s*) {*for a production version,*
>   *this test should be removed*}
>   **then** *SET_LCEL*(*s, CELL*(*x, NIL_CEL, NIL_CEL*))
>   **else** *ERROR*(...)
>   **end** {*SET_LFT*}.

For tree objects,
the primitive *TREE* may
be hidden.

It is probably reasonable, not to implement the operation *TREE* (but to treat it as a hidden operation) because of its substantial inefficiency.

In the following chapter we shall generalize the concept of binary trees.

EXERCISES

Theoretical exercises

T7.1   Prove that the axioms (7.1)–(7.8) form a sufficiently complete specification of binary trees.

T7.2   Prove the correctness of the program

> **function** *DEPTH*(*t:Bitree*):*Integer;*

given in section 7.2.

T7.3   Using *VALID* and *ABSTR*, prove that the implementation given in section 7.3 is correct.

T7.4   Draw the (parse) tree for the following expressions

> (a) $a * (b + c/((x - 1) * (y + 4))) + x*x - 24$
> (b) $a_0 + x * (a_1 + x * (a_2 + x * a_3))$).

T7.5   Trace the program *EXPRESSION* for recursive descent parsing for the following expression:

> $14 + (x * (2 + (x * 7)))$.

HINT: start with the expression *term1* + *term2*, where *term1* = 14 and *term2* = $(x * ...)$.

T7.6   Find an axiomatic specification for the function

> **function** *COMP_LEVEL*(*t:Bitree*):*Integer;*

that finds the number of the lowest complete level of a given tree *t*. This is the greatest number *n* such that *LEVEL*(*t,n*) has 2^{n-1} elements. Which of the functions defined in this chapter is most similar to *COMP_LEVEL*?

T7.7   Prove that axioms (7.36)–(7.61) on page 202 are sufficiently complete.

T7.8   From axioms (7.26)–(7.31) on page 192 show that

> $INSERT(x, INSERT(y,s))$ and $INSERT(y, INSERT(x,s))$

are equivalent with respect to *MEMBER* and *ISMT_SET*.

Problems T7.9–T7.12 concern *ABSTR* and *VALID* for search trees *without sites* representing sets.

T7.9   Prove that

$$VALID(t) \text{ implies}$$

for all labels x of tree t, $MAXL(t) \geq x \geq MINL(t)$.

T7.10   Prove that

$$VALID(INSERT(x,t)) \textbf{ if } VALID(t).$$

T7.11   Once an abstract data type has been implemented, there are two versions for each of its operations: one on the level of abstraction and one on the level of implementation. Denoting by f' the operation that implements f, we have, for example

$$INSERT'(x:Item; t:Bitree):Bitree;$$

and

$$INSERT (x:Item; s:Set):Set;$$

If and only if *INSERT'* is properly programmed with respect to *ABSTR*, the following must hold:

for all t of type *Bitree, $VALID(t)$* implies
$$ABSTR(INSERT'(x, t)) = INSERT(x, ABSTR(t)).$$

Prove that this relationship is, indeed, true for the given code of *INSERT*.

T7.12   Prove that the axioms (7.26)–(7.31) are satisfied by the functions *NIL_SET*, etc. given in the text (page 191 ff).

Problems T7.13–T7.17 are concerned with sets implemented by trees *with sites* (see Section 7.6).

T7.13   Prove that

$$INSRT'(x, TREE(y,lt,rt), LT(lt,s))$$
$$= TREE(y, INSRT'(x, lt, s), rt)$$

and that

$$INSRT'(x, TREE(y,lt,rt), RT(lt,s))$$
$$= TREE(y, lt, INSRT'(x, rt, s)).$$

T7.14   Prove that

$$VALID(INSERT'(x,t)) \textbf{ if } VALID(t).$$

T7.15   Prove that

$$MEMBR'(x,TREE(y,lt,rt), LT(lt,s))$$
$$= MEMBR'(x,lt,s).$$

T7.16   Prove that

for all t of type *Bitree {with sites} $VALID(t)$* implies
$$ABSTR(INSERT'(x, t)) = INSERT(x, ABSTR(t)).$$

T7.17   Prove that

  for all *Bitrees t*, *VALID*(*t*) implies
    MEMBER'(*x*, *t*) = *MEMBER*(*x*, *ABSTR*(*t*)), that is, that
      MEMBER'(*x*,*INSERT'*(*y*,*t*))
      = if (*x* = *y*)
        then true else *MEMBER'*(*x*,*t*).

T7.18   Give an axiomatic specification for trees

  (a)   with a point of interest and
  (b)   with traces. Finding a suitable set of primitives for these types is part of the problem.

T7.19   Determine an upper bound for the expected value for the depth of a random tree (see Lemma 7.12 on page 175).

  HINT: If a set is partitioned at random into two subsets, then these subsets are usually of different size. Let M be the size of the original set and L the expected value of the size of the larger subset. Then L/M depends on M. From an upper bound of L/M compute an upper bound for the expected value of the depth of a random binary tree.

T7.20   Design a set of primitive operations for a binary tree that allows labels of different types of items (a tree that has a "mixed bag" as its root item). Give an axiomatic specification of your operations.

Programming exercises

For each of the following problems write two programs: one for tree values and one for tree objects. Use sites for tree objects. Derive the tree-object program from the corresponding tree-value program making minimum modifications. Select a suitable treatment for all special cases.
  Prove the correctness of each of the tree-value programs.

P7.1   Write a program (a function) that computes the number of labels in a given binary tree.

  Syntax:
    function *N_O_LABELS*(*t*:*Bitree*):*Integer*.

P7.2   Write a program that returns the subtree (the site) with the greatest root label. Suppose that the labels in the tree are integer numbers. As header for your program use
    function *MAX_LABEL*(*t*:*Bitree*):*Bitree*{*Site*}.

P7.3   Write the program *COMP_LEVEL* defined in problem T7.6.

P7.4   Write a program that finds the greatest leaf in a given tree *t*.
  Syntax;
    function *MAX_LEAF*(*t*:*Bitree*):*Item*;
  with **type** *Item* = *Integer*.

P7.5   Write a program that finds the greatest label on the kth level of a given tree.

Syntax:

> **function** *MAX_ON_LEVEL(t:Bitree; k:Integer):Item;*

with **type** *Item = Integer.*

P7.6   Write a program that finds the highest level of a tree t (the level closest to the root of t) with two equal labels; the value "0" is to be computed if such a level does not exist. In other words, the program is to find the smallest value k such that *LEVEL(t,k)* contains two equal values.

Syntax:

> **function** *EQ_LABEL(t:Bitree):Integer;*

HINT: Create a data type "list of trees" ("list of sites").

P7.7   Write a program that finds the highest level in a given tree t that contains two subtrees of equal depth (if t is not empty, then such a level always exists. Why?).

Syntax:

> **function** *EQ_DPTH(t:Bitree):Integer.*

P7.8   Write a program that produces a tree t' from a given tree t according to the following rule: t' is a copy of t except that for every subtree s in tree t for which *ISMT_TREE(LEFT(s))* or *ISMT_TREE(RGHT(s))*,s is replaced by the leaf *TREE(ROOT(s), NEW_TREE, NEW_TREE)*.

Syntax:

> *function*   *TRUNK_COPY(t:Bitree):Bitree;*

or

> **procedure** *TRUNK_COPY(var t2:Tree_obj; t1:Tree_obj).*

P7.9   Implement the primitives for trees with a point of interest (see T7.18 above). For the implementation of *MOVE_LFT, MOVE_RGT* and *MOVE_BACK* use the principle of link modification developed for sequences in section 6.3.3 (page 155).

P7.10   Implement the tree primitives designed and specified in T7.20 using variant records. Find out about variant records from a Pascal manual, for example, from the Wirth-Jensen Report [JW74].

        Specify the functions *VALID* and *ABSTR* for your implementation and prove that your implementation is correct.

P7.11   Read about threaded trees in, for example, [KN68], listed in the bibliography and compare them with circularly linked lists described in 6.3.2 (page 154).

8 *N*-ary Trees and General Trees

The concept of binary trees, discussed in Chapter 7, can be generalized in two ways:

(i)   to so-called *n*-ary trees and

(ii) to general trees.

Binary trees are n-ary trees where n = 2.

While a binary tree has exactly two (possibly empty) subtrees, an *n*-ary tree has exactly *n*. These could be called *FIRST, SECOND, THIRD*, etc. or a single subtree function might be provided with a second parameter that tells which subtree to select. Of course, instead of viewing the *n*-ary tree as a generalization of a binary tree we may as well view a binary tree as a special *n*-ary tree, namely one for which *n* equals 2.

n-ary trees are related to general trees as vectors to sequences.

The difference between *n*-ary trees and general trees is similar to the difference between vectors (one-dimensional arrays) and sequences. Since we are familiar with vectors as so-called structured types built into Pascal and since we are familiar with sequences from Chapter 6, let us study the difference between these two types first. The newly acquired understanding may then easily be applied to trees.

8.1   VECTORS AND SEQUENCES

Vectors are provided by almost all programming languages in the form of one-dimensional arrays. If we had to specify them by algebraic axioms, we would arrive at the following definition for vectors as values:

Type Vector

Sets: Vector, Item, Index {some finite set, e.g. the subrange 1..k}

Syntax:

> **function** *NEWVECTOR*: *Vector*;
> **function** *CHANGE*(*v*:*Vector*; *i*:*Index*; *x*:*Item*):*Vector*;
> **function** *VALUE*   (*v*:*Vector*; *i*:*Index*):*Item*;

Axioms: for all *v* in *Vector*, *i*, *j* in *Index*
   and *x* in *Item*–{*error*}

$$VALUE(NEWVECTOR, i) = error; \tag{8.1}$$
$$VALUE(CHANGE(v, i, x), j) \tag{8.2}$$
$$= \textbf{if } (i = j)$$
$$\quad \textbf{then } x$$
$$\quad \textbf{else } VALUE(v, j).$$

Pascal treats
vectors as mutable
objects.

Interpreting vectors as mutable objects (where *NEWVECTOR* and *CHANGE* are procedures), we can translate the above notation to the notation of Pascal as follows:

1. If an array *A* is introduced by a declaration of the form

   var *A*: *array*[...] of ...

then there is no operation that corresponds to *NEWVECTOR* unless we want to identify it with this declaration. Otherwise *NEWVECTOR* corresponds to Pascal's procedure *NEW*(*P*).

2.   *CHANGE*(*v*,*i*,*x*) corresponds to *v*[*i*] : = *x*, and

3.   *VALUE*(*v*, *i*) corresponds to *v*[*i*].

With a slightly different definition we can eliminate the set *Index* by introducing several versions of the *CHANGE* and *VALUE* operations:

Type *Vector 1*

Sets: *Vector, Item*

Syntax:

> **function** *NEWVECTOR*:*Vector*;
> **function** *CHANGE*_1(*v*:*Vector*; *x*:*Item*):*Vector*;
>   .
>   .
>
>   .
> **function** *CHANGE*_*n*(*v*:*Vector*; *x*:*Item*):*Vector*;
> **function** *VALUE*_1 (*v*:*Vector*): *Item*;
>   .
>   .
>
>   .
> **function** *VALUE*_*n*(*v*:*Vector*):*Item*.

Vectors with named components correspond to Pascal records.

With this definition the second axiom now has the following form

$$VALUE\_i(CHANGE\_j(v, x))$$

$$= \textbf{if } (i = j)$$

$$\textbf{then } x \textbf{ else } VALUE\_i(v).$$

(8.3)

This form of a vector, where the components are selected by names instead of indices, corresponds to Pascal's *record* type, and as with records, it allows different types of items for its different components.

While vectors allow random access to their components, ...

Both forms, arrays and records, have the common property that the items held by any given vector are associated with a predetermined set of components. These correspond either to the members of an index set or to the *VALUE–CHANGE* pairs in the set of operations. Thus, the number of items held by a vector is predetermined and fixed. As a consequence, we can never remove an item from a vector without putting some other items into its place.

While the names $VALUE\_1$, ..., $VALUE\_n$ may suggest that the items in a vector are organized sequentially, this organization does not prevent us from accessing items in a vector at random. That is to say, we do not need to pass by k items in order to find the $k + 1$st one; if we know its index, we can retrieve an item in one step.

Now we compare vectors with sequences. In a similar way to vectors, sequences store items in a sequential fashion. For any given sequence we can construct a one to one correspondence between the items in the sequence and a suitable index set. However, the association of items and index values is not as strong as it is with vectors. For example, if an item is added to the front of a sequence, the indices of all items already in the sequence are changed: the first item becomes the second, the second becomes the third, and so forth. Hence the operation

function $VALUE(s:Sequence;\ i:Index):Item$

... sequences may grow and shrink.

does not make as much sense for sequences as it does for vectors. On the other hand, since the number of items in a sequence is not fixed, items can be added to a sequence without others being eliminated and items can be removed without being replaced.

In short, while both vectors and sequences provide a sequential arrangement of items, they achieve this result by different means: vectors use a fixed template while sequences form an open ended chain that can grow and shrink.

8.2   DEFINITION OF *N*-ARY TREES AND GENERAL TREES

The definitions of "*n*-ary tree" and "general tree" are now very simple:

Definition: n-ary tree

The set of all *n*-ary trees is the smallest set which contains the empty *n*-ary tree and all those ordered pairs whose first component is a member of the set *Item* and whose second component is a vector of *n* components which are *n*-ary trees.

Definition: general tree

The set of all general trees consists of all ordered pairs whose first component is a member of the set *Item* and whose second component is a (possibly empty) sequence of general trees.

General trees are never empty.

So, *n*-ary trees have a vector of *n* (*n*-ary) subtrees while general trees have a sequence of subtrees. But there is a second difference: *there is no such thing as an empty general tree!*

This seems to be curious! Is this just the result of a whim of the inventor of general trees, or is there a compelling reason to have empty *n*-ary trees but not empty general trees?

In order to answer this question let us examine the function of the empty *n*-ary tree. We observe that, by the definition of *n*-ary trees, the set of *n*-ary trees would be void if we did not require that the empty tree be in it. For the sake of this argument, drop the requirement for an empty tree and suppose that the set of *n*-ary trees is empty. Then, clearly, there is no pair consisting of an item and a vector of *n* *n*-ary trees! Thus, the assumption that the set is empty is consistent. Admittedly, with a different assumption the set would not be empty, but the definition calls for the smallest consistent set, which is the empty set. We conclude that we definitely need the empty *n*-ary tree.

The set of general trees contains at least the tree formed as a pair of an item and an empty sequence of trees. Hence the empty tree is not a concept necessary to make the definition of general trees meaningful.

In other words, the base of the recursive definition of *n*-ary trees is the empty tree while the base of the definition of general trees is the tree with an empty list of subtrees. Using an analogous base for *n*-ary trees is not possible because there are no empty vectors; a vector of *n* components always has *n* compartments, each of which must contain something, even if it is only an empty tree.

We shall devote the remainder of this chapter to general trees because the specification, implementation, and the typical algorithms for *n*-ary trees are so similar to those for binary trees that the reader can easily develop them for himself.

8.3 SPECIFICATION OF GENERAL TREES

Type G_tree

Sets: <u>*G_tree*</u>, <u>*Forest*</u>, *Item, Boolean*
    {*a Forest is a sequence of G_trees;*
       note that there are two carrier sets}

Syntax:

    function *GTREE(x:Item; s:Forest):G_tree*
    function *ROOT (t:G_tree):Item;*
    function *SUBS   (t:G_tree):Forest;*

    function *NULSEQ: Forest;*
    function *IS_NUL(s:Forest):Boolean;*
    function *PUSH(t:G_tree; s:Forest):Forest;*
    function *POP   (s:Forest):Forest;*
    function *TOP   (s:Forest):G_tree;*

Axioms: for all *t* in *G_tree* − {*error*}, *s* in *Forest* − {*error*},
       and *x* in *Item*

$$ROOT(GTREE(x,s)) = x; \tag{8.4}$$
$$SUBS\ (GTREE(x,s)) = s; \tag{8.5}$$

$$IS\_NUL(NULSEQ) \tag{8.6}$$
$$\textbf{not}\ \ ISNUL(PUSH(t, s)) \tag{8.7}$$
$$POP(NULSEQ)\ \ = error; \tag{8.8}$$
$$POP(PUSH(t, s)) = s; \tag{8.9}$$
$$TOP(NULSEQ)\ \ = error; \tag{8.10}$$
$$TOP(PUSH(t, s)) = t. \tag{8.11}$$

We see that the specification consists of two parts, one concerned with trees and the other concerned with sequences of trees. From the many different specifications of sequences we have chosen the one for stacks. Depending upon the intended use of the type *G_tree*, one may select any other specification, for example, that for queues or one that provides a point of interest. The reduced form of tree expressions turns out to be as follows:

    GTREE(x, s) is reduced if *s* is a reduced sequence expression;
    NULSEQ   is a reduced sequence expression, and
    PUSH (t, s)   is a reduced sequence expression
         if   *t* is a reduced tree expression and
             s is a reduced sequence expression.

With this as a hypothesis, we can easily prove that the specification is sufficiently complete. The reader may do this as an exercise.

    Which of the two sets, *G_tree* or *Forest,* is considered to be the primary one is a matter of taste. There are good arguments in support of each approach. One could claim that one needs a tree before one can have a forest and, consequently, consider *G_tree* as the primary set. On the other hand, one could argue from a standpoint of mathematical simplicity that the primary set should provide the base case for the recursive definition. With this choice the forest would be considered primary. In any case, with the two concepts, *G_tree* and *Forest,* our definition becomes very simple:

A *Forest* is either empty or it is a sequence of *G_trees;*
A *G_tree* is an ordered pair of an Item and a Forest.

8.4 TYPICAL APPLICATIONS OF GENERAL TREES

While family
trees are general
trees, ...

General trees occur naturally in a wide variety of contexts. For example, there is the *family tree.* The root of such a tree is labeled with the name, *"A"*, of a person, and this name is associated with a *"family forest"* consisting of one family tree for each of *A*'s children.

... pedigrees
are binary trees.

Note that a Family Tree is a general tree while a Pedigree is, due to the nature of reproduction, a binary tree.

Other examples
include organization
charts, ...

Consider next the organization of a company or some other institution. We could define such an organization to consist of, for example, a president (or a person, to be more general) and a forest of organizations. If this forest happens to be empty, then the person is an employee without supervisory functions.

... other
hierarchies, ...

Frequently, one refers to such a tree-like organization as a hierarchy. To continue our list of examples, we observe that books are often organized hierarchically and this structure is reflected by their table of contents.

... and
game trees.

Furthermore, board games, such as Checkers or Chess can be described totally by means of a general tree called a game tree. The root of such a tree is a board position; the forest of subtrees is the set of trees of all those positions that the current player can produce from the root position by his next move. If no further move is possible, the position, which must be a winning one, a losing position, or a drawing position, constitutes a leaf of the tree. The perfect game-playing program operates in the following way.

First it classifies each position in the tree as a winning position (a position from which there is a move to another winning position), a drawing position (from which there is a move to another drawing position though not to a winning position), or as a losing position (where neither such move exists). During the course of the game, the program hopes to reach a winning position after a mistake by its opponent (unless the opening position is a winning position). Note that the program cannot actively move to a winning position unless it is already at another one; however, it can improve the probability of a mistake by its opponent by moving to a (losing) position where most of its opponent's moves lead to a winning position. Of course, if the opponent has the same intelligence, the mistake will never happen! Once a winning position has been reached, there is, by definition, always a move that will take the game to another winning position.

Complete game
trees are awfully big!

We hasten to add that, for interesting games, the complete game tree is often so large that an actual representation of it is out of the question. For example, a typical chess game consists of thirty to forty pairs of moves and in most game positions many pieces may be moved, each in a number of different ways. Let us assume that there are twenty possible moves for each player whenever it is his turn to move (this is about right for the opening move of a chess game, but quite conservative in general). Then a pair of moves gives us $20*20 = 400$ new positions. The total number of positions after thirty pairs of moves is, therefore,

$$N \geq 400^{30} \geq 10^{78}$$

In order to get some idea of the magnitude of this number assume we would squeeze the representation of a chess position into the volume of, say, a cubic millimeter, that is, about the size of a grain of sand. The volume of all N chess positions would then be a cube whose side measures more than a million light years or more than ten times the diameter of our galaxy! So, do not try to write the perfect chess program! Actual game-playing programs (as well as human players) use only minute parts of the game tree in order to decide which move to make next.

8.5   OPERATIONS AND ALGORITHMS FOR GENERAL TREES

Many of the operations discussed for binary trees can be meaningfully used with general trees. For example, preorder and postorder traversal may be defined as follows.

Definition: Preorder traversal of general trees

(a)   To traverse a general tree in preorder, visit the root and traverse the forest of subtrees in preorder.

(b)   To traverse a forest in preorder, do nothing if the forest is empty, otherwise, traverse, in turn, all trees of the forest in preorder.

The definition of postorder traversal is analogous. Some authors define inorder traversal of general trees as the process that traverses the first subtree in inorder, visits the root, and traverses the remaining subtrees in inorder.
Programs that manipulate general trees can usually be decomposed into two parts that, by invoking each other, form a recursive process. One part is concerned with the tree aspect, that is, the root and the sequence of subtrees. The second part processes the sequence item by item, that is, subtree by subtree, again involving the first part for the detailed manipulation of the subtrees. The following program illustrates this kind of structure.

An example   The purpose of the program is to construct a general tree from input data that represent the tree as follows:

<label of root><sequence of subtrees>.

The period at the end of the previous line is part of the notation. The *<sequence of subtrees>* is given as the representation of all of the subtrees juxtaposed. For example, let the labels be single letters. Then the general tree with the root label *"a"* that does not have subtrees is represented by

    a.

If the tree has two subtrees (denoted by *b.* and *c.*), then the whole tree is denoted by

    a b. c..

A more complex example is given by Figure 8.1.

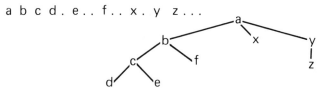

Figure 8.1   A Linear Representation of a General Tree

The program that reads such data and constructs the proper tree is surprisingly simple:

```
function READ_TREE(var input:text):G_tree;

    var labl: Char;

    begin
        READ(input, labl)
        if labl = '.'
            then ERROR(...)
            else  READ_TREE : =
                    GTREE(labl, READ_SEQ(input))
    end;

function READ_SEQ(var input:text):Forest;

    var period: Char;

    begin
        if input ↑ = '.'                                    {1}
            then begin
                    READ(input, period);                    {2}
                    READ_SEQ : = NUL                         {3}
                end
            else
                READ_SEQ : =                                 {4}
                PUSH(READ_TREE(input), READ_SEQ(input))
    end.
```

For the construction of the sequence in *READ_SEQ* we could have used a "**while**-loop" instead of the recursive invocation of *READ_SEQ*. We have chosen recursion in order to demonstrate how one constructs an inductive argument for the correctness of a program with mutual recursion. We will develop this argument now.

Verification of a program with nested recursion

In the following argument we use the term "tree expression" for a character sequence of labels and periods properly assembled to describe a general tree. If we remove the first label from a tree expression, we obtain a character string that describes a forest; hence we call it a "forest expression". The number of labels in a tree or forest expression determines its length. Hence a tree expression is at least of length 1 while a forest expression may be of length 0.

The theorem that we wish to prove is: *READ_TREE* reads a tree expression including the terminating period and returns the corresponding tree.

We prove this by induction over the length of the tree expression. We observe that *READ_TREE* works correctly for tree expressions of length $n+1$ if *READ_SEQ* works for forest expressions of length n, that is, if *READ_SEQ* reads a forest expression of length n including the terminating period and returns a sequence consisting of all trees in the forest expression.

Since this observation is based on the statements in *READ_TREE* there is no more information to be gained from its code unless we wish to observe that *READ_TREE* rejects tree expressions that begin with a period.

We now consider the code of *READ_SEQ* and try to compose an inductive proof for it over the length of the remaining forest expression. By means of lines 1, 2 and 3, *READ_SEQ* reads a forest expression of length 0 and returns the appropriate forest, the null sequence. Notice that the period is, indeed, read from the file.

Now suppose that *READ_SEQ* reads a forest expression with period of length n and returns the appropriate forest. By our analysis of *READ_TREE* we may immediately conclude that, because of this assumption, *READ_TREE* reads tree expressions of length $n+1$. Now, we give *READ_SEQ* a forest expression of length $n+1$ (which does not start with a period since it consists of at least one tree expression). *READ_SEQ*, by means of lines 1 and 4, correctly reads the first tree expression (with its terminating period) from the forest expression and converts it into a tree. It then pushes the tree onto the sequence that is built from the remaining forest expression by the recursive invocation of *READ_SEQ*.

Both of the partial processes, one reading the leading tree and the other reading the trailing forest expression, are covered by the induction hypothesis. The leading tree expression cannot be longer than $n+1$ if the whole forest expression is of length $n+1$, and since the leading tree expression consists of at least one label, the trailing forest expression cannot be of length greater than n. □

8.6 IMPLEMENTATION OF GENERAL TREES

Besides the obvious implementation of general trees ...

The implementation of general trees seems to be straightforward. We simply use a cell with two compartments, one for the label and one for the sequence of subtrees. Since we know how to implement sequences, further discussion appears to be unnecessary.

... there is one that is much more efficient.

However, there is an implementation that uses storage space more efficiently than the method outlined above. This method works with cells with three compartments: one for the label, one for the list of subtrees and one that is only used if the tree is on a list of subtrees. This latter compartment contains the remaining list of subtrees. The method is defined by the following definition of *ABSTR* and is illustrated by Figure 8.2.

binary tree

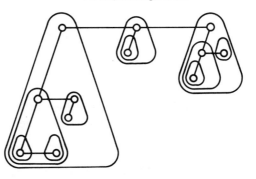

corresponding Forest

Figure 8.2 A Forest Represented by a Binary Tree

With *NIL_CEL* and *CELL* as defined in Chapter 5 but extended to accommodate three fields, we obtain for forests:

function *ABSTRf(c:Cells):Forest;*

$$ABSTRf(NIL\_CEL) = NUL;$$
$$ABSTRf(CELL(x,s,t))$$
$$= PUSH(GTREE(x,ABSTRf(s)), ABSTRf(t)).$$

According to this definition, a cell represents a forest rather than a single tree. But how is a tree represented? It seems that a cell wears two hats, so to speak, because it also represents a tree. The corresponding function *ABSTRt* has the form

> **function** *ABSTRt*(*c*:*Cells*):*G_tree;*

> *ABSTRt*(*CELL*(*x*,*s*,?)) = *GTREE*(*x*,*ABSTRf*(*s*)).

As a result, the function *TOP* that retrieves the first tree from a forest does not perform any real transformation; it only performs a ceremonial change of hats:

> **function** *TOP*(*f*:*Forest*):*G_tree;*

> **begin** *TOP* := *f* **end.**

This implementation shows that there is a simple bijection between binary trees and forests of general trees (Figure 8.2). A binary tree can uniquely be interpreted as a forest of general trees as follows:

(i)   the root label and the left subtree of the binary tree correspond to the root label and the forest of subtrees of the first general tree in the forest;

(ii) the right subtree corresponds to the rest of the forest.

EXERCISES

Theoretical exercises

T8.1   Prove that the axioms (8.1)–(8.8) form a sufficiently complete specification of general trees.

T8.2   Give an axiomatic specification of the function *COMP_LEVEL* (as defined in T7.6 on page 212) modified for the case of general trees.

T8.3   Design a specification for general trees with sites.

T8.4   Solve the problems described on page 214 in T7.18 and T7.20 for general trees.

Programming exercises

P8.1—P8.9

For general trees, solve the problems described in P7.1–P7.10 except P7.8 (page 214).

P8.10   Code the operations for general trees using binary trees to represent forests.

9 Sets, Dictionaries and Graphs

Sequences and trees on the one hand and sets on the other differ in the way the items they store are organized. For sequences, as well as for trees, the order in which items are arranged matters; for sets it does not. This has several consequences for both the specification and implementation of sets.

Among the many applications of sets, two stand out: sets as dictionaries and sets as graphs. But after this short preview of what is to come we shall start, as usual, with the specification.

9.1 SPECIFICATION OF SETS

Let us examine the following to see if it specifies the mathematical concept of a set.

Sets: *Sets, Item, Integer, Boolean*

Syntax:

>**function** *NEW_SET*: *Sets;*
>**function** *ISMT(s:Sets):Boolean;*
>**function** *INSERT(x:Item; s:Sets): Sets;*
>**function** *DELETE(x:Item; s:Sets):Sets;*
>**function** *MEMBER(x:Item; s:Sets):Boolean;*
>**function** *UNION(s,t:Sets):Sets;*
>**function** *INTERSECT(s,t:Sets):Sets;*
>**function** *CARD(s:Sets):Integer;*

Axioms: for all *s*, *t* in *Sets* and *x,y* in *Item*

$$ISMT(NEW\_SET) \tag{9.1}$$

$$\textbf{not} \quad ISMT(INSERT(x,s)) \tag{9.2}$$

$$DELETE(x, NEW\_SET) = NEW\_SET \qquad (9.3)$$
$$DELETE(x, INSERT(y, s)) \qquad (9.4)$$
$$= \textbf{if } (x = y)$$
$$\textbf{then } DELETE(x, s)$$
$$\textbf{else } INSERT(y, DELETE(x, s))$$

$$\textbf{not } MEMBER(x, NEW\_SET) \qquad (9.5)$$
$$MEMBER(x, INSERT(y, s)) \qquad (9.6)$$
$$= (x = y) \textbf{ or } MEMBER(x, s)$$

$$UNION(s, NEW\_SET) = s \qquad (9.7)$$
$$UNION(s, INSERT(x, t)) \qquad (9.8)$$
$$= INSERT(x, UNION(s, t))$$

$$INTERSECT(s, NEW\_SET) = NEW\_SET \qquad (9.9)$$
$$INTERSECT(s, INSERT(x, t)) \qquad (9.10)$$
$$= \textbf{if } MEMBER(x, s)$$
$$\textbf{then } INSERT(x, INTERSECT(s, t))$$
$$\textbf{else } INTERSECT(s, t)$$

$$CARD(NEW\_SET) = 0 \qquad (9.11)$$
$$CARD(INSERT(x, s)) \qquad (9.12)$$
$$= 1 + CARD(DELETE(x, s))$$

Reduced set expressions ...

Clearly, reduced set expressions consist of the operations *NEW_SET* and *INSERT*. Again, the reader may verify that this is a consistent assumption and that the above set of axioms is sufficiently complete.

So far so good. But how can we determine that two sets are equal? Set theory states that two sets are equal if they consist of the same elements. Thus,

$$s = t \text{ iff } ISMT(s) \textbf{ and } ISMT(t) \textbf{ or }$$
$$\text{for all } x \ . \ MEMBER(x, s) \text{ iff } MEMBER(x, t).$$

.... denoting equal sets ...

This condition is similar, for example, to the one for stacks. However, for stacks we can show that two stacks are equal if and only if their reduced expressions are equal while for sets we find that different reduced expressions may, indeed, define the same set. This is disturbing because, for sets, our system does not seem to provide expressions that we can identify with the abstract sets. (This we were able to do for all of our previous data types, and we took advantage of this, especially for the definition of the implementation descriptor *ABSTR*). Such an identification works only if there is a *bijection* between the two collections. While, for every reduced set expression, there is exactly one abstract set that this expression describes, we find that, for every abstract set, there are a great number of different expressions that describe it.

... are not always equal.

An example may illustrate the problem. Consider

$$s1 = INSERT(x, INSERT(y, NEW\_SET))$$

and

$$s2 = INSERT(y, INSERT(x, NEW\_SET)).$$

Clearly, both expressions are in reduced form and both describe the same set. Formally,

$$MEMBER(z, s1) = MEMBER(z, s2) \text{ for all } z$$

follows directly from axioms (9.5) and (9.6).

This observation seems to indicate that our axioms may not be sufficiently complete after all! They do not express that two sets are equal if and only if they consist of the same elements. According to the axioms, sets are equal only if they consist of the same elements inserted in the same order.

Does this really mean that the axioms are not sufficiently complete? If so, then we would be in deep trouble because we would have to abandon our way of proving completeness as unreliable. Short of finding a better one, we would have to question the value of our method of specification. Because of the gravity of this problem, we must try to resolve it now!

Earlier, we said that a set of axioms is sufficiently complete if all expressions that can be formed with the operations defined by the axioms can be completely analyzed using these axioms, provided that the values of all variables are known. This is certainly a proper definition of completeness in the light of our objective that a user (or implementer) must be able to infer from the axioms what exactly the operations (are supposed to) do. Since our method of proving completeness was based exclusively on this definition, it must be correct. In order to regain our confidence, we may convince ourselves that the axioms given above do indeed allow the analysis of all expressions over *NEW_SET*, *INSERT*, etc.

So, what is wrong with these axioms? The answer is: while they are sufficiently complete, they define a data type that does not sufficiently approximate the mathematical concept of "set". In order to repair this deficiency, we need one additional axiom, namely

$$INSERT(x,INSERT(y,s)) \qquad\qquad (9.13)$$
$$= \textbf{if } (x = y)$$
$$\qquad \textbf{then } INSERT(x,s)$$
$$\qquad \textbf{else } INSERT(y,INSERT(x,s)).$$

This axiom permits us to permute the order of insertions arbitrarily and to introduce or eliminate duplicate elements without changing the meaning of the expressions. Now our type *Sets* has the right properties; yet it still does not provide expressions that can be identified with the abstract sets. Axiom (9.13) simply states that the set denoted by a reduced expression does not depend on the order in which the different instances of the function *INSERT* are applied. Thus, (9.13) still leaves us with many representations for a single set.

In mathematics, such a problem is usually resolved by selecting *one* of the many representations of an abstract value as the "normal" representation. In our particular case, this means that, from the different orders in which elements can be inserted, one is to be selected as the normal one. Then the corresponding expression may be termed a (set) expression in normal form. The particular order must, of course, be unique so that two expressions in normal form denote the same set if and only if they are identical. NOTE: This requires, of course, that item expressions contained in such a normal form are also reduced or normalised. For values that we can represent by some kind of code (that is, for values that we can store in the computer) we can always find such an ordering, and this ordering can then be used as the normal order of insertion.

Thus we may assume that, for any two items x and y, one of the following is true:

$$x > y, \; x < y, \; \text{or } x = y.$$

We can incorporate the concept of normal form into the axiomatic definition of sets by way of the hidden function

$$ADJUNCT(x{:}Item; \; s{:}Sets){:}Sets$$

and define

$$INSERT(x,NEW\_SET) = ADJUNCT(x,NEW\_SET) \qquad (9.13a)$$
$$INSERT(x, ADJUNCT(y, s)) \qquad\qquad\qquad (9.13b)$$

> $= \textbf{if } (x = y)$
> > $\textbf{then } ADJUNCT(y, s)$
> > $\textbf{else}$
> > > $\textbf{if } x < y$
> > > > $\textbf{then } ADJUNCT(x, ADJUNCT(y, s))$
> > > > $\textbf{else } \; ADJUNCT(y, INSERT \quad (x, s)).$

We might consider adding the condition that

$$x \geq y \text{ implies } ADJUNCT(x,ADJUNCT(y,s)) = error$$

as an axiom, but *ADJUNCT*, being a hidden function, enters into expressions only by transformations based on (9.13a,b) which ensure that elements are added in descending order and that duplications are eliminated. By (9.13b), $ADJUNCT(y,s)$ can be viewed as being derived from $INSERT(y,s)$; hence, by (9.6),

$$MEMBER(x,ADJUNCT(y,s)) \qquad\qquad\qquad (9.14)$$
> $\text{iff } x = y \textbf{ or } MEMBER(x,s).$

Axiom (9.13) and (9.13a,b) each ensure that set expressions can be transformed into one another if and only if they denote equal sets, but (9.13a,b) supplies a specific method for testing equality.

More precisely: Axiom (9.13) states that changing the order of successive insertions does not change the meaning of a set expression. Thus, in order to find out if two set expressions mean the same thing (denote the same set) we must try to transform one into the other by (possibly repeated) application of (9.13). The particular method of finding the common form (or of showing that such a form does not exist) is up to us; the axiom does not give us any hint.

Axiom (9.13a,b) on the other hand specifies how to transform an expression that contains instances of *INSERT* into one that is built exclusively with *ADJUNCT*. Two expressions built with *INSERT* denote the same set if the corresponding expressions built with *ADJUNCT* are identical.

If we insist that the reduced forms of set expressions are bijectively related to the sets denoted, then we have to opt for axiom (9.13a,b) and declare an expression as reduced if it is built exclusively from *ADJUNCT* and *NEW_SET*.

Expressions that represent the same set form an equivalence class.

If we opt for axiom (9.13), the situation is a little more complex but still tractable. Let us call two expressions that can be transformed into one another (and hence denote the same set) "equivalent". Now the set of all expressions may be subdivided into disjoint subsets of equivalent expressions. Such a subset is called an *equivalence class*. Since all expressions denote the same set if they are in the same equivalence class and since all expressions are in the same equivalence class if they denote the same set, there is a bijection between the equivalence classes of expressions and the sets denoted. This means that sets *S1* and *S2* are equal if they are denoted by expressions that are equivalent though not necessarily identical.

If we opt for (9.13), which we shall do for the purpose of our discussion here, we may still use (9.13a,b) as a means for showing equivalence since, from (9.13), we can prove the following theorem.

Theorem: There exists a function *ADJUNCT* such that (9.13a,b).

The proof of this theorem is not difficult but it is lengthy. Its objective is to show that transforming an expression *E1* built with *INSERT* to an expression *E2* built with *ADJUNCT* and back to an expression *E3* again built with *INSERT* always ensures that *E1* is equivalent to *E3*.

NXT_EL and REST facilitate scanning a set.

Sometimes we wish to examine or process all of the elements of a given set. For this purpose we would like to have an operation that retrieves the *next* element of a set *S*. Which element is picked is not important as long as every member of the set is eventually produced and produced once only. We will accomplish this using two operations:

function *NXT_EL*(s:*Sets*):*Item* {*retrieves next element*},

and

function *REST*(s:*Sets*):*Sets* {$s - \{NXT\_EL(s)\}$}.

We might be tempted to specify *NXT_EL* and *REST* by

$$
\begin{aligned}
NXT\_EL(NEW\_SET) &= error \\
REST(NEW\_SET) &= error \\
NXT\_EL(ADJUNCT(x,s)) &= x \\
REST(ADJUNCT(x,s)) &= s.
\end{aligned}
$$

Yet, this would be a mistake.

Specifications should
not restrict the
implementer
unnecessarily.

To be sure, this specification is precise and complete. In fact, it is too precise, or more accurately, too restrictive. It requires that elements be picked in a particular order while, of course, the order is not important. By prescribing a specific order this definition does not become incorrect, but, to be satisfied, it may force the implementer to select a rather costly method. On the other hand, if the specification does not imply an order, then the implementer is free to pick an order that results in the most efficient algorithm. We may acknowledge the implementer's freedom of choice by introducing the nondeterministic proposition *ISD*, meaning "implementer so decides", into our specifications. Of course, we can never tell if this proposition is true or false, and any conclusion derived from axioms that contain *ISD* must be shown to be independent of the actual value of *ISD*. For a moment, let us suppress our understandable uneasiness with this concept until we have seen how it is applied:

for x in *Item* and s in *Sets* – {*NEW_SET, error*}

$$NXT\_EL(NEW\_SET) = error; \qquad\qquad (9.15)$$
$$REST \quad (NEW\_SET) = error; \qquad\qquad (9.16)$$
$$NXT\_EL (ADJUNCT(x,s)) \qquad\qquad (9.17)$$
$$\quad = \textbf{if } ISMT(s) \textbf{ or } ISD \text{ \{implementer so decides\}}$$
$$\qquad \textbf{then } x \textbf{ else } NXT\_EL(s)$$
$$REST \quad (ADJUNCT(x,s)) \qquad\qquad (9.18)$$
$$\quad = \textbf{if } NXT\_EL(ADJUNCT(x,s)) = x$$
$$\qquad \textbf{then } s \textbf{ else } ADJUNCT(x, REST(s)).$$

Axioms (9.15) and (9.16) state the obvious error conditions. An alternative to (9.17), (9.18), and the use of *ISD* is the following pair of assertions:

for nonempty sets s,
$$MEMBER(NXT\_EL(s), s) \qquad\qquad (9.17a)$$
and
$$MEMBER(x, REST(s)) \qquad\qquad (9.18a)$$
$$\quad = MEMBER(x,s) \text{ and } x \neq NXT\_EL(s).$$

But these do not have the familiar form of other axioms, which define the effect of a new operation upon reduced expressions of the carrier set. As an example of the use of *ISD* in a proof, we will now show that (9.17) implies (9.17a), that is, we will show that (9.17a) is true for the function *NXT_EL* defined by (9.17).

Since, in (9.17a), s is nonempty, it must be of the form $ADJUNCT(z,t)$. Now

$$MEMBER(NXT\_EL(ADJUNCT(z,t)), ADJUNCT(z,t))$$
$$\text{iff } NXT\_EL(ADJUNCT(z,t)) = z$$
$$\quad \text{or } MEMBER(NXT\_EL(ADJUNCT(z,t)), t) \text{ \{by 9.14\}}$$
$$\text{iff } (\textbf{if } ISMT(t) \textbf{ or } ISD$$
$$\qquad \textbf{then } z = z \qquad\qquad\qquad\qquad \{a\}$$
$$\qquad \textbf{else } NXT\_EL(t) = z)$$

or

> **(if** *ISMT*(*t*) **or** *ISD*
> **then** *MEMBER*(*z*,*t*)
> **else** *MEMBER*(*NXT_EL*(*t*), *t*)). {*b*}

Now, by induction over the length of expression *t*:

> **if** *ISMT*(*t*) {*base case*} *MEMBER*(...) = (*z* = *z*), {*by line a* }

> **else,** with the induction hypothesis that

> > *MEMBER*(*NXT_EL*(*t*), *t*) for *length*(*t*) = *n*–1,

> > *MEMBER*(*NXT_EL*(*t'*), *t'*) {*with t'* = *ADJUNCT*(*z*,*t*),

> > > *thus length*(*t'*) = *n*}

> > = **if** *IDS* **then** {*line a*} (*z* = *z*)
> > > **else** {*line b*} *MEMBER*(*NXT_EL*(*t*), *t*). □

9.2 IMPLEMENTATION OF SETS

Sets can be represented by bit vectors or by aggregates such as sequences or trees.

There are two fundamentally different ways of implementing sets.

One method represents a set by a bit vector where every component (bit) of the vector corresponds to an element in the universal set *Item*. In fact, *Item* may be viewed as the index set of the vector. If an item *x* is or is not to be in the set represented by the vector *V*, then *V*[*x*] is assigned true or false, respectively.

The other method assembles all members of the set *Item* that are to be members of a set *S* into some structure (for example into a sequence or a binary tree) and uses this structure to represent *S*. The two methods are illustrated in Figure 9.1.

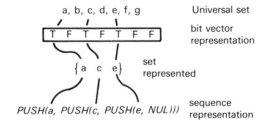

a, b, c, d, e, f, g   Universal set

| T | F | T | F | T | F | F | bit vector representation

{a c e}   set represented

PUSH(a, PUSH(c, PUSH(e, NUL)))   sequence representation

Figure 9.1 Bit vector and sequence representation of sets

Both methods have their advantages and disadvantages. Which method is better for a particular application depends on a number of things, in particular on the ratio of the number of elements in *Item* and the expected number of elements in the sets S constructed. Since sequences are usually represented by linked lists, a comparison of the space efficiency of the two methods requires that we know how pointers (addresses) are represented in the computer. Suppose that N bits are needed to represent a pointer. Then the first method (which, by the way, is built into Pascal) is usually better as long as the number of elements in a set S is, on average, greater than about $1/(k*N)$ of the number of elements in *Item*, where k is the number of pointers required to represent a member using the second method. Otherwise the second method is usually preferred. The number k depends on the structure used for the second method; for sequences implemented as singly linked lists k equals 2, for binary trees k equals 3.

9.2.1   Sets implemented by bit vectors

Suppose that we use Pascal's pointers to represent sets. With the assumption that the type *Item*

(i)   is a scalar but not of type *Real*
(ii)   has been defined previously, and
(iii)   has *FIRST ITEM* and *LAST ITEM* as its first and last element,

we define:

> **type** *Bit_vector* = *array*[*Item*] *of Boolean;*
>   *Myset*   = $\uparrow$ *Bit_vector.*

With these definitions we obtain for the implementation descriptors:

> **function** *ABSTR*(*s*:*Myset*):*Sets* {*the abstract sets*};

> $ABSTR(s)$
>   = **if** $(s = nil)$
>   **then** *NEW_SET*
>   **else** *ABSTRa*(*s, FIRST_ITEM*)

where

> $ABSTRa(s,i)$
>   = **if** $(i = LAST\_ITEM)$
>   **then**
>   **if** $s\uparrow[i]$
>   **then** *ADJUNCT*(*i, NEW_SET*)
>   **else** *NEW_SET*
>   **else**
>   **if** $s\ [i]$
>   **then** *ADJUNCT*(*i, ABSTRa*(*s, succ*(*i*)))
>   **else** *ABSTRa*(*s, succ*(*i*));

function *VALID*(*s*:*Myset*):*Boolean;*

VALID(*s*) iff {*s is defined and* for all *i* in *Item*
s↑[*i*] *is defined*}.

Notice how introducing the auxiliary function *ABSTRa* makes the definition of *ABSTR* possible without the use of a loop construct.

We will not discuss the implementation of the different set operations because they are straightforward. We observe, however, that the operations *MEMBER*, *INSERT* and *DELETE* yield O(1) algorithms, a fact that makes this implementation method very attractive.

9.2.2 Sets implemented by sequences

With very large universal sets, bit vectors cannot be used.

As the size of the universal set *Item* grows larger in comparison to the average size of the sets that we wish to represent, bit vectors become inefficient and eventually utterly impractical. Suppose, for example, that *Item* is the set of all identifiers built with up to eight letters. This set contains more than $2*10^{11}$ elements. A single bit vector over this universal set would fill a whole disk drive. For identifiers with sixteen letters a bit vector would fill as many disk drives as there are bits on one drive.

Thus, to represent a subset of a large universal set, we store, in some aggregate, exactly those elements of *Item* that we want to have in the subset. Both sequences and trees are suitable aggregates. Let us discuss sequences first.

Clearly, the nul-sequence *NUL* corresponds to *NEW_SET*. The operation *INSERT* could be implemented as either *PUSH* or *QUEUE*. For the implementation of *DELETE*, a "point of interest" with the operation *SHRINK* provides a convenient solution. The implementation descriptors for sets implemented by sequences may be specified as follows:

function *ABSTR*(*s*:*Sequence*):*Sets;*

ABSTR(*NUL*) = *NEW_SET*;

For all *x* in *Item* and *s* in *Sequence,*
ABSTR(*PUSH*(*x*,*s*)) = *INSERT*(*x*,*ABSTR*(*s*)).

Since all sequences over the set *Item* are valid representations of sets the predicate *VALID* is **true** for all sequences.

If sets are represented by sequences, MEMBER is O(n).

The implementation of the various set operations is straightforward and will not be discussed. We observe, however, that the time complexity of *INSERT* is O(1) while the complexity of *MEMBER* and *DELETE* is O(*n*) where *n* is the number of elements inserted into the set being considered. *UNION* can be implemented as concatenation, that is, for sets treated as mutable objects, by an O(1) algorithm. *INTERSECT* and the comparison of sets for equality are rather costly operations; their complexity is O(*n*∗*n*) unless we keep sequences sorted. But maintaining sorted sequences leads to $O(n)$ for *INSERT* (we have to search for the proper place of the new item), and *UNION* (we have to merge sequences properly rather than linking them back to back). Which implementation is better depends on the relative importance of the speed of the different operations for the application envisaged.

For many applications the most important operation is *MEMBER*. Unfortunately, with sequences representing sets, *MEMBER* is $O(n)$. Keeping the sequence sorted (for example in ascending order) does not improve the complexity, but, everything else being equal, it saves about half of the time if *MEMBER*(x,s) is **false** (why?). Since this is not a very significant improvement, let us look for something better.

If sets are represented by sorted vectors, *MEMBER* is $O(\log(n))$, ...

We might consider representing a set by a sorted vector of items. This is different from the bit vector representation in which every element of *Item* has a dedicated bit which is turned on or off to indicate that the element is present or absent. Similarly to a sequence, a sorted vector contains only items that are present in the set. In order to record how much of the vector (array) is currently being used a length value (integer) must be maintained together with the vector. This method has, of course, the disadvantage that the prearranged size of the vector limits the size of the represented set if sets are treated as objects. If they are treated as values, then inserting and deleting requires copying the entire set (see the array implementation of stacks in 4.2.4). On the other hand, *MEMBER* can now be implemented by an $O(\log(n))$ algorithm using the binary search. For details, review Section 2.5.

... but updating is expensive.

Because updating such vectors is very expensive, this method is useful only if this operation is rarely performed. For example, your telephone directory is usually updated once every year, and your dictionary of the English language even less frequently. Thus both are excellent candidates for this approach.

Clearly, we would like to have a scheme that strikes a reasonable compromise between the speed and the memory efficiency provided by vectors and sequences. Such a scheme does, indeed, exist, and it is even faster, on average, than the vector method and about as space efficient as the sequence method.

9.2.3   Hashing

The basic idea behind this method is to replace one long sequence by many short sequences. This is accomplished by:

(i)   subdividing the set *Item* into k disjoint subsets of about equal size, and

(ii)   associating a sequence with each of these subsets.

This sounds simple enough. But, in practice, how can we determine which of the sequences to use for storing, retrieving, or deleting a given item? We need a function that maps each item to one of our k sequences by returning, for example, a number between 1 and k or 0 and $k-1$.

HASH transforms an item into a number between 0 and $k-1$.

Let us look at this method in some more detail by first assuming that we already have such a function defined as

function $HASH(x{:}Item){:}Sqs$

where **type** $Sqs = 0..k-1$.

We do not care too much about specific properties of *HASH* except for one: let x be an item chosen at random and let $k > i \geq 0$; then the probability that $HASH(x) = i$ should be $p_i = 1/k$.

Figure 9.2 shows how a set S is now represented. There is a vector of k sequences such that the ith sequence contains exactly those members x of *SC Item* for which $HASH(x) = i$.

$$\{a,b,c,d,e,f\}$$

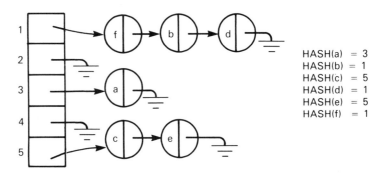

$$
\begin{aligned}
HASH(a) &= 3 \\
HASH(b) &= 1 \\
HASH(c) &= 5 \\
HASH(d) &= 1 \\
HASH(e) &= 5 \\
HASH(f) &= 1
\end{aligned}
$$

Figure 9.2   A set represented by a hash table

The implementation descriptors are best specified by a two level definition. The first level consists of *ABSTRs* and *VALIDs* where *ABSTRs* is defined as *ABSTR* for sequences, thus

$ABSTRs(NUL) = NEW\_SET$
$ABSTRs(PUSH(x,s)) = INSERT(x,ABSTRs(s))$.

VALIDs has two arguments, i and s, and it is true if all items x in s yield $HASH(x) = i$; thus

$VALIDs(i,NUL);$
$VALIDs(i,PUSH(x,s)) = (HASH(x){=}i)$ and $VALIDs(i,s)$.

With these functions we obtain, with

type $Vect = $ **array**$[0..k-1]$ **of** $Sequence$ and $v \in Vect,$

$ABSTR(v) = ABSTRa(v,0)$

$ABSTRa(v, i)$
  $= \textbf{if } (i = k)$
      $\textbf{then } NEW\_SET$
      $\textbf{else } UNION(ABSTRs(v[i], ABSTRa(v, i+1))).$

$VALID(v) = VALIDa(v,0)$
$VALIDa(v,i)$
  $= (i = k)$
      $\textbf{or } VALIDs(v[i]) \textbf{ and } VALIDa(v, i+1).$

The implementation of *HASH* ...

Now we come back to the function *HASH*. What kind of function will give us the desired property, namely that for randomly chosen items all values between 0 and $k-1$ have an equal probability ($1/k$) of occurring?

If the *Items* were numbers, then there would be an obvious choice: the *MOD* function.

$n\ MOD\ k$

... is usually based on *ORD*, ...

has a value between 0 and $k-1$ and, if n is chosen at random, then none of these values is preferred. We could use the same means for, say, character strings if we had some method of converting character strings to numbers before applying *MOD* . There are clearly many methods by which this can be accomplished. As a basic tool, Pascal provides the function *ORD* that maps single characters to numbers. A string can now be converted by combining the letters in some reasonable fashion. Assuming that we have string operations which give us a point of interest within the string by means of functions

$NEXT(s:String):String,$
$CURNT(s:String):Char$, and
$EOS(s:String):Boolean$
  $\{is\ point\ of\ interest\ at\ end\ of\ sequence?\};$

we could write *HASH* as follows:

type $Subrng = 0..k - 1;$

function $HASH(s:String):Subrng;$

  const $c = 26$
  var *number*: *Integer*;

  begin
  $number: = 0;$
  while not $EOS(s)$ **do**
      begin
{a} $number: = c*number + ORD(CURNT(s));$
              $s : = NEXT(s)$
          end;
  $HASH : = number\ MOD\ k$
  end.

The purpose of line {*a*} is to give all *numbers* an almost equal chance of occurring. The constant *c* has been set to 26 on the assumption that items are mostly strings of letters. We shall not go into a deep discussion of the proper choice for *c*. We mention, however, that *c* = 1 leads to a distribution that gives a much greater chance of occurrence of numbers in the middle of the possible range of *number* than to numbers near its extremes.

... and must deal with the possibility of overflows.

Another issue, however, commands our attention. The function above has a flaw, because it does not deal with possible overflows in line {*a*}. Unfortunately, there are now uniform rules about how Pascal compilers handle integer overflow. One of the following two methods is usually applied. Either,

$$SUCC(MAXINT) \; = \; error \; \{execution \; terminates\}$$

or

$$SUCC(MAXINT) \; = \; - \; MAXINT-1.$$

If the first method has been adopted, then we need to test if line {*a*} could cause an overflow at the next evaluation. A possible corrective action is suggested by the following code segment:

```
var temp: Integer;
begin
      temp    : = 0;
      number : = 0;
      while not EOS(s) do
            begin
            if {possible overflow}
                  then begin
                              temp : = temp −number;
                              NUMBER : = 0;
                              if temp < 0
                                    then temp : = −temp;
                        end
            number : = c∗number + ORD(CURNT(s));          {a}
            s : = NEXT(s);
            end;
            number : = ABS(number − temp)                  {b}
      end.
```

If the second method has been adopted, then *number* may become negative. Since

$$number \; MOD \; k$$

is negative if *number* < 0 and *k* > 0 while the *HASH* value is required to be positive, we need line {*b*} above to ensure an acceptable result.

The efficiency of hashing

The time complexity of *MEMBER*, *INSERT* and *DELETE* for sets implemented by means of a hash table, is, strictly speaking, $O(n)$. However, if we can put some upper bound on n, the cardinality of the set, then we can choose k, the size of the hash table, so that the time complexity is $O(1)$. These seemingly contradictory results are obtained as follows.

Evaluating $HASH(x)$ is assumed to be independent of the cardinality n of the set *Item* and is therefore $O(1)$. The result $h = HASH(x)$ leads us in one step to the sequence of all items z for which $HASH(z) = h$. Now we have to search this sequence. The average length of the sequence is n/k, and so proportional to n if k is assumed constant. So, the search is $O(n)$.

On the other hand, if we know an upper bound N for n (as we usually do) then we can choose k so that N/k is some small number, such as one or two. Now, the average search will take no more than N/k steps as long as n does not exceed N.

But even if we do not know this upper bound N on n, we can keep the complexity of the operations *MEMBER*, *INSERT* and *DELETE* to $O(1)$ if we reorganize the table from time to time by adjusting the value of k to the current value of n so that n/k is sufficiently small. Details of this method can be found, for example, in Aho, Hopcroft, and Ullman [AH74].

The complexity of union is $O(n)$. It is also easy to see that the complexity of intersection is $O(n)$ provided that the representations of the two intersecting sets use the same value of k and the same function *HASH*. Otherwise intersection is $O(n*n)$.

9.2.4   Implementation of sets by search trees

Most of the details of this implementation have already been described in Section 7.4.4. We remind the reader that the time complexities for the basic operations *MEMBER*, *INSERT* and *DELETE* are $O(\log(n))$.

For the implementation of *UNION* and *INTERSECT* the procedure *SPLIT* and the function *FUSE* are very useful.

Given a search tree t and an item x, *SPLIT* produces two trees, $t1$ and $t2$, and a boolean value *xin*. The tree $t1$ ($t2$) contains the labels of t that are less (greater) than x, and *xin* is **true** if x is equal to a label of t.

Given two trees, $t1$ and $t2$, *FUSE* constructs a tree that contains the labels of both $t1$ and $t2$. If any of the trees is empty, *FUSE* returns the other tree. If both trees are nonempty, *FUSE* returns a tree that has $MAXL(t1)$ as its root label and $DELETE(MAXL(t1),t1)$ and $t2$ as its left and right subtree, respectively.

With *SPLIT* and *FUSE*, *UNION* and *INTERSECT* are easy to program:

```
function UNION(t1,t2:Bitree):Bitree;

    var t3,t4:Bitree; xin:Boolean;

    begin
        if ISMT_TREE(t1)
            then UNION := t2
            else
        if ISMT_TREE(t2)
            then UNION := t1
        else begin
          SPLIT(t2, ROOT(t1), t3, t4, xin);
          UNION := TREE(ROOT(t1),
                           UNION(LEFT(t1), t3),
                           UNION(RGHT(t1), t4))
        end;

function INTERSECT(t1,t2:Bitree):Bitree;

    var t3, t4:Bitree; xin:Boolean;

    begin
      if ISMT_TREE(t1) or ISMT_TREE(t2)
        then INTERSECT := NIL_TREE
        else begin
          SPLIT(t2, ROOT(t1), t3, t4, xin);
          if xin
            then
              INTERSECT
                := TREE(ROOT(t1),
                        INTERSECT(LEFT(t1), t3),
                        INTERSECT(RGHT(t1), t4))
            else
              INTERSECT
                := FUSE(INTERSECT(LEFT(t1), t3),
                        INTERSECT(RGHT(t1), t4))
        end
    end.
```

SPLIT and *FUSE* are coded as follows:

```
procedure SPLIT(t:Bitree; x:Item; var t1, t2: Bitree;
                    var xin:Boolean);
    begin
        if ISMT_TREE(t)
            then begin
                t1 := NIL_TREE; t2 := NIL_TREE;
                xin := false
                end
```

```
                                         else
                           if x = ROOT(t)
                               then begin
                                       t1 := LEFT(t); t2 := RGHT(t);
                                       xin := true
                                       end
                                   else
                           if x < ROOT(t)
                               then begin
                                       SPLIT(LEFT(t), x, t1,t2, xin);
                                       t2 := TREE(ROOT(t), t2, RGHT(t))
                                       end
                                   else begin
                                       SPLIT(RGHT(t), x, t1,t2, xin);
                                       t1 := TREE(ROOT(t), LEFT(t), t1)
                                       end
                       end.

            function FUSE(t1,t2:Bitree):Bitree;

                begin
                  if ISMT_TREE(t1)
                  then FUSE := t2
                     else
                       if ISMT_TREE(t2)
                          then FUSE := t1
                          else FUSE :=
                             TREE(MAXL(t1),DELETE(MAXL(t1),t1),t2)
                end.
```

It is not difficult to show that $FUSE(t1,t2)$ as well as the trees $t3,t4$ computed by $SPLIT(t,x,t3,t4,xin)$ are search trees provided that $t1$, $t2$ and t are search trees and $MAXL(t1) < MINL(t2)$.

The Time needed for UNION and INTERSECT is proportional to the total number of elements involved.

Analyzing the complexity of *UNION* and *INTERSECT* for search trees as sets is rather complicated and goes beyond the scope of this book (methods for analyzing algorithms of this sort can be found in Aho, Hopcroft, and Ullman [AH74]). However, such an analysis shows that both algorithms have an average time complexity of not worse than $O(n+m)$ where n and m are the number of nodes in the two operand trees.

Figures 9.3 and 9.4 show how *SPLIT* and *UNION* work.

9.2.5   Tree Balancing

While a degenerate tree ...

For sets implemented as trees, the worst case behavior of *MEMBER*, *INSERT* and *DELETE* is, unfortunately, $O(n)$ rather than $O(\log(n))$. The

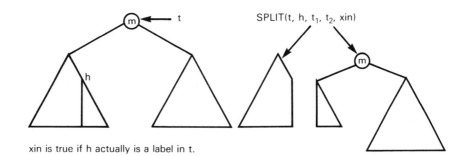

xin is true if h actually is a label in t.

Figure 9.3 The procedure SPLIT

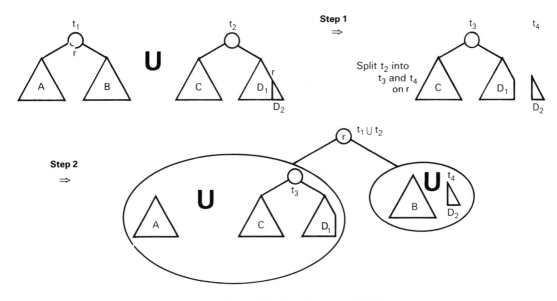

Figure 9.4 The function UNION

worst case occurs if the search tree is (nearly) degenerate, that is, if it is (almost) a sequence rather than a tree. More precisely, a *degenerate binary tree* is either empty or one of its subtrees is empty and the other subtree is degenerate.

... is unlikely to occur with random insertions,

    Although it is very unlikely that we would obtain a degenerate tree by random insertions, we always obtain such a tree by insertion of items in sorted order. Whatever the case may be, tree balancing should be considered if there is any reason to worry about the occurrence of degenerate trees (either because they occur, for some systematic reason, more frequently than they would with random insertions, or because any risk of their occurrence, however slight, is intolerable due to the nature of the application).

... tree balancing
is sometimes necessary.

With the operation *SPLIT*, balancing a binary tree is rather straight-forward. Using *SPLIT* we pivot the tree *t* around its middle element (the element *x* for which the number *i* of elements smaller than *x* and the number *j* of elements larger than *x* differ by not more than 1) obtaining the tree *t'*, and balance both the left and right subtree of *t'*. The fact that empty trees are trivially balanced is used to terminate the recursion.

The complexity
of balancing based on
SPLIT ...

The complexity of this algorithm depends on the complexity of finding the middle element. Clearly, we can always do this in O(*n*) time by traversing the tree in "inorder", where we encounter the labels in ascending order. Counting as we go and starting with zero, we reach the middle element when the count reaches *n*/2, where *n* is the total number of labels in the tree. This leads to a complexity of O(*n*log(*n*)) for the balancing act, which is rather expensive.

The method can be improved to O(*n*) by traversing the tree only once and storing extra information. This information is the relative position of each label of the tree in the sorted sequence of all labels. The information could be stored with the labels in the tree; however, this would require a field that can hold a natural number $i < n$ with every label (node) of the tree. As an alternative, the information could be stored in a temporary array of tree sites so that the array position *i* contains the site of the label with the relative position *i*.

... is, on the
average, O(*n*), and at
worst O(*n*log(*n*)).

Using the first method we find the middle element, on the average, in log(*n*) steps; using the second we find it in just one step (since we can compute the array location that contains the site of the desired label by means of a simple arithmetic expression). In either case, the average performance of balancing is O(*n*) and, in the worst case, it is O(*n*log(*n*)).

With the **function** *MIDDL*(*t*:*Bitree*):*Item* which finds the middle element and the procedure *INIT_MIDDL*(*t*:*Bitree*) that collects information used to speed up *MIDDL* in a single traversal, we obtain for the function *BALANCE*:

```
function BALANCE(t:Bitree):Bitree;
  function BLNCE(t:Bitree):Bitree;
    var x:Item; t1,t2:Bitree; xin:Boolean;
    begin
      if ISMT_TREE(t)
        then
          BLNCE := NIL_TREE
        else begin
          x := MIDDL(t);
          SPLIT(t, x, t1, t2, xin);
          BLNCE := TREE(x, BLNCE(t1), BLNCE(t2))
        end
    end;
```

> **begin**
>   *INIT_MIDDL*(*t*);
>   *BALANCE* := *BLNCE*(*t*)
> **end.**

The cost
of balancing ...

In order to assess their true costs, we need to analyze our balancing activities over an extended period of time.

    Suppose that we rebalance trees after a total of i insertions and/or deletions. Starting with n labels and inserting and/or deleting i labels we will end up with m labels where

$$n - i \leq m \leq n + i.$$

Rebalancing the tree after i operations will therefore cost

$$k = O(m) \leq O(n + i)$$

... per insertion
or deletion ...

steps. Hence the cost per insertion/deletion is

$$k/i \leq O(1 + n/i)$$

and, with $i = c*n$,

$$k/i \leq O(1 + 1/c).$$

If we set some lower bound for c, that is, if we make i dependent on n so that $i/n > C_o > 0$ for some constant C_o, then the cost per operation is

$$k/i = O(1).$$

... is very small,
indeed!

Since the complexity of *INSERT* and *DELETE* is $O(\log(n))$, the overall cost of this strategy of rebalancing becomes less noticeable as n increases.

Depth balancing
...

    There is another kind of balancing that yields trees for which *MEMBER*, *INSERT* and *DELETE* are also always $O(\log(n))$. It is called height balancing or depth balancing. In order to accentuate the difference, we juxtapose the definitions of ordinary balancing and depth balancing:

    With **function** *LBLS*(*t*:*Bitree*):*Integer* which returns the number of labels of a given tree, we have, for balanced trees,

> *BALANCED*(*t*) iff
>   *ISMT_TREE*(*t*) **or**
>   (*BALANCED*(*LEFT*(*t*)) **and** *BALANCED*(*RGHT*(*t*)) **and**
>   *ABS*(*LBLS*(*LEFT*(*t*)) − *LBLS*(*RGHT*(*t*))) ≤ 1),

and for depth-balanced trees

> *DEPTH_BAL*(*t*) iff
>   *ISMT_TREE*(*t*) **or**
>   (*DEPTH_BAL*(*LEFT*(*t*)) **and** *DEPTH_BAL*(*RGHT*(*t*)) **and**
>   *ABS*(*DEPTH*(*LEFT*(*t*)) − *DEPTH*(*RGHT*(*t*))) ≤ 1).

Thus, while for (ordinarily) balanced trees the *number of labels* in the subtrees may differ by at most one, for depth-balanced trees the *depths* of the subtrees may differ by at most one.

... causes a small
delay for every
insertion ...

It turns out that depth-balancing can be maintained with very little extra effort. This extra effort involves some bookkeeping along the search path of *INSERT* or *DELETE* (i.e. costs of $O(\log(n))$ per operation) and an occasional rearranging of not more than five links when a disturbed balance is restored. The reader may enjoy rediscovering the details of this method (see Exercise T9.2 and P9.1).

Nevertheless, a comparison of the overall costs for ordinary balancing and depth balancing shows an advantage for ordinary balancing because here the expense per operation is constant while there it is $O(\log(n))$.

... instead of
occasional extended
delays.

Still, choosing depth-balancing may be indicated for interactive or so called realtime applications where the occasional interruptions caused by the somewhat lengthy process of ordinary balancing may be intolerable. These interruptions may delay a response to an outside request so much that it comes too late when it eventually occurs. On the other hand, adding little delays to every *INSERT* and *DELETE* operation as required by depth balancing may not cause any problems although the combined time of these delays may substantially exceed the time needed for ordinary balancing.

9.3   FUNCTIONS, DICTIONARIES, SYMBOL TABLES

Functions viewed
as sets of ordered pairs,
...

A function from some domain X to a codomain Y may be viewed as a set of pairs (x,y) with x in X and y in Y with exactly one such pair for every element in X. Since, by this definition, a function is just a special kind of set, the abstract data type *Funktion* that we are about to discuss should be very similar to the data type *Sets*.

NOTE: In order to avoid a name conflict with the Pascal term **function,** we use the German spelling *Funktion* for distinction.

The sets involved are the carrier set *Funktion* and the sets *Domain* and *Codomain*. The latter two contain items of some sort that we do not need to specify further. As for the set *Item* used in previous definitions any reasonable types may be substituted for *Domain* or *Codomain*. We only require that *Codomain* contain the distinguished element *default*. The new type *Funktion* has four operations:

(1)   *NEW_FUN* creates a function on *Domain* that everywhere assumes the value *default*.

(2)   *ADD* takes a function f and a pair (x,y) and returns a function f' that maps x to y but otherwise behaves like f.

(3)   *DLT* takes a function f and a value x and returns a function f' that maps x to *default*.

(4)   Finally, *APPLY* takes a function f and a value x and returns the value y of the pair (x,y) in f.

NOTE: The value *default* is quite different from the value *error* introduced earlier. In practice, an occurrence of the value *error* is equivalent to the termination of a computation due to an error condition. The value *default*, on the other hand, is an actual value. In fact, it may be any suitable value in the codomain of a function. $APPLY(f,x)$ returns *default* if the expression that defines f does not contain a term $ADD(x,y,f')$ except, possibly, $ADD(x,default,f')$.

Formally we have:

Type Funktion

Sets: *Funktion, Domain, Codomain*
{*Codomain contains the distinguished member "default"*}

Syntax:

function *NEW_FUN:Funktion;*
function *ADD(x:Domain; y:Codomain; f:Funktion):Funktion;*
function *DLT (x:Domain; f:Funktion):Funktion;*
function *APPLY(f:Funktion;x:Domain):Codomain;*

Axioms: for all x,z in *Domain*,
y in *Codomain* − {*default*},
and f in *Funktion*

$APPLY(NEW\_FUN, x)$	$= default;$	(9.20)
$APPLY(ADD(x,y,f), z)$		(9.21)

$\quad = \textbf{if } x = z$
$\qquad \textbf{then } y$
$\qquad \textbf{else } APPLY(f, z);$

$ADD(x,default,NEW\_FUN) = NEW\_FUN;$		(9.22)
$ADD(z,w,ADD(x,y,f))$		(9.23)

$\quad = \textbf{if } x = z$
$\qquad \textbf{then } ADD(z,w,f)$
$\qquad \textbf{else } ADD(x,y,ADD(z,w,f));$

$DLT(z, NEW\_FUN)$	$= NEW\_FUN;$	(9.24)
$DLT(z, ADD(x,y,f))$		(9.25)

$\quad \textbf{if } x = z$
$\qquad \textbf{then } DLT(z,f)$
$\qquad \textbf{else } ADD(x,y,DLT(z,f))$

end {*Funktion*}.

... have special properties ...

Comparing the type *Funktion* with the type *Sets,* we find similarities between *NEW_FUN* and *NEW_SET, ADD* and *INSERT, DLT* and *DELETE*, and, to a lesser extent, between *APPLY* and *MEMBER*. Nonetheless, there are two substantial differences: (i) A function always contains as many pairs as there are elements in *Domain*. Therefore, *NEW_FUN* is not the empty set but the set of pairs (*x,default*) for all *x* in *Domain*. (ii) Even if they are different, pairs with the same domain component cannot simultaneously be members of the same function (the reader may analyze how this rule is enforced by the axioms). Thus, as far as their set membership is concerned, pairs with like domain components behave as if they were equal. So, *ADD* is actually a replacement operation and *DLT*(*x,f*) gives the same result as *ADD*(*x,default,f*). Thus we should and will eliminate *DLT* and rename *ADD* as *REPLACE*. As a bonus, the axioms (9.24) and (9.25) are no longer needed, and the specification becomes simpler. To make sure that this change is consistent with the original definition, replace *w* in (9.23) by default and *ADD*(*u,default,g*) by *DLT*(*u,g*) and observe that axioms (9.22) and (9.23) become (9.24) and (9.25).

... that are rather complex to formalize.

These differences between *Sets* and *Funktion* make our original view of *Funktion* as a special case of *Sets* rather tenuous. The restrictions that must be imposed on sets in order to make them behave as functions are severe and noticeably more complex than the specifications of either *Sets* or *Funktion* individually. In fact, the respective sets of axioms show more similarity between *Sets* and *Funktion* than one might expect considering the harsh restrictions needed to derive functions from sets.

However, sets viewed as functions ...

Searching for a way to formulate the obvious relationship between the two types more naturally we explore the other direction: we interpret the type *Sets* as a special case of the type *Funktion*. Now things are simple. Basically, we consider a set derived from the universal set *Item* to be a function from *Item* to *Boolean* where *false* assumes the role of *default*. In order to make sure that sets and predicates (functions to Boolean) may be identified in this way, we have to demonstrate that there is a bijection between them. This is easy. Let *Item* be both the domain of predicates *p* and the universal set of which all sets *s* are subsets. Then each such set *s* defines, and is defined by, the predicate *p* with the property

$$\text{for all } x \text{ in } Item. \ p(x) \text{ iff } x \text{ in } s.$$

are easy to formalize ...

This predicate is called the *characteristic function* of the set *s*. With the concept of the characteristic function, the abstract type *Sets* can now be viewed as the abstract type *Funktion* with *Boolean* as *Codomain* where the value *false* takes on the role of *default*. Consequently, *NEW_FUN* becomes *NEW_SET*, *REPLACE*(*x,true,s*) (alias *ADD*) becomes *INSERT*(*x,s*), *REPLACE*(*x,false,s*) becomes *DELETE*(*x,s*), and (!) *APPLY*(*s,x*) becomes *MEMBER*(*x,s*).

Clearly, for this "new" type *Sets*, we can construct additional operations, such as *UNION*, by defining

$$MEMBER(x, UNION(p,q)) = APPLY(p,x) \textbf{ or } APPLY(q,x),$$

and so on.

Dictionaries and
symbol tables are
functions.

At this point we should mention that our type *Funktion* is frequently also called *dictionary, symbol table,* or *directory.* This is because the type *Funktion* (although not always formally specified as such) is customarily used in assemblers and other translators to record the mapping from identifiers (character strings) to addresses, types, or other information associated with identifiers. Also, on mass storage media, the names of files are associated with their physical location by so called directories, which are, of course, also functions.

Finally, for functions we sometimes need a pair of operations similar to *NXT_EL* and *REST* with the important difference that the order in which the elements are produced is specified. For example, we may want operations

  function *MIN_X(f:Funktion):Domain,*

and

  function *MIN_REST(f:Funktion):Funktion,*

that return, respectively, the domain value x for which $f(x)$ is the minimum of f, and the function g for which $g(x) = default$ and $g(z) = f(z)$ for all $z \neq x$. Thus,

  $MIN\_X(NEW\_FUN) = error;$

  $MIN\_X(REPLACE(x,y,f))$
   $= \textbf{if } f = NEW\_FUN$
    then x
    else if $y < f(MIN\_X(f))$
     then x
     else $MIN\_X(f);$

  $MIN\_REST(f)$
   $= \textbf{if } f = NEW\_FUN$
    then *error*
    else $REPLACE(MIN\_X(f), default, f).$

9.3.1   Implementation of the type *Funktion*

Implementation
methods for sets can
be adapted to
functions.

The implementation techniques developed for the type *Sets* are easily generalized to the type *Funktion* by replacing the set *Boolean* by the set *Codomain.* Hence, the implementation by bit vectors becomes an implementation by vectors of type *Codomain.* The implementations by sequences, hash tables, and search trees must be modified slightly: in each record we must store the pair (x,y) rather than just x. Before, it was sufficient to store x rather than $(x,true)$ since the pair $(x,false)$ was realized by not storing x at all. Thus, if *MEMBER* found the value x, it returned **true** otherwise it returned **false**. Now, if $APPLY(f,x)$ finds a pair (x,y), it returns y, otherwise it returns *default.*

For functions, the storage and retrieval of the pair (x,y) must be exclusively based on x. Because of this, the values x of the set *Domain* are frequently called "retrieval keys" or simply "keys".

9.4   GRAPHS AND RELATIONS

In Section 9.3 we have discussed functions of one variable. The generalization to several (in particular, to two) variables is not difficult. We only need to consider domains that consist of pairs of values rather than single values. The specification of this kind of function is no different from the one given previously. But what does this have to do with graphs and relations?

We must first answer a more fundamental question: What are graphs and relations?

A relation ...

Let us start with relations: Intuitively, given two sets A and B, a relation specifies which elements in A are related (for whatever reason) to which elements in B. Relations may also be defined for more than two sets. If they deal with exactly two sets, then they are called *binary relations*. As a practical example of a binary relation consider the set of human beings and the set of dogs with the relationship "master of". For every human h and dog d we can state the (usually false) proposition "h is the master of d".

... is a subset of
a cartesian product.

Mathematically, we may view the relationship "master of" as a subset of the set (human beings) $\times$ (dogs) where the subset contains all those ordered pairs (h,d) for which "h is the master of d" is a true proposition. This (sub)set may now be represented by its characteristic function

master_of: (human beings) $\times$ *(dogs)* $\rightarrow$ *Boolean*

that is true for the pairs in the subset and false for the rest of the cartesian product.

Frequently, we encounter relations where the two factors of the cartesian product are the same set. The relation "$>$" between integer numbers is an example. Such a relation is called a (binary) relation *on* a set. Figure 9.5 depicts the relation "$>$" for a subset of the integers.

Figure 9.5   The relation "$>$" for some numbers

Another way of depicting a binary relation on a set A is as follows: for each element in A, draw a point (a vertex) and draw an arrow from the point

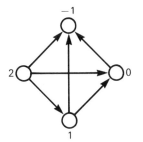

Figure 9.6   The graph of relation "$>$" on $-1..2$

of element x to the point of element y if the pair (x,y) is in the relation. This "graph" for the relation ($>$) of Figure 9.5 is depicted in Figure 9.6.

A graph is a binary relation on a set of vertices.

Indeed, we may define a graph as a binary relation on a set. Usually the elements of the set are called the *vertices* (singular: vertex) of the graph, and the ordered pairs of the relation are called the (directed) *edges* of the graph.

For some relations R on sets A we find that

for all x,y in A. (x,y) in R iff (y,x) in R.

Such a relation is called symmetric. The family relation "sibling of" is an example: Jim is a sibling of Sue iff Sue is a sibling of Jim.

An undirected graph is a symmetric relation.

If the underlying relation of a graph is symmetric, then for all pairs of vertices a and b that are related there is a directed edge from a to b as well as one from b to a. For simplification we interpret such a pair of edges as one undirected edge (graphically, a and b are connected by a single line rather than by a pair of arrows), and call the graph undirected. Many authors call undirected graphs simply "graphs" and directed graphs "digraphs". If there is no risk of confusion, we leave out the attribute "directed" or "undirected".

The edges of a graph may be labeled.

Sometimes the edges of a graph are associated with elements (labels) of some other set, L. Such a graph can be viewed as a two-place function (that is, a function with two arguments) with the codomain L. Thus, with the set V of vertices, a labeled graph is defined by a function

$$g: V \times V \rightarrow (L \cup \{default\}),$$

that, for every pair of vertices, returns the label of the connecting edge or the value *default* if such an edge does not exist.

We summarize: relations can be viewed as functions (predicates) of several variables; graphs (and binary relations *on* a set) represent the special case where the functions have two independent variables taken from the same set.

The following set of operations for labeled graphs corresponds to the minimal set $\{NEW\_FUN, ADD, DLT, APPLY\}$ of operations for functions:

Type Graph

Sets: <u>*Graph*</u>, *Vertex, Labl {Item}*

Syntax:

> **function** *NEW_GRAPH*: *Graph;*
> **function** *ISMT_GRAPH*(*g:Graph*):*Boolean;*
> **function** *ADD_EDGE*(*v1,v2:Vertex*; *l:Labl*; *g:Graph*):*Graph;*
> **function** *DLT_EDGE*(*v1,v2:Vertex*; *g:Graph*):*Graph;*
> **function** *EDGE_LBL*(*v1,v2:Vertex*; *g:Graph*):*Labl;*

Axioms: for all *g* in *Graph, a,b,c,d* in *Vertex,* and *x,y* in *Labl*

> *ISMT_GRAPH*(*NEW_GRAPH*);
> **not**   *ISMT_GRAPH*(*ADD_EDGE*(*a,b,x,g*));
>
> *EDGE_LBL*(*a,b,NEW_GRAPH*) = *default;*
> *EDGE_LBL*(*a,b,ADD_EDGE*(*c,d,x,g*)) =
> > **if** $a = c$ **and** $b = d$
> > > **then** *x*
> > > **else** *EDGE_LBL*(*a,b,g*);
>
> *ADD_EDGE*(*a,b,x,ADD_EDGE*(*c,d,y,g*)) =
> > **if** $a = c$ **and** $b = d$
> > > **then** *ADD_EDGE*(*a,b,x,g*)
> > > **else** *ADD_EDGE*(*c,d,y,ADD_EDGE*(*a,b,x,g*));
>
> *DLT_EDGE*(*a,b,NEW_GRAPH*) = *NEW_GRAPH;*
> *DLT_EDGE*(*a,b,ADD_EDGE*(*c,d,g*)) =
> > **if** $a = c$ **and** $b = d$
> > > **then** *DLT_EDGE*(*a,b,g*)
> > > **else** *ADD_EDGE*(*c,d,DLT_EDGE*(*a,b,g*))
> **end** *{Graph}*.

9.4.1   A programming example

A spanning tree of a graph *g* ...

Here we will not try to do justice to the great practical importance of graphs. Such an endeavor would go far beyond the scope of this book because it would force us to review the mathematical theory of graphs in some details. In order to demonstrate how graph operations work together in a program, we will be content to discuss one of the simpler examples. This example deals with the construction of a *spanning tree* of a given (undirected) graph, a concept which is discussed next.

... has the same vertices as *g* but no cycles.

Let *v1* and *v2* be two vertices in some undirected graph *g*. Then there may be a train of one or more edges leading from *v1* to *v2*. If for each pair of vertices (*v,w*) there is such a train of edges, then the graph is called *connected*. If there is exactly one, then the graph is called a (free) tree, if there is at most one, then it is called a forest.

A graph g' is called a *spanning forest* of a graph g if g' is a forest that has the same vertices as g.

It is rather obvious that for every graph there exists at least one spanning forest and, if the graph is connected, that there exists at least one spanning tree. In order to construct a spanning tree for a given connected graph g, we proceed as follows.

First, for the vertex set V of g we construct a graph g' without any edges (using *NEW GRAPH*). Then, considering each edge in g (using an operation such as *NXT_EL*), we add a corresponding edge (v, w) to g' if and only if there is not yet a path between v and w in g'. One can show that the resulting g' is a spanning tree for g.

The test for a connection can be sped up by additional bookkeeping.

This algorithm is quite simple except for the operation that tests whether two vertices v and w are connected. Since performing this test by a search through g' is rather slow, we decide to do some additional bookkeeping in order to speed it up. For this we wish to program a function, $REP(v: Vertex): Vertex$, that returns a common representative vertex for all vertices in a connected part of a graph. Thus, v and w are connected iff $REP(v) = REP(w)$. It follows immediately that $REP(REP(v)) = REP(v)$.

It turns out that REP can be expressed in terms of a rather simple function f as follows:

$$REP(v) = \textbf{if } (v = f(v)) \tag{9.30}$$
$$\textbf{then } v$$
$$\textbf{else } REP(f(v)).$$

So, f represents the knowledge of how the vertices are connected. Now our plan is to start with a trivial version of f and update f as we gain knowledge about the connectivity of the graph. Suppose that f is the identity; that is, for all vertices v we have $f(v) = v$. By (9.30) this means that, for all vertices v, $REP(v) = v$. Thus no two vertices are connected, and so all vertices are isolated. Now suppose that for some function f, v is the representative of some connected part A of the graph, and w, distinct from v, is that of a second connected part B (think of A and B as the sets of vertices that have, respectively, v and w as their representatives). Now consider the graph described by f' where

$$f' := REPLACE(v, w, f); \tag{9.31}$$

that is, consider REP to be based on f' rather than on f. For all vertices x in B, we still have $REP(x) = w$. But for all vertices y in A, we now have $REP(y) = w$ as well. Thus f' describes the state of connectivity in the graph obtained from the previous one because of the edge planted between part A and part B. Thus, with statement (9.31) we can update f and keep track of the state of connectivity in g' as we build it.

We are now almost ready to write our spanning tree program except for a small technicality: since the operation $NXT\_EL(g: Graph): Edge$ will return an edge (a pair of vertices) as a unit, we need two unpacking functions $FRST(e: Edge): Vertex$ and $SCND(e: Edge): Vertex$ that return the two end points (vertices) of the edge *e*. With *FRST*, *SCND*, and the (predefined) identity function *ID* on the type *Vertex* we obtain the program:

function *SPAN(g:Graph):Graph;*

   function *SPN(g:Graph; f:Funktion):Graph;*

   var *v,w: Vertex;*

     begin
      if *ISMT(g)*
        then *SPN* := *NEW_GRAPH*
        else **begin**
          v := *FRST(NXT_EL(g))*;
          w := *SCND(NXT_EL(g))*;
          if *REP(v)* = *REP(w)*
           then *SPN* :=*SPN(REST(g), f)*
           else *SPN* :=
             ADD_EDGE(v, w, EDGE_LBL(v,w,g),
                SPN(REST(g),
                    REPLACE(REP(v),REP(w),f)))
        end
      end;

   begin *SPAN* := *SPN(g, ID)* **end.**

The related problem of finding the minimal weight spanning tree is solved with a minor modification of the above program. The problem occurs with edge labeled graphs; it involves finding a spanning tree where the sum of all (edge) labels is minimal. The above program, with *NXT_EL* and *REST* replaced by *MIN_X* and *MIN_REST*, respectively, suitably generalized to graphs, returns the minimal weight spanning tree.

9.4.2   More operations on graphs

If we need to
traverse a graph ...

Some other operations on graphs are very desirable. Frequently, we wish to travel through a graph by moving from one vertex to another following available edges. For this purpose, we would like to have a function which, given a graph and a vertex, returns the set of all adjacent vertices. We can derive this operation from the function *EDGE_LBL* by the following process.

   The function *EDGE_LBL(v1,v2:Vertex; g:Graph):Labl* can be viewed as a set of ordered pairs of the form

$$((g,a,b),x) \text{ with } g \text{ in } Graph, a,b \text{ in } Vertex, \text{ and } x \text{ in } Labl.$$

What would happen if we rearranged the elements in each pair in the new form

$$((g,\ a),(b,x))?$$

... we may construct a function ...

Of course, such a structure would associate the elements of (*Graph* $\times$ *Vertex*) with the elements of (*Vertex* $\times$ *Labl*); however, it would not be a function! The reason is that for each pair (g,a), there would be, in general, more than one pair (b,x). But we do not need to give up the idea. All we have to do in order to obtain a function again, is to collect all pairs (b,x) that are associated with the same pair (g,a) into a set and consider the mapping

$$((g,a),\ \{(b_i,x_i)\ \big|\ ((g,a,b_i),x_i)\ \text{in}\ EDGE\_LBL\}).$$

In other words, instead of considering a function

$$(Graph\ \times\ Vertex)\ \rightarrow\ (Vertex\ \times\ Labl),$$

we consider one of the form

$$(Graph\ \times\ Vertex)\ \rightarrow \mathrm{P}(Vertex\ \times\ Labl).$$

... that maps each vertex to the set of its neighbors.

Recall that $\mathrm{P}(S)$ is the powerset (the set of all subsets) of S.

We call this new function

function *NEIGHBORS*(v:*Vertex*; g:*Graph*):*V_L*.

V_L is either a set type over the universal set (*Vertex* $\times$ *Labl*) or a function type with the domain Vertex and the codomain *Labl*. With the latter choice we obtain the axioms for *NEIGHBORS*:

NEIGHBORS(a, *NEW_GRAPH*) = *NEW_FUN*;
NEIGHBORS(a, *ADD_EDGE*(b,c,x,g)) =
    if $a = b$
        then *REPLACE*($c,x,NEIGHBORS$(a,g))
        else *NEIGHBORS*(a,g).

9.4.3   Implementation of graphs

Since they are functions (*Edge*$\rightarrow$*Boolean* or *Edge*$\rightarrow$*Labl*), graphs are implemented in the same way as functions and so further discussion of the subject seems to be redundant.

If we need to traverse a directed graph in both directions, ...

Yet there is one case that deserves special attention. Suppose that we wish to specify two neighbor functions, one that associates a vertex v with all vertices w that can be reached from v by an edge (v,w), and another that associates v with all vertices u that can reach v by an edge (u,v). In other words, suppose that we wish to be able to travel through a directed graph not only in, but also against, the specified direction of the edges. With the assumption that the graph in question has many more edges than it has vertices, this pair of neighbor functions can be implemented with about the same space requirements as a single neighbor function if we are prepared to degrade the execution time.

Assuming that vertices and edges are represented by pointers, we find that the number of pointers needed for a single neighbor function is about twice the number of edges. This follows because the constituent pair of the neighbor function, $(v, \{ w_1, w_2, ..., w_k \})$, requires $2*k$ pointers, k to represent the vertices w_i, and k additional pointers to organize these vertices into a set. Now consider the following representation.

First, implement two functions, *NXT_OUT* and *NXT_IN*, from edges to edges: for an edge (v, w_1), *NXT_OUT* returns its clockwise neighbor (v, w_2) emanating from v, while *NXT_IN*, for an edge (v_1, w), returns its clockwise neighbor (v_2, w) arriving at w.

These functions can be implemented by allocating a record with the fields *N_OUT* and *N_IN* for each edge in the graph. The pointers to these records now represent the edges. The fields *N_OUT* and *N_IN* are set so that $e\!\uparrow\!.N\_OUT$ and $e\!\uparrow\!.N\_IN$ have the values of *NXT_OUT*(e) and *NXT_IN*(e), respectively. Thus space for $2*N$ pointers is required where N is the number of edges. Figure 9.7 shows how edges connect to each other.

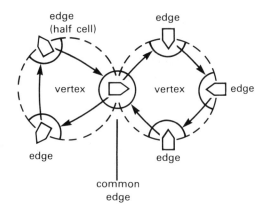

edge
(half cell)   edge

vertex   vertex   edge

edge   edge

common
edge

Figure 9.7 The interconnection of edges for the ring implementation of graphs

... we may consider
implementation by *ring
structures*.

Because of its circular linking of the edges, this implementation of graphs is usually called implementation by *ring structures*.

A closer inspection of the graph segment in Figure 9.7 reveals that the graph has a rather special structure: a node is either the target or the source of edges but never both. In addition, a node, represented only by a ring of edges, has no storage space associated with it that could, for example, be used to store a label if that was desired. But these deficiencies are easily repaired: we interpret *two neighboring rings* as a node of a graph with the connecting edge representing the node (Figure 9.8). Clearly, this special edge needs to be distinguished by some sort of distinct label. Now, arbitrary graphs can be

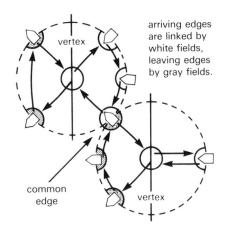

arriving edges
are linked by
white fields,
leaving edges
by gray fields.

vertex

common
edge

vertex

Figure 9.8 Ring structure implementation for arbitrary graphs

represented and each node of a graph is associated with an actual space in memory. The total space requirement for this representation is $2*(N + M)$ where N is the number of edges and M is the number of nodes.

It remains to be demonstrated that the functions *NXT_OUT* and *NXT_IN* do, in fact, describe the desired graph completely and that they permit us to travel through the graph in either direction.

Both questions can be answered affirmatively because (i), given a vertex v (that is, given a specially labeled edge), we can find, by *NXT OUT* and *NXT IN*, all edges originating from, and arriving at, v, and (ii), given an edge (v,w), we can find the special edges representing v or w (repeatedly using *NXT OUT* or *NXT IN*, respectively); that is, we can find the vertices that are connected by (v,w). Thus we can determine whether there is an edge between two given vertices (hence the graph is completely described), and, given a vertex v, we can find all adjacent vertices connected to v by leaving and by arriving edges.

EXERCISES

Theoretical exercises

T9.1   Prove the theorem stated in 9.1 (page 231): there exists a function *ADJUNCT* such that (9.13a,b).

T9.2   Prove that the number of nodes in a height-balanced tree of depth d is, at least $F(d + 1) - 1$ (where $F(n)$ is the nth element in the Fibonacci sequence).

Programming exercises

P9.1   Develop the operations *INSERT* and *DELETE* for a set represented by a depth-balanced tree.

P9.2   Design and implement a type *Funktion* that is sufficiently general to be used for the implementation of *Sets, Directory,* or *Graph* (see also page 246).

P9.3   Use the type *Funktion* developed in P9.2 to implement a type *Sets* whose members are names (character strings).

P9.4   Use the type *Funktion* developed in P9.2 to implement a telephone directory.

P9.5   Use the type *Funktion* developed in P9.2 to implement a model of a road network. A road network can be modeled by a directed graph as follows: intersections correspond to vertices, one way roads to single (directed) edges, and two way roads to pairs of edges going in both directions. The edges are labeled by the length of the corresponding road segment and, possibly, by the name of the road.

P9.6   For the road map of problem P9.5 write a program that finds the shortest route between two given intersections. Encode the answer as a sequence of intersections.

P9.7   Write the program for problem P9.6 assuming that the *NEIGHBORS* function is among the primitives of the type *Graph*.

P9.8   The transitive closure of a graph g is a graph g' with the same set of vertices as g that has an edge $(v1, v2)$ whenever there is a directed path (connection) from $v1$ to $v2$ in g. Write a function that computes the transitive closure of a given graph.

10 Storage Management

10

"new" and "dispose" ...

Direct and linked implementation of all data types require the allocation and deallocation of storage space at run-time (also called "dynamic allocation and deallocation"). For this purpose Pascal provides the operations *new* and *dispose*. We have seen in Chapter 5 that these operations can also be implemented by the user. Thus having them provided by the programming language is convenient and promotes efficiency, but it is not essential.

... are adequate for mutable objects but not for values.

While *new* and *dispose* are (almost) adequate for the implementation of mutable objects, they are insufficient for the economic implementation of values. Recall that the use of values leads to the proliferation of inaccessible storage cells (so called garbage cells) which, in turn, depletes the number of usable cells. As a result programs frequently terminate prematurely for lack of available cells. Therefore, proper support for the use of values must provide means that either permit the collection of garbage cells once the pool of available cells is exhausted or that prevent the occurrence of garbage in the first place.

Objects may cause garbage, too.

We hasten to add that garbage may also occur with mutable objects. If an object is no longer needed and is abandoned, its storage locations are permanently lost unless they are returned to the pool of available space. For two reasons we may not wish to assign this task to the programmer. First, he may not know whether the same object is still being used elsewhere, and secondly, in an effort to separate levels of concern, we may not wish to burden him with the mundane activity of attending to storage economy.

Thus some form of automatic deallocation of storage, usually called *storage management*, is desirable for mutable objects and is indispensable for values.

Themes of this chapter:

In this chapter we will deal with three strategies for storage management:

Reference counts,

garbage collection

and garbage
compaction.

(i)   The prevention of garbage cells by the use of reference counts;

(ii)   garbage collection (commonly used when all cells are of equal size);

(iii)   garbage compaction (commonly used when the sizes of cells may
        differ).

If reference counts are used with cells of varying size, an occasional
compaction step improves the performance of the system by preventing the
premature termination of a program due to what is called *storage
fragmentation*. We shall discuss this problem in more depth at the end of the
next section.

10.1   REFERENCE COUNTS

We cannot always dispose of a cell that is no longer needed in some part
of a program, because we may not know whether some other part has a claim
to it. Hence the conservative policy is not to delete cells. Frequently, however,
this leads to inefficiencies — but it never leads to errors.

Recording
arriving pointers ...

We can apparently improve the situation and always dispose exactly of
those cells that are about to become inaccessible, if we keep track of the
number of references to each cell. This requires (i) an extra field, the so called
reference count, in every cell, and (ii) extra code that updates these fields as
references change and that disposes of a cell as soon as its reference count
drops to zero.

... does not
cost much storage
space.

The extra field does not need to be very large. An eight-bit field (a byte)
is more than enough. To be sure, there can be cells that are referenced more
often, but these can be marked "permanent" by setting the reference count to
some special value set aside for this purpose. These cells, then, would never
be deleted. This, in turn, may eventually cause some unsalvaged garbage but
this will not cause errors (as explained earlier) and, it is very unlikely to occur
due to the great popularity of these "permanent" cells.

Unless provided
by the compiler,
reference counts
demand the
programmer's
cooperation.

The additional code needed for updating the reference counts should,
of course, be hidden inside the cell operations so that higher level programs
are not burdened with these details. This is nearly possible except for two
prescriptions that the programmer has to accept: (i) The assignment operator
": =" may no longer be applied with values or objects implemented by cells;
instead a special procedure *ASSIGN* must be used. (ii) All variables used for
such values or objects must be initialized, for example, to **nil** before they may
be used.

In order to keep the description of the additional code simple, we base it
on two procedures that increment and decrement the reference count of a
given cell. These procedures also take care of the disposal of a cell if the count
drops to zero and of marking a cell "permanent" if the count reaches a given
maximum. These procedures, called *INC_REF* and *DEC_REF*, are
programmed as follows.

procedure *INC_REF*(*c*:*Cells*);
   begin
      if $c <> $ **nil**
         then
            if $c\uparrow.ref < permanent$
               then $c\uparrow.ref := c\uparrow.ref + 1$
      end;

procedure *DEC_REF*(*c*:*Cells*);
   begin
      if $c <> $ **nil**
         then
            if $c\uparrow.ref = 1$
               then dispose(*c*)
               else **if** $c\uparrow.ref < permanent$
                  then $c\uparrow.ref := c\uparrow.ref - 1$
   end.

ASSIGN updates
reference counts.

The new operation *ASSIGN*(*v*,*w*) is used to perform the assignment

$$v := w.$$

At the same time, it is required to update the reference counts of the cells accessed by both *w* and the old value of *v*. The reference count of *v* is decremented by one and that of *w* is incremented by one. Thus we obtain for *ASSIGN*:

procedure *ASSIGN*(**var** *v*:*Cells*; *w*:*Cells*);
   begin
      DEC_REF(*v*); *INC_REF*(*w*); $v := w$
   end.

CELL and *SET_NXT*
update reference
counts.

If only cell value operations are needed, then only the function *CELL* needs to be changed. Since *CELL* plants a new pointer to each argument of type *Cells*, the reference count of each of these arguments needs to be incremented. If cell objects are used, then all procedures that assign a new value to a pointer field within a given cell (for example, *SET_NEXT* in Section 5.1) need to be modified, too. They must perform what amounts to *ASSIGN*(*pointer_field*, *new_value*).

Reference counts
cannot handle circular
lists, but ...

There seems to be a deficiency inherent in the method of reference counts: circular structures cannot be dissolved because the reference counts in such a structure are never reduced to zero. This property of reference counts will not cause problems if values and objects are implemented properly, for the following reasons.

... circular lists never
occur with values, ...

(a) In order to build a circular structure, we must change at least one pointer field in a cell that already exists (why?). Thus, with values, circular structures never occur because a cell, once created, is never changed.

... and usually
not with objects ...

(b) With objects, only head cells need to have a reference count; cells within an object can be deleted by the primitive operation that removes the cell from the object. Furthermore, the reference count of a head cell should only count references to the object from the outside but not references from the interior cells of the object back to the head cell. This is so because the interior references are properly maintained, again, by the primitive operations of the data type.

... unless objects may contain themselves.

(c) We introduce the danger of circularity only if we allow an object to contain itself directly or indirectly as an item. Some applications require this. One example is the representation of context free grammar rules by means of sequences. But, at least with this example, the problem is solvable systematically: the theory of formal languages provides criteria to determine whether or not a rule is useless. Thus the identification of sequences (rules) that should be eliminated is on a higher level of concern; it is the user's problem. To solve this problem, the user needs an operation that deletes an object regardless of its current reference count.

Storage fragmentation

Simultaneous use of cells of different size ...

The method of reference counts described above, salvages a cell by evoking *dispose*. The operation *dispose* (similar to *DELETE* described in Chapter 5) arranges deleted cells in one or more lists of available space. Several lists are sometimes used with cells of varying size, such that each list contains all available cells of a particular size. This avoids the necessity of lengthy searches for suitable cells which would occur if cells of all sizes were kept on the same list.

... may lead to storage fragmentation.

Fragmentation, that is, the depletion of large available cells and the proliferation of small ones, has a simple cause. Frequently, there are no cells available that exactly match the size of the cell requested. In such a case a larger available cell must be found and divided in order to obtain a cell of the desired size. The remaining part is added back to the pool of available cells. Since this process only divides large cells and never fuses small ones, the pools of larger cells inevitably become depleted. Thus, at some point it may happen that a request for a cell of a certain size cannot be satisfied, although the combined space of available cells would be more than sufficient to do so. In this case, termination occurs, not because the available space is exhausted, but because it is too fragmented. In this case storage compaction, which shifts all available cells to one end of the cells space and thereby fuses all available cells into one large cell, can prevent premature termination. Some details of this method are described in Section 10.3.

If storage compaction is provided by the compiler, fragmentation does not cause problems.

For programs written in Pascal (and similar languages) the enhancement of reference counts by compaction is rather impractical. While the prescriptions imposed on the programmer by the implementation of reference counts are tolerable, those needed for user implemented compaction are so awkward that the latter is of questionable utility. On the other hand, if compaction can be triggered automatically (that is, managed by the compiler) when *new* cannot satisfy a request, then the compaction process would be completely invisible (transparent) to the user.

10.2 GARBAGE COLLECTION

Garbage collection requires that each cell has an extra marker bit for the exclusive use of the garbage collector. This bit is inaccessible or taboo to the user. Garbage collection, now, proceeds in two steps: the first step identifies (marks) the cells that are currently in use, and the second step organizes the remaining (the garbage) cells into a new list of available space. This second step is a rather simple process. It examines all cells in the cell space (which can be thought of as an array), unmarks all marked cells (so that they can be marked again later when garbage collection is invoked another time) and disposes of the cells that are not marked.

The process that finds and marks the cells in use is a little trickier. To be sure, the basic concept is not difficult; the garbage collector, in traversing all structures built by and currently accessible to the user, visits every cell possibly in use and marks it. But there are a number of details that need to be clarified.

(i)   The marking procedure can traverse all structures only if it has a list of all locations, other than cells, to which the user may currently refer, and which contain pointers to the user's cell structures. Such a list can be maintained — without the user's conscious cooperation on all levels of his program — only by code generated by the compiler. This makes garbage collection a feature of the implementation of a language; attempts to add garbage collection in the form of a (user written) procedure have, to my knowledge, always led to rather awkward constructs that prevent the proper separation of levels of concern within programs that use them.

(ii)   The marking procedure must be able to traverse ring structures without the danger of infinite looping.

(iii) Since its main part is a traversal process, the marking procedure is most conveniently written as a recursive program. However, the implementation of recursion requires storage space (a stack) to keep track of local variables, temporary results, and return addresses. However, at precisely the time when garbage collection is needed, storage space is not available. Thus, some way must be found to avoid the need for this space.

Accepting the fact that garbage collection should be a part of the implementation of the language itself, we shall not consider (i) further.

In order to avoid infinite looping of the marking process we can apply a simple strategy. We mark a cell as soon as we reach it and treat a pointer to a marked cell in the same way as **nil**. Hence, the traversing process will only pass through a cell once (that is, enter it and continue searching by following the pointers stored in the cell). This clearly avoids infinite looping, but does it mark all accessible cells? We need to define our process more precisely in order to answer this question.

Let us assume that we have (i) a

procedure *SET_MARK(c:Cells)*

that marks cell *c*, (ii) a

function *MARKED(c:Cells):Boolean*

that tells if cell *c* is marked, and that we are working with cells that have, besides information fields for items other than pointers (cells), two pointer fields: *LEFT* and *RGHT*. The generalization of this procedure to more than two pointers is straightforward. We program the procedure *MARK* that is supposed to mark all cells accessible from *c* as follows:

The recursive version of the marking program is simple ...

```
procedure MARK(c:Cells);
    label 0,1,2;

0:  begin
        if c<>nil
            then
                if not MARKED(c)
                    then begin
                        SET_MARK(c);
                        MARK(LEFT(c));
1:                      MARK(RGHT(c))
2:                  end {the purpose of the labels is
                            explained in the text below}
    end.
```

Now we assert the following

Theorem: *MARK(c)* terminates and marks every cell *c'* not yet marked that is accessible from *c* either directly or through unmarked cells.

... and easy to verify; ...

Proof (by induction over *n*, the number of cells accessible from *c*):

Base case: *n* = 0, that is, *c* = **nil**. No cell needs to be marked; *MARK* terminates immediately.

Induction hypothesis: the theorem holds for *n* ≤ *k* cells accessible from *c*.

Inductive step: Suppose we are given a pointer *c* from which *k* + 1 cells can be accessed. Then the number of cells, not counting the cell directly accessed by *c*, is *k*. We denote the set of unmarked cells accessible through unmarked cells from *LEFT(c)* by *A*, the set accessible through unmarked cells from *RGHT(c)* by *B*, and the set of cells marked or accessible only through marked cells by *C*.

Since *MARK* treats pointers to marked cells in the same way as the **nil** pointer, we may replace all pointers to cells in *C* by **nil** without changing the marking or the termination behavior of *MARK*. Furthermore, if there are references from *A* or *B* to the top cell *c*, then these may also be replaced by **nil**, for *c* is marked first and may be viewed as a member of *C* when marking proceeds to *LEFT(c)* and *RGHT(c)*. To complete the proof we must show that all cells in *A* and in *B* are being marked. We distinguish two cases.

(a) In the simpler case, A and B are disjoint. Here the induction hypothesis ensures that all cells in A and B will be marked.

(b) In the second case A and B overlap, that is, there are cells which may be accessed both through $LEFT(c)$ and $RGHT(c)$. Here the induction hypothesis is directly applicable to A, but not to B since marking A modifies B (B contains marked cells after A is marked). Now consider the set $B-A$. We observe that (i) $A \cup (B - A) = A \cup B$; thus marking $(B - A)$ completes the job, (ii) all cells in $(B - A)$ are accessible from $RGHT(c)$ without involving cells in A, (iii) no cell in $(B - A)$ is marked, and (iv) all pointers from $(B-A)$ to cells in A are pointers to marked cells that, by our earlier reasoning, may be replaced by **nil**. Thus $MARK(RGHT(c))$ marks all cells in $(B - A)$. $\square$

Corollary 1: if none of the cells accessible from c is already marked, then $MARK$ terminates and marks all cells accessible from c.

Corollary 2: if none of the cells accessible from

$\quad c_1$ or $\ldots$ or c_k

is already marked, then

$\quad MARK(c_1);\ldots;MARK(c_k)$

terminates and marks all of them.

… but it must be modified …

Since, at the time when garbage collection is needed, stack space required for executing recursive programs is usually unavailable, we have to develop code for $MARK$ that does not need stack space.

… to avoid the need for stack space.

In the recursive code of $MARK$, stack space is needed to retain the (pointer to the) current cell and the return address, that is, the value of label 1 or label 2. We will now modify the code of $MARK$ so that this stack space is no longer needed.

First modification: avoid stacking the parameter 'c'.

The first modification keeps track of the current cell without requiring stack space. For this we introduce the function $BACK$ that undoes the effect of both $LEFT$ and $RGHT$. Thus $BACK(LEFT(c)) = BACK(RGHT(c)) = c$. We shall not yet worry about how $BACK$ can be programmed. With these functions we can rewrite the segment

$\quad SET\_MARK(c);$
$\quad MARK(LEFT(c));$
$\quad MARK(RGHT(c));$

as

$\quad SET\_MARK(c);$
$\quad c := LEFT(c); MARK(c); c := BACK(c);$
$\quad c := RGHT(c); MARK(c); c := BACK(c).$

What have we accomplished? First, note that this code segment restores the value of the variable c.

Since there are no other statements in $MARK$ that change the value of *c*, we conclude that *MARK*, so modified, restores the value of *c*. Hence there is no danger in making *c* global. We hasten to say that, under normal circumstances, global variables should be avoided because of the hazards of potential side effects that make programs difficult to analyze and, as a consequence, may cause errors that are hard to find. However, since *MARK* does not change *c*, it does not produce a side effect on *c*.

Since the new program does not have a parameter, we give it the different name *MARKC* for distinction. We obtain the following code:

```
procedure MARKC;

    label 0,1,2;

0:      begin { the variable c is global }
            if c<>nil
                then
                    if not MARKED(c)
                        then begin
                            SET_MARK(c);
                            c := LEFT(c); MARKC;
1:                          c := BACK(c);
                            c := RGHT(c); MARKC;
2:                          c := BACK(c)
                        end
    end.
```

Second modification: avoid stacking the return address. Now only the return label requires stack space. We eliminate this requirement by another code modification. First we observe that we only need to retain a count that tells us which pointer field has been processed. With only two pointer fields, *LEFT* and *RGHT*, this count can be stored in one bit: 0 (1) indicates that control is returning from *MARKC* applied to the first (second) pointer field (we assume that *BACK(c)* = **nil** is satisfied when *MARKC* is completely finished and, thus, must return to the program that called it in the first place). Instead of storing the count information on a stack, we require that there be space of it in every cell.

NOTE: The count information stored in a cell *c* is used only temporarily while the descendents of *c* are being processed. Hence a stack, which stores a count only as long as it is needed, yields a better *average* utilization of storage. But, since there is no difference in the *worst case*, providing a counter for each cell may be a necessity. Thus we may as well place these counters into the cells.

Suppose that the operations *SET_R(c)*, *CLR_R(c)* and *R_BIT(c)* allow us to set, clear and test this bit, respectively. With these, the final code for *MARKC* is quite different from what we have used so far. Since we handle the return jumps explicitly, the recursive calls also become jumps. While jump instructions (goto statements) are usually considered harmful, the disciplined use in the following program does not cause any problem, as we shall see:

```
procedure MARKC;
    label 0,1,2;
0:  begin
        if c< >nil                                    {a}
        then
            if not MARKED(c)
            then begin
                SET_MARK(c); SET_R(c);                {b}
                c := LEFT(c); goto 0{ call MARKC};    {c }
1:              c := BACK(c); CLR_R(c);               {d}
                c := RGHT(c); goto 0 {call MARKC};    {e}
2:              c := BACK(c)                          {f }
            end;
        if BACK(c)< >nil                              {g }
        then if R_BIT(BACK(c))
            then goto 1 {recursive return}
            else goto 2 {recursive return}
    end.
```

We shall now prove the following theorem that ensures the correctness of *MARKC*:

Theorem: let c contain **nil** or a pointer to a cell; then, except for the effect of *SET_R* and *CLR_R*, the code of *MARKC* entered at label "0" will perform the same task as *MARK(c)* restoring c. *MARKC* will return if *BACK(c)* = **nil** or transfer control to label "1" or label "2" if *R_BIT(BACK(c))* is **true** or **false,** respectively.

Since we have not formalized the semantics of the **goto**, we will have to appeal to the reader's intuition. But, as we will see, the following proof is quite simple otherwise because it utilizes the already established correctness of the code taken from the program *MARK*.

Proof: by induction over n, the number of cells marked by *MARK(c)*.

Base case: if $n = 0$ (c contains **nil**), then control is immediately transferred to {g}. The code at {g} switches control in the way described in the theorem.

Induction hypothesis: Suppose that the theorem holds if not more than $n \leq k$ cells are marked by *MARK(c)*.

Inductive step: Now consider a structure $c = CELL(x,l,r)$ with $n = k+1$ cells marked by *MARK(c)*; thus, since cell c is marked immediately, not more than k cells are marked (by *MARK(c)*) through either l or r.

    (a) if cell c is already marked, *MARK(c)* returns without changing anything, and *MARKC* only performs the code at {g}.

(b) Otherwise, *MARKC* transfers control to {b}. Here it marks *c* (duplicating the action of *MARK*(*c*)) and sets $R\_BIT(c)$; next *c* is changed to *LEFT*(*c*), that is, to *l* and control is transferred to "0". By the induction hypothesis, *MARKC* now performs the task of *MARK*(*l*), that is, of *MARK*(*LEFT*(*c*)) and transfers control to label 1 (since $R\_BIT(BACK(l))$ is set). Now *c* is restored by *c* : = *BACK*(*c*), $R\_BIT(c)$ is cleared, *c* changed to *RGHT*(*c*), that is, to *r*, and control goes to "0". Again, the task of *MARK*(*RGHT*(*c*)) is performed, and control goes to "2" since $R\_BIT(c)$ is **false**. At 2, *c* is restored to its original value and control is properly switched by the return code segment {g}. □

The implementation of *BACK* is accomplished by reversing pointers.

We still have to give the code of *BACK*. We will use the method described earlier for singly linked sequences with a point of interest (Figure 6.9 on page 155), that is, we will reverse pointers in order to find our way back to the point of departure. This requires, that we also change the code for *LEFT* and *RGHT* so that pointers are properly reversed. We accomplish all this by introducing a second global variable "*b*", that always points to the previous cell. Now it is convenient to replace the statements *c* : = *LEFT*(*c*) etc. by procedure calls of the form *GO_LEFT*(*b,c*) etc. that properly update *b* and *c*. Furthermore, the operation *BACK* is advantageously split into the two procedures *UP_LEFT* and *UP_RGHT*. Since we have direct access to the previous cell through the new global variable "*b*", the tests "*BACK*(*c*) = **nil**" and "$R\_BIT(BACK(c))$" become "*b* = **nil**" and "$R\_BIT(b)$", respectively. With this the code of *MARKC* changes to:

```
      procedure MARKC;
            label 0,1,2;
      0:    begin
               if c<>nil                                          {a}
               then
                  if not MARKED(c)
                  then begin
                        SET_MARK(c); SET_R(c);                    {b}
                        GO_LEFT(b,c); goto 0 {recursive call};    {c}
      1.                UP_LEFT(b,c); CLR_R(c);                   {d}
                        GO_RGHT(b,c); goto 0 {recursive call};    {e}
      2:                UP_RGHT(b,c)                              {f}
                     end;
               if b<>nil                                          {g}
                  then if R_BIT(b))
                        then goto 1 {recursive return}
                        else goto 2 {recursive return}
            end.
```

Before *MARKC* is called, *b* is set to **nil** to ensure proper termination through line {g}. *UP_LEFT* and *UP_RGHT* must be written in such a way that the segments

$GO\_LEFT(b,c)$; $UP\_LEFT(b,c)$ and
$GO\_RGHT(b,c)$; $UP\_RGHT(b,c)$

leave b and c unchanged. We will not prove that the transformed *MARKC* is
still correct. A proof to establish correctness could proceed by adding some
other minor modifications which allow the identification of the ordered pair
(b,c) of the transformed program with the global variable c in the original
version.

We obtain the following code for GO_LEFT GO_RGHT, UP_LEFT,
and UP_RGHT:

procedure *GO_LEFT*(*b*,*c*: *Cell*);

    var *temp: Cell;*

    begin
        temp := *c*;
        c := *LEFT*(*c*);
        SET_LEFT(*b*,*temp*) { *the analog to SET_HD of*
                              section 5.3, page 111}
        b := *temp*
    end;

procedure *GO_RGHT*(*b*,*c*: *Cell*);

    var *temp*: *Cell*;

    begin
        temp := *c*;
        c := *RGHT*(*c*);
        SET_RGHT(*b*,*temp*);
        b := *temp*
    end;

procedure *UP_LEFT*(*b*,*c*: *Cell*);

    var *temp: Cell;*

    begin
        temp := *b*;
        b := *LEFT*(*b*);
        SET_LEFT(*c*,*temp*);
        c := *temp*
    end;

procedure *UP_RGHT*(*b*,*c*: *Cell*);

    var *temp: Cell;*

    begin
        temp := *b*;
        b := *RGHT*(*b*);

$$SET\_RGHT(c,temp);$$
$$c := temp$$
end.

10.3   GARBAGE COMPACTION

Compaction proceeds
by marking and then
moving all accessible
cells, but ...

As with garbage collection, garbage compaction first has to identify the garbage cells by marking the cells which the user can access. The second step of garbage collection, namely linking the unmarked cells together to form a new list of available space, is so simple that no further explanation is required. With garbage compaction things are different.

Recall that garbage compaction moves all garbage cells to one end of the cell space. This obviously implies that it must move all non-garbage cells to the other end. The compaction process itself is not difficult to understand. Two addresses are maintained, the source address and the target address. At the beginning of every copy operation, the source address refers to the cell to be copied, and the target address refers to the location to which the cell is to be copied. Both addresses are initialized to, say, the smallest address value in the cell space. The source address is incremented until the first marked cell is found. Then this cell is copied to the target address. Now the target address is incremented so that it refers to the first location that follows the copy, while the source address is advanced to the next marked cell. This process is repeated until the source address reaches the other end of the cell space. At this point, the target address marks the beginning of the compacted garbage area, that is, of the new area of available space.

For the proper incrementation of the source address we need a method for finding the first location of the next cell. Thus, if cells vary in size, each must carry information from which its type (and size) can be inferred.

... the chief problem is
updating pointers
properly.

But this is not all. Cells, as we know, are accessed by pointers, which refer to certain locations in memory. Thus, by moving the cells to different places we destroy the whole structure of cells and links unless — we make sure that all pointers in use are modified so that they refer to the new locations of their cells. This sounds like a formidable task! It turns out that algorithms which perform this task are rather complicated but not too inefficient. In fact, the entire compaction process can be performed in $O(n)$ time, where n is the total number of cells. In the rest of this section we will sketch two of these algorithms.

Compaction aided by 'forwarding addresses'

Pointers can be
updated by providing a
forwarding address for
every cell, ...

Suppose that our cells are, on the average, rather large so that an extra address (pointer) field in each cell for the exclusive use of the garbage compactor can be justified. We shall call this new field the forwarding address of the cell. Now we can proceed as follows. After marking, we first only pretend to compact without actually moving any cell. By this step we find out where cells are going to be copied, and we place into the forwarding address field of each cell the pointer to the place where this cell is going to be after compaction. Next we replace every pointer by the forwarding address of the cell accessed by the pointer. In this step we must process all pointers located in cells as well as those stored in variables outside of the cell space. This does not cause additional problems, since the pointers outside of the cell space are needed for the marking step anyway. Finally, compaction can proceed as described earlier.

Compaction aided by reversing pointers

... or, again,
by reversing pointers in
a suitable way.

This second method is mentioned only because of its great efficiency. Describing the method in any detail would go beyond the scope of this book, so we refer the interested reader to the literature [MA82]. The basic idea of the method is to reverse pointers systematically in such a way that the cell which needs to be moved next is not the target of any pointer. It turns out that reversing the pointers can be combined with the marking step, and restoring them with the compaction step. This method is particularly well suited if cells contain a specific field (for example, a header field) that is never used for storing pointers. It has been shown that this method is even more efficient than garbage collection, provided that a large fraction of the cell space is likely to be garbage when garbage collection/compaction is initiated. While the exact percentage for which compaction becomes superior depends on certain parameters such as cell size and number of pointer fields per cell, a rough figure is about 60 percent. With the extensive use of values over mutable objects, this percentage is easily reached for most of the runs of the garbage compactor that occur during the execution of a program.

EXERCISE

T10.1   Compare the efficiency of reference counts and garbage collection by distributing the costs over the operations that allocate new cells. More precisely, compute how many load and store operations are executed on the average in order to salvage a cell. Make the following assumptions about the program that uses the cells:

(i)   At any time, there is a fraction $q < 1$ (say $q = .6$) of all cells accessible to the user.

(ii)   A cell has two pointer fields.

(iii)   Over its life time, a cell is referenced, on average, by k pointers.

(iv)   Accessing the field of a cell costs one load operation.

(v)   Updating a field of a cell costs a load and a store operation.

(vi)   Load and store operations need an equal amount of time.

BIBLIOGRAPHICAL NOTES

The names, books, and journal articles mentioned below are not meant to form a comprehensive bibliography. However, I believe that through this list of references the interested reader can retrieve most of the relevant works published prior to 1982.

Ideas of data abstraction go back at least to the late 1960s. Most notable is the contribution of the programming language SIMULA [DA67].

The interpretation of data types as algebraic structures was suggested by Morris [MO73]; the method of algebraic specification was developed by Guttag, Zilles, and Goguen in 1975/6. The book [YE78] contains chapters by Guttag and Goguen, and contributions from a number of other researchers, as well as a comprehensive bibliography of 217 titles.

Horowitz and Sahni wrote the first text book on abstract data types in 1976 [HS76].

The concept of the implementation descriptors is due to Hoare [HO72].

Most of the implementation methods were developed in the 1960s; descriptions and references are found in Knuth [KN68].

The efficient method of representing queues as values (illustrated in Figure 6.5), was found by Burton [BU82].

The value implementations of stacks and binary trees were used by programmers for quite some time. The author has taught this material in graduate and undergraduate courses since 1979 [MA79].

An excellent reference on the complexity analysis of algorithms is the book by Aho, Hopcroft, and Ullman [AH74].

Storage management using reference counts was first described by Collins [CO60].

Garbage collection methods were developed in the 1960s. The marking algorithm that does not require stack space is known as the Schorr-Waite algorithm [SW67]. The method of garbage compaction aided by reversing pointers during the marking phase is described by Martin [MA82].

There are many excellent books on Pascal. Welsh and Elder [WE82] and Jensen and Wirth [JW74] are just two examples.

[AH74] Aho, A. V. *et al.*, *The design and analysis of algorithms,* Addison-Wesley 1974.

[BU82] Burton, F. W. "An efficient functional implementation of FIFO queues," *Information Processing Letters*, Vol 14, 5 (July 1982) pp 205-6.

[CO60] Collins, G. "A method for overlapping and erasure of lists," *CACM* Vol 3,12 (Dec. 1960) pp 655-7.

[DA67] Dahl, O-J. *et al.* "The SIMULA 67 common base language," *Publication S-22*, Norwegian Computing Center, Oslo.

[HO72] Hoare, C. A. R. "Proof of correctness of data representation," *Acta Informatica 1* (1972) pp 271-81.

[HS76] Horowitz, E. and Sahni, S. *Fundamentals of data structures,* Computer Science Press, Inc. 1976.

[JW74] Jensen, K. and Wirth, N. *Pascal, user manual and report,* Springer-Verlag 1974.

[KN68] Knuth, D. E. *The art of computer programming I: fundamental algorithms,* Addison-Wesley, 1968.

[MA79] Martin, J. J. "Foundations of data structures," technical report, Dept of Computer Science, VPI&SU, Blacksburg Va, 1979.

[MA82] Martin, J. J. "An efficient garbage compaction algorithm," *CACM* Vol 25,8 (1982), pp 571-81.

[MO73] Morris, J. H. "Types are not sets," Proceedings of First ACM Symposium on Principles of Programming Languages, ACM, New York, pp 120-4.

[SW67] Schorr, H. and Waite, W. "An efficient machine-independent procedure for garbage collection in various list structures," *CACM* Vol 10, 8, (Aug 1967) pp 501-6.

[WE82] Welsh, J. and Elder, J. *Introduction to Pascal,* 2nd edition, Prentice-Hall International, 1982.

[YE78] Yeh, R. T. (Editor), *Current trends in programming methodology IV: data structuring,* Prentice Hall 1978.

INDEX

In order to make the index more useful, the following types of occurences of index terms have been distinguished.

(1) bold: definitions or introductory discussions
(2) roman: other occurences
(3) italic: occurences in exercises